ARISTOTLE
ON THE
PERFECT LIFE

ARISTOTLE
ON THE
PERFECT LIFE

Anthony Kenny

CLARENDON PRESS · OXFORD

1992

Oxford University Press, Walton Street, Oxford OX2 6DP

Oxford New York Toronto
Delhi Bombay Calcutta Madras Karachi
Petaling Jaya Singapore Hong Kong Tokyo
Nairobi Dar es Salaam Cape Town
Melbourne Auckland
and associated companies in
Berlin Ibadan

Oxford is a trade mark of Oxford University Press

Published in the United States
by Oxford University Press, New York

British Library Cataloguing in Publication Data
Data available

Library of Congress Cataloging in Publication Data
Kenny, Anthony John Patrick.
Aristotle on the perfect life / Anthony Kenny.
p.   cm.
Includes bibliographical references and index.
1. Aristotle.   2. Happiness—History.   3. Ethics, Ancient.
4. Contemplation—History.   I. Title.
B485.K46   1992   171'.3—dc20   92-4507
ISBN 0-19-824017-1

Typeset by Joshua Associates Ltd., Oxford
Printed in Great Britain by
Biddles Ltd, Guildford & King's Lynn

ΤΟ ΑΝΘΡΩΠΙΝΟΝ ΑΓΑΘΟΝ ΨΥΧΗΣ ΕΝΕΡΓΕΙΑ ΓΙΝΕΤΑΙ
ΚΑΤ ΑΡΕΤΗΝ ΕΙ ΔΕ ΠΛΕΙΟΥΣ ΑΙ ΑΡΕΤΑΙ ΚΑΤΑ ΤΗΝ
ΑΡΙΣΤΗΝ ΚΑΙ ΤΕΛΕΙΟΤΑΤΗΝ ΕΤΙ Δ ΕΝ ΒΙΩΙ ΤΕΛΕΙΩΙ

Inscription around the dome of the rotunda in
Rhodes House, Oxford

PREFACE

THIS book is a contribution to a debate on the nature of happiness in Aristotle which has exercised many scholars in recent decades, and to which my own first contribution was made twenty-five years ago in a paper read to the Aristotelian Society entitled 'Happiness'. In its present form it is a development of four lectures given in a seminar 'The Good Life: Luck, Choice, and Vocation' under the auspices of the Greater Philadelphia Philosophy Consortium in April 1991. I am grateful to the organizers and members of that seminar, and in particular to my hosts Professor Michael Krausz and Professor Brice Wachterhauser.

Earlier brief treatments of the topics I have here addressed are to be found in papers contributed to two joint volumes: 'Aristotle on Moral Luck' in the Urmson Festschrift *Human Agency* (Stanford, 1988) and 'The Nicomachean Conception of Happiness' in the Lloyd Festschrift *Aristotle and the Later Tradition* (Oxford, 1991).

Much of the present book is concerned with Aristotle's less well-known treatise, the *Eudemian Ethics*. I have had the advantage, in preparing for publication, of being able to use the new Oxford Classical Text (OCT) of the treatise, edited by R. R. Walzer and J. M. Mingay. It has been a great boon to be able to draw on the apparatus of that volume. However, I have not always agreed with the editors' reconstruction of the text. In the case of the text which I have chosen to study in greatest detail, the section on fortune in the final book of the treatise, I have set out my differences from the Oxford editors in an appendix. I am grateful for permission to reprint the text in order to do so.

In my book *The Aristotelian Ethics* (Oxford, 1978) I set out the case for believing that the three books which are best known as the fifth, sixth, and seventh books of the *Nicomachean Ethics*, and which are also assigned by the manuscript tradition to the *Eudemian Ethics*, originally belonged in the *Eudemian* and not the *Nicomachean Ethics*. I argued also that, whatever might be the original date of the *Nicomachean Ethics*, the *Eudemian* had a solid claim to be a late and definitive statement of Aristotle's ethical position. I have taken this opportunity, in an appendix, to revisit the relationship between the two treatises, and in the light of scholarship since 1978 to defend those conclusions of my book which have been wrongly criticized, and to recant or modify those which criticism showed to be untenable in their original form.

In the present book, as in the previous one, I have used the abbreviations *NE* and *EE* for the undisputed books of the Nicomachean and Eudemian treatises, using arabic numerals for the books of the *NE* and roman for those of the *EE*. I have used the abbreviation *AE* (*Aristotelian Ethics*) for the disputed or common books, and have referred to the individual books by the letters A, B, and C. Thus 'C' refers to the book which is best known as book 7 of the *Nicomachean Ethics*, but is also the sixth book of the *Eudemian*. In referring to manuscripts of the *Eudemian Ethics* I have adopted the sigla of the OCT.

A.J.P.K.

Rhodes House
August 1991

CONTENTS

THE ENDS OF LIFE

THROUGHOUT his philosophy, Aristotle is concerned with the question 'Why?' Everywhere, he looks for answers to why-questions; but before that he seeks to identify and distinguish between different kinds of why-questions. In his practical philosophy he is above all concerned with the whys and wherefores of human action. 'Why are you doing this?' 'Why did she do that?' Aristotle, like all moral philosophers, is of course interested in the question 'What shall I do?' But the answer to that question, according to his own account, demands reflection on the more basic question why human beings do anything at all.

If a human agent is asked 'Why are you doing that?' the answer must set out some good which the action embodies. The good may be an intrinsic good of some kind, a good which has value in itself, or it may be an instrumental good, a good whose value is its role in the production of some different, intrinsic good. The answer to the question 'Why are you doing that?' may set out the agent's practical reasoning. Practical reasoning is reasoning which reasons out the good, as theoretical reasoning is reasoning which reasons out the truth. The conclusion of a piece of theoretical reasoning is a truth to be believed; the conclusion of a piece of practical reasoning is a good to be brought about. By setting out my theoretical reasoning I may explain why I believe a certain proposition; by setting out my practical reasoning I may explain why I am performing a certain action.

Of course, not every proposition which I believe as a result of theoretical reasoning is in actual fact true: my deduction may be faulty, or one of my premises may be false. Equally, not every action which I perform as a result of practical reasoning is objectively a good action; here too, my deduction may be flawed or I may have started from vicious premises. None the less, the point of practical reasoning is the achievement of good, just as the point of theoretical reasoning is the acquisition of truth.

Aristotle was the first philosopher to attempt a systematic account of practical reasoning, just as he was the first philosopher to systematize theoretical logic. But his account of the practical syllogism lacks the elegance and rigour of his theoretical syllogistic. There are many reasons for this. Some of the reasons are accidental and contingent, but some of them are rooted in the essential differences between practical and theoretical reasoning, which make the codification of practical reasoning an intrinsically more difficult matter.

The most important difference between the two kinds of reasoning can be stated as follows. If a theoretical proposition is true, then it cannot conflict with any other true theoretical proposition. But sound practical premisses may conflict with each other: that is to say, a premiss expressing the goodness of a certain value or course of action may very well conflict with another premiss expressing the goodness of a different value or incompatible course of action. From true premisses, by valid deductive procedures, one cannot draw a false conclusion. But if we think of practical reasoning as being quite parallel to theoretical reasoning, then it seems that starting from a good premiss one may in the course of deduction derive a bad conclusion: that is to say, a course of action which is genuinely an appropriate means to a good end may be (because of its relationship to other ends or norms) an objectively bad action.

Accordingly, if we are to construct a logic of practical reasoning, it is not sufficient to describe a scheme which will provide guidance in concluding from ends to means. We will need also some rules about the prioritization of ends: if the pursuit of different ends seems to call for different, and incompatible, courses of action, how are we to determine which end should be pursued?

Aristotle often writes as if he is more concerned with chains of reasoning from ends to means than with the comparative evaluation of ends. It is not that he is uninterested in evaluating ends: this is one of the major concerns of his ethical treatises. But he is inclined to present discussions of competing intrinsic values as if they were discussions of means to a single overarching end.

The opening of the *Nicomachean Ethics* (*NE*) is concerned with the hierarchy of the ends of action and choice, the series of goods chosen for the sake of other goods. From one point of view, this can be seen as an account of means–end reasoning. The first point to be made is that all such chains of reasoning must halt somewhere: they must terminate in an end, for if there were no ends there could be no means either. At 1094^{a}20 Aristotle says that if we choose everything for the sake of something else, then there will be an infinite regress and appetite will remain idle and void. Later in the same book, at 1096^b17 and 1097^b1, Aristotle gives lists of things which we choose for their own sakes, such as pleasure, honour, wisdom, sight, virtue, and happiness. Any choice which we make, he tells us, must be made for the sake of good (1094^a2). But according to the *NE*, as we learn in the second book, there are three kinds of good: the pleasant, the useful, and the noble (1104^b31).

To explain a choice, an agent will have to specify the good pursued. In doing so, he will show how his action is related, directly or indirectly, to an ultimate end. Asked to give a reason for an action, an agent may either explain that the action is a means to some end, or say that it is valued for its own sake. In the former case the action will be characterized as in some way useful, and in the latter case it will be characterized as either pleasant or noble. What is useful must, in terms of this trichotomy, be useful for pleasure or useful in the pursuit of what is noble. Not everything can be chosen as a means to some other end, and whenever our reasoning comes to a stop with something which is chosen for its own sake we can once again ask: is it because it is pleasant or because it is noble that this end is pursued? Ultimately, therefore, in terms of the Nicomachean classification of goods, all actions are done for the sake of pleasure or nobility.

There may, of course, be different kinds of pleasure and different forms of nobility; there is certainly much room for discussion about the fundamental nature of pleasure and what, for human beings, constitutes true nobility. None the less, it seems true within the Nicomachean system that every chain of practical reasoning must at some point lead to a characterization of a good pursued as pleasant, or a characterization of a good pursued as noble. Now are these to be regarded as independent, potentially conflicting, ends; or are they to be regarded as means to some other, overarching end? Does the chain of reasoning, having traced back the value of the action under consideration to its contribution to pleasure or nobility, come to a halt?

A doctrine common to all Aristotle's ethical treatises is that the halting-point of a person's practical reasoning—the ultimate end which motivates action—reveals the agent's moral status or character (e.g. 1139^a33). For instance, if an action is characterized as pleasant, then we can ask whether the agent has a general policy of pursuing what is pleasant or not. If so, then we have the vice of *akolasia*: the choice manifests the moral character of intemperance. If not, then what is the reason for the present pursuit of pleasure? If a reason is given (e.g. 'Even the hardest working politician needs a break sometimes'), this will reveal something about the agent's ultimate goal in life. If no reason is given, then the agent's present pursuit of pleasure is not the result of choice: what we have is the impulsive action of the incontinent (*akratēs*). If the action performed is characterized on the other hand not as pleasant but as noble, then the agent's action is performed for the sake of virtue, as the brave man performs his brave actions for the sake of what is noble (1116ᵃ28). Of course an agent in characterizing his action as noble may be mistaken: this would be the case, for instance, of the intemperate (*akolastos*) man whose idea of the good life is the pursuit of pleasure: Antony, for instance, telling Cleopatra 'the nobleness of life is this'.[1]

Among ultimate ends, in all the Aristotelian ethical treatises, *eudaimonia* or happiness has a very special role. The *Eudemian Ethics* (*EE*) begins with a solemn introduction which leaves us in no doubt that the subject of the work is happiness. The first point of enquiry is what a good life is and how it is to be acquired (1214ᵃ15). Immediately we are presented with five candidate answers to the second question (by nature, by learning, by training, by grace, and by luck) and three candidate answers to the first (wisdom, virtue, and pleasure). At the beginning of the *NE* we are told that the subject-matter of ethics is the good for man, the end of action for the sake of which all else is desired. Most people would agree that this supreme good is happiness, however much they may disagree about what precisely happiness consists in (1097ᵇ22). Aristotle goes on to expand the general view that the supreme good is happiness by outlining the three traditional lives—the life of philosophy, that of virtue, and that of pleasure.

There is an important difference in structure between the *EE* and the *NE* in that whereas the *EE* begins with the concept of happiness, and discusses the nature of goodness while commenting on a traditional definition of happiness, the *NE* begins by taking the subject-matter of ethics to be the supreme good, and goes on to consider happiness as the most popular answer to the question 'What is the supreme good?' But from this difference of structure, by itself, one cannot conclude to a difference of doctrine. We need to examine the two sets of texts more closely.

In the *NE* Aristotle prepares the ground for his own account of happiness by saying that the good we are looking for must be an end

---

[1] See Kenny, *Will, Freedom, and Power*, 16–17; *Aristotle's Theory of the Will*, 99.

with two special properties. First, it must be a specially 'endy' (*teleion*) end: it must—to use a more traditional translation—be perfect[2] by comparison with other ends. That is to say, it must be something sought always for its own sake and never for the sake of anything else. Secondly, it must be self-sufficient—that is, it must be something which taken on its own makes life worth while and lacking in nothing.

Happiness,[3] Aristotle says, has both these properties (1097^a15-^b21). What then *is* happiness? To elucidate this we must consider the *ergon* or function of man. Man must have a function because particular types of men (e.g. sculptors) do, and parts and organs of human beings do. What is it? Not life, not at least the life of growth and nourishment, for this is shared by plants, nor the life of the senses, for this is shared by animals. It must be a life of reason concerned with action: the activity of the soul in accordance with reason. So the good of man will be his good functioning: the activity of soul in accordance with virtue. If there are several virtues, it will be in accordance with the best and most perfect virtue ($1097^b22-1098^a18$).

Thus far the familiar account in the *NE*. If we turn to the *EE* we find an account which resembles this in some ways, but which also displays important differences. The most important of these is that while the *NE*, in book 1, leaves open the possibility that happiness is to be identified with a single dominant end, namely, the activity of the highest virtue, the *EE* views happiness as an inclusive end, the activity of all the virtues of the soul—the rational soul in the broadest sense of the word. The *NE* says that the good for man is 'activity of soul in accordance with virtue, and if there are several virtues, in accordance with the best and most perfect'. In the last chapter of the book we are told that there are indeed several virtues—there are, for instance, moral and intellectual virtues—and hence, we conclude, unconditionally, that happiness is activity in accordance with the best and most perfect of these many virtues. In book 10 we learn that the best and most perfect virtue is *sophia* or understanding,[4] and

---

[2] Thus I translate the Greek word τέλειος to avoid begging the question whether in particular contexts Aristotle means by it 'complete' or 'supreme'. Most published translations of *NE* 1.7 assume one or other of the contested interpretations. In Appendix 2 I have tried to give a non-tendentious translation of the passage.

[3] I use this translation of εὐδαιμονία because it is traditional and convenient. I am well aware that the meaning of the Greek and English words overlaps rather than coincides.

[4] I thus translate the Greek σοφία in preference to the traditional translation 'wisdom', which is much more appropriate as a translation of the Greek word φρόνησις. In *Aristotle's Theory of the Will* I used the infelicitous translation 'learning'.

that the activity of this virtue, *theōria* or contemplation, is therefore to be identified with happiness.

In the *EE* we are told that happiness is 'activity of perfect life in accordance with perfect virtue'. In this context 'perfect' means not 'supreme' but 'complete'; for the word has just been unambiguously glossed when we are told that 'life is either perfect or imperfect, and so also virtue—one being whole virtue, another a part' (1219ᵃ35–9). So that when Aristotle goes on in the *EE* (as he did in the *NE*) to distinguish parts of the soul and virtues, we know that their activities are all supposed to be parts of happiness. The virtue which figures in the definition of the end of man is the virtue constituted by several virtues of different parts of the soul.

The account just briefly enunciated I first put forward in a paper on 'Happiness' in 1966, and developed further in the course of the comparison which I undertook between the *NE* and the *EE* in my book *The Aristotelian Ethics* in 1978. In writing thus I was taking sides on a disputed question, the question whether, in the terminology introduced by W. F. R. Hardie,[5] Aristotle's conception of happiness in the *NE* was 'dominant' or 'inclusive': that is, whether he saw supreme happiness as consisting in a single activity, or in the exercise of several independently valued pursuits. My thesis might be stated by saying that in the *NE* Aristotle proposed a dominant view of happiness, in the *EE* an inclusive view.[6]

During the twenty-five years since Hardie introduced his distinction the correct interpretation of the *NE* has been a matter of vigorous debate which shows no signs of diminishing.[7] Contributors to this

[5] See Hardie, 'The Final Good in Aristotle's Ethics', and *Aristotle's Ethical Theory*.

[6] Devereux, 'Aristotle on the Essence of Happiness', argues that the contrast between the inclusive and the dominant models is misguided, because Aristotle does not believe that the intrinsic goods are separable. It is true that Aristotle does not think that the moral virtues are separable from wisdom. But that leaves two, and only two, models of happiness: the (intellectualist) one which makes it consist in contemplation; and the (inclusive) one which makes it consist in wisdom plus moral virtues.

[7] A list of the treatments of the topic since 1965 would have to include, among others: Kenny, 'Happiness'; Ackrill, *Aristotle on EUDAIMONIA*; Cooper, *Reason and Human Good*; Clark, *Aristotle's Man*; Kenny, *The Aristotelian Ethics*; Price, 'Aristotle's Ethical Holism'; Devereux, 'Aristotle on the Essence of Happiness'; Irwin, 'Permanent Happiness' and 'Stoic and Aristotelian Conceptions of Happiness'; Cooper, 'Contemplation and Happiness'; Heinaman, 'Eudaimonia and Self-sufficiency'; Roche, 'ERGON and EUDAIMONIA'; White, 'Aristotelian Happiness'.

These contributions can be crudely classified as being on one side or other of the 'dominant vs. inclusive' debate. For the dominant view: Kenny, Clark, Heinaman; for the inclusive view: Ackrill, Irwin, Price, Devereux. Cooper, having in 1975 defended a qualified version of the dominant view (*Reason and Human Good in Aristotle*), in 1987

debate principally concentrate on the interpretation of *NE* 1 and 10, and in particular on chapter 7 of each book. In this book I want to restate my own account of the *NE* in a way which takes account of the abundant contributions of recent years, but I want also to place the argument in the broader context of the Aristotelian ethical system as expounded in the *EE* as well as the *NE*.

The argument essentially concerns Aristotle's view of the hierarchy of choice: that is to say, the structure to be given to the pattern, in human life and striving, of one thing's being done for the sake of another, of A's being chosen for the sake of B.

Aristotle is sometimes thought to have imposed a strict pyramidical shape on the pattern of these choices. That is, his doctrine of the supreme good in the *NE* is sometimes thought to present as a logical truth the thesis that every one, in every choice, aims at a single end which is common to the choices of all.

It is indeed a necessary truth that one cannot choose everything for the sake of something else: chains of reasoning about means and ends must come to a halt somewhere. As we have seen, Aristotle alludes to this truth on the first page of the *NE* (1094^{a}18–21):

> If, then, there is some end of the things we do, which we desire for its own sake (everything else being desired for the sake of this), and if we do not choose everything for the sake of something else (for at that rate the process would go on to infinity, so that our desire would be empty and vain), clearly this must be the good and the chief good.

This passage has been taken to contain a fallacious transition from 'Every series whose successive terms stand in the relation *chosen for the sake of* has a last term' to 'There is some one thing that is the last term of every series whose successive terms stand in the relation *chosen for the sake of*'. That is to say, Aristotle has been accused of arguing from 'Every chain of practical reasoning comes to a halt at some end' to 'There is some single end at which every chain of reasoning comes to a halt'. But commentators commonly acquit Aristotle of this fallacy: the second if-clause, they maintain, is a consequence of, not a reason for, the first.[8]

If the passage stood on its own, it would, I think, be most naturally read as involving the fallacious argument. The principal reason for

defends a nuanced form of the inclusive view ('Contemplation and Happiness'). White takes a judicious position between the two.

[8] See e.g. Williams, 'Aristotle on the Good'; von Wright, 'The Good of Man'.

denying that it does is that Aristotle elsewhere makes statements which are incompatible with there being only a single end of all human action. But it must be admitted that it is not easy to make consistent the various passages in the early books of the *NE* in which Aristotle appears to give an answer to the question 'Is there a single end for the sake of which everything else is desired?'

On the one hand, there are passages where it looks as if Aristotle gives a positive answer: Yes, there is a single end for the sake of which everything else is desired, namely happiness. For instance, he sums up his account of happiness in book 1, just before moving on to the treatment of virtue, in the following words: 'Happiness is among the things that are prized and perfect: it seems to be so also from the fact that it is a first principle; for it is for the sake of this that we all do everything else' (1102ª-4).

On the other hand, there are passages where he seems to be giving a negative answer: No, there is no single end for the sake of which everything else is desired; there are ends, other than happiness, which we pursue for their own sake. At 1097ª23 he says that if there is a single end of everything that is done, then this will be the good achievable by action; but if there be more than one such end, then it will be these. He at once goes on to say 'there is obviously more than one end' and to exclude from consideration those ends which are not perfect (*teleia*), i.e. things such as flutes, wealth, etc., which are always sought in virtue of some other end. But it is not even the case that there is only one perfect end: there are some things which are sought both for themselves and for another end. Honour, pleasure, under-standing, and virtue we choose for their own sake (for we would choose them even if nothing resulted from them), but we choose them also for the sake of happiness, hoping to achieve happiness through them (1097ᵇ1-5).

Perhaps the way to reconcile these two strands is as follows. Every-thing other than happiness can be, and sometimes is, chosen for the sake of happiness: in that sense we can be said to do everything else for the sake of happiness. But it is not the case that every single action of every agent has happiness as its ultimate end: some actions are the result of chains of practical reasoning which halt elsewhere—in honour, perhaps, or understanding or pleasure.

However this may be, there is a further problem of reconciling what is said about happiness with the trichotomy of goods in *NE* 2. If every choice is for the sake of some good, and every good must be either useful, or pleasant, or noble, and useful goods are by definition instrumental, then intrinsic goods must be either in the category of pleasant, or in the category of noble (or perhaps in both). No doubt virtue comes in the category of the noble; and perhaps also understanding and honour are pursued as noble goals—the first correctly, the second incorrectly. In which category will the supreme good come? If happiness is the supreme good, is that because it is the supremely noble thing, or because it is the supremely pleasant thing?

In both *NE* and *EE* the answer, ultimately, is that it is both. The *NE* says (1099^a25-8) 'happiness is the best, noblest, and most pleasant thing—the attributes are not severed as in the inscription at Delos: "Most noble is that which is justest, and best is health; | But pleasantest is it to win what we love."' The Delian epigram is made the introductory text for the *Eudemian Ethics*, and the task of the book is stated as to show that happiness is at once the noblest and best of all things and also the pleasantest (1214^a1-8).

However, the relationship between this thesis of the omnivalence of happiness and the doctrine of the hierarchy of choices is not the same in the two ethical treatises. To see the difference, we have to look closely at the final book of the *EE*, where Aristotle discusses the comprehensive virtue of *kalokagathia*.[9] Here we find a new, and subtler, division of goods in place of the tripartition of the noble, the pleasant, and the useful.

Among goods, Aristotle says, those are ends which are chosen for their own sake. And of these, those are noble which are praiseworthy, such as justice and just actions, and temperance and temperate actions. Health and strength, on the other hand, riches and honour, power and fortune, though goods, are not objects of praise and therefore not noble. Indeed, though they are naturally good, they may in an individual case be harmful, materially or morally.

Aristotle sees these goods as good only provisionally: he calls them 'goods *simpliciter*' (*haplōs agatha*). This does not mean that they are absolute goods, things that are good come what may; it means just the opposite, that they are only prima-facie goods which may, in the concrete, not be goods at all. Their goodness depends on the goodness of their possessor: it derives from their being used by a good person.

---

[9] 1248^b10: I read καλοῦμεν, with Bf vocamus, Jackson, and Woods, against the MSS and Barnes ἐκαλοῦμεν.

They are not goods when used by a bad man, since for him they are not instruments of virtuous action (1248^{b}27–34).[10]

These provisional goods are indeed the ones most competed for and are thought of by many as the greatest goods, but they can be harmful to those of bad character. If you are foolish or unjust or intemperate you will not benefit from them, any more than a sick man will benefit from a robust diet, or a weak man will be able to make use of the armour of the strong.

If the natural goods are to be good for you, you have already to be good. But—for the first and only time in the ethical treatises—Aristotle in this last chapter of the *EE* makes a distinction between two types of good people: those who are just plain good (*agathos*), and those who are both good and noble (*kalos kagathos*).

The distinction between these two kinds of people depends on the distinction made above between the two kinds of intrinsic goods. Those goods that are praiseworthy are not merely good but noble. Nobody can be good without performing the virtuous actions which deserve praise. But it is possible to perform these actions for more than one motive. The actions may be done for their own sake; or they may be done with a view to gaining and retaining the non-praiseworthy goods. The character of the person who ranks praiseworthy acts below non-praiseworthy goods is described by Aristotle as follows.

There is also the civic disposition, such as the Laconians have, and others like them might have. This is a state of the following kind: there are people who think that one should possess virtue, but only for the sake of the natural goods. Such men are therefore good (for the natural goods are good for them), but they do not possess nobility as well as goodness (*kalokagathian*). For the things that are noble do not belong to them for their own sake. (1248^{b}38–1249^{a}3)

This important passage is not altogether clear.[11] Do these people actually possess virtue, in Aristotle's eyes? On the one hand, they are good people, and good people are people who have virtues; it is difficult not to read the passage as implying that they are genuinely virtuous, but virtuous for the wrong reason. But if they do the

---

[10] Here I am much indebted to the excellent treatment of this passage in Broadie, *Ethics with Aristotle*, 376.

[11] One minor puzzle, to which I do not know the answer, is this. Why is this disposition called 'civic' (πολιτική)? Does Aristotle mean that there are several civic dispositions, one of which is the Spartan one (so apparently Woods, *Aristotle's* Eudemian Ethics, 44), or that there are several dispositions, of which the one about to be described is the one which specially, and perhaps solely, deserves the name 'civic' (so apparently Barnes, *Complete Works*)?

appropriate actions, but do not do them for their own sake, or because they are noble actions, are they really virtuous?

The passage which I have translated 'The things that are noble do not belong to them for their own sake' can be translated, and sometimes is translated, 'They do not possess the things that are noble in themselves'.[12] But that translation is difficult to reconcile with the interpretation we have given: for these people do possess virtues, and virtues are noble in themselves, therefore they possess the things that are noble in themselves. The point surely is that they have acquired these noble things not *qua* noble, but *qua* useful, useful for the acquisition of the natural competitive goods.

It is instructive to compare the doctrine of *NE* 2. There we are told that it is possible to do just acts without being just, and temperate acts without being temperate. For just and temperate acts to be done justly and temperately, the agent has to act knowingly, he has to choose the acts and choose them for their own sake, and the action must proceed from a firm and unchangeable character ($1105^{a}31$-4). According to this, would a Laconian doing just acts have the virtue of justice? Not if he does not choose them for their own sake but for the material advantages they bring. Whereas according to the Eudemian final chapter, the Laconian is indeed just, even if it should turn out that his justice is something that is merely good and not noble.

In the common book B there is a passage which touches on the same topic and which resembles the account in *NE* 2.

As we can say that some people who do just acts are not, for all that, just—e.g. if they do the acts the law prescribes either unwillingly or by mistake or for some other reason and not for their own sake, even though they do what they ought and all the things the good man should—similarly there is a state which enables one to do these things in such a way as to be good, i.e. one must do them as a result of choice and for the sake of the acts themselves. ($1144^{a}13$-20)

According to the description here no less than in *NE* 2, it would seem that the Laconian person falls short of being good if he performs just acts for the sake of competitive advantage. Performing the acts for the sake of the acts themselves is, according to *AE* B, a necessary condition not just for *kalokagathia*, but for simple goodness.

Is there a real conflict here between the Eudemian final chapter and the other two passages? No: the conflict arises from the assumption that the Laconian, when he chooses to perform a particular just action,

---

[12] So Woods, *Aristotle's* Eudemian Ethics, 44.

does so for the sake of wealth or power or other natural goods. But that is not what Aristotle means in *EE* VIII. The Laconian, like any virtuous man, performs virtuous actions for their own sake, because they are the acts that virtue requires; where he differs from the noble person is in the answer he gives to the second-order question 'What is the point of being virtuous?' The *kalos kagathos* gives the answer 'Because virtue is splendid, fine, and noble'; the Laconian gives the answer 'Because virtue pays'.

The matter is very well put by Sarah Waterlow Broadie:

> The point concerns different *reflective* attitudes to virtue and virtuous actions *in general*. The noble person prizes these because they are noble in themselves. The merely good man certainly cares about virtue: he seeks to inculcate it in his children; he deplores its absence in others; in each situation he wants to know what is right to do so as to act upon it; and he may put even his life on the line in doing what he sees himself called upon to do. He behaves as if good conduct matters most, and his behaviour itself is a judgment to this effect. But when asked why virtue matters, the answer he gives, if he makes anything at all of the question, is that it is for the sake of the natural goods. We should note that for a person to count as good and as living a life of virtue, it is not necessary that he have any general view about why virtue is important. Nor is it necessary that he think about his own virtues or about his actions as exercises of virtue. He may simply make and stand by good decisions, each as it comes along.[13]

The Laconian, then, has the virtues, and performs virtuous actions virtuously—that is, for their own sake; his character and his actions are alike good. But are his virtues noble, and does he act nobly? A few lines later Aristotle gives an answer to the second question. At 1249^{a}15 we are told that the person who thinks the virtues are for the sake of exterior goods does noble things only *per accidens*. (It is not suggested that he does *good* things only *per accidens*.) But what of the actual virtues themselves? They are noble in themselves (1248^{b}21–5), but are they noble in the Laconian? Perhaps Aristotle's final answer would be that they are noble by nature, but not noble in the case of the Laconian, just as wealth is good by nature but not good in the case of the vicious.[14]

---

[13] Broadie, *Ethics with Aristotle*, 379.

[14] Against this, Woods says: 'Things may be described as fine [noble] which can be recognized as having merit appropriate to the kind of thing that they are, when viewed from an impersonal standpoint; whereas in Greek thought, when something is called "good" the question "good for whom?" always seems to be in place' (*Aristotle's* Eudemian Ethics, p. 186).

Aristotle goes on to give us a contrast between the Laconian and the truly noble person:

The *kaloi kagathoi* choose noble things for their own sake; and not only these, but also the things which are not noble by nature, but merely good by nature, are noble for them. For things are noble when the reason for which people do them and choose them is noble, and that is why to the noble person the natural goods are noble. (1249ª3-7)[15]

The noble person possesses the things that are noble in themselves, namely the virtues; and he does the things that are noble (namely virtuous actions); and he does them for the sake of their own nobility, not for the sake of the non-noble goods which are the highest value of the Laconian (1248ᵇ34-7). But in the case of the noble person it is not only virtuous acts and dispositions which are noble: the natural goods, which for the vicious person are evil, and for the Laconian person are merely good, are for him noble too. These natural goods are ennobled by the noble purposes for which the noble person uses them. It is just and fitting that the noble person should have such things as wealth, high birth, and power, since when they are his they are noble (1249ª4-14). The nobility of these objects of course is not intrinsic nobility, but derivative nobility, a nobility deriving from the noble purposes of the noble person.

Aristotle says:

To the *kalos kagathos* what is useful is also noble; but for the many there is not this harmony between the useful and the noble, for things prima facie good are not good for them, as they are for the good man; to the *kalos kagathos* they are also noble, for he does many noble deeds by means of them. (1249ª10-15)

We may paraphrase as follows: For the noble person, the noble and the useful are in harmony. (It is not that the two coincide, as some

---

[15] At 1249ª2 there is a serious crux. The MS tradition reads: οὐ γὰρ ὑπάρχει αὐτοῖς τὰ καλὰ δι' αὐτά, καὶ προαιροῦνται καλοὶ κἀγαθοί. As Woods says, the MS readings involve an intolerable shift from those who are not to those who are καλοὶ κἀγαθοί. Dirlmeier and Woods suppose a lacuna. Solomon and Ross alter to καλὰ κἀγαθά. The alteration, though adopted by OCT, is unacceptable because καλὸς κἀγαθός is never used of things but only people. OCT makes a further emendation, taking a cue from the Latin version 'quibuscumque autem existunt propter ipsa'. It proposes that ὅσοις δ' ὑπάρχει δι' αὐτά has dropped out, after τὰ καλὰ δι' αὐτά, so that the passage would mean something like 'Those to whom noble things belong by themselves choose good and noble things'. The construction would be very contorted, and a much simpler emendation would give a better text. If a second τὰ καλὰ δι' αὐτά has dropped out by haplography, the original text would read: οὐ γὰρ ὑπάρχει αὐτοῖς τὰ καλὰ δι' αὐτά. τὰ δὲ καλὰ δι' αὐτὰ προαιροῦνται καλοὶ κἀγαθοί. This is the text translated above.

translators make Aristotle say; not everything that is noble is useful, but everything that is useful is noble.) However, this harmony is highly exceptional. Most people are not good, let alone noble, and so for most people what is useful (i.e. what is prima facie good) is not even good: it is useful only to their own bad purposes. In the case of the good but not noble person, the useful and the good overlap, and whatever is useful is good. But instead of what is useful being ennobled by noble purposes, as it is in the case of the noble person, in the merely good person what is noble—namely virtue—is downgraded by being treated, in the utilitarian manner, as useful for non-noble ends.

In various places in Aristotle's ethical treatises we are told that the virtuous man performs virtuous actions 'for their own sake' or 'because they are noble'. One of the things we learn from the final chapter of the *EE* is that these two expressions are not equivalent. The Laconian performs virtuous actions for their own sake (otherwise he would not be good); but he does not perform them because virtue is noble (otherwise he would be a *kalos kagathos*).

In the *EE* itself the virtuous action is described as action in pursuit of the noble: thus at 1229ª1–2 we are told 'Courage is a following of reason, and reason commands to choose what is noble'; and the courageous man is one who is 'fearless for the sake of the noble'. Again, more generally, at 1230ª27–9: 'virtue makes a man choose everything for the sake of some object, and that object is what is noble.' Here virtue is being described in terms which, as the final chapter of the book will reveal, are strictly appropriate only for the virtuous person who is not only good, but noble. The new character who is introduced in the final book is not the *kalos kagathos* but the mere *agathos*, the 'Laconian' character who performs virtuous actions for their own sake but not because they are noble.[16] He—like the continent and incontinent persons discussed in *AE* C and from time to time in the *EE*—occupies a position intermediate between the virtuous and vicious characters who are presented in an exaggeratedly well-defined trichotomy by the doctrine of the mean.[17]

The introduction of the Laconian, however, does mark two sig-

---

[16] Broadie, *Ethics with Aristotle*, 434, claims that the good man does each particular deed for the sake of the noble. She notes that this is difficult to reconcile with the statement at 1249ª14–16 that the merely good man does noble things *per accidens*.

[17] In my book *The Aristotelian Ethics* I claimed (p. 206) that the Laconian performed virtuous actions as a means to an end, in a utilitarian manner. Having read Broadie I now believe that if the Laconian is to be compared to a utilitarian, it is to a rule-utilitarian rather than an act-utilitarian.

nificant elements in which the Eudemian ethical system differs from the Nicomachean.

First, the attitude to natural goods, such as health and wealth, is very different. In the *NE* wealth is quickly dismissed as a candidate for the supreme good. 'The life of money-making is one undertaken under compulsion, and wealth is evidently not the good we are seeking; for it is merely useful and for the sake of something else' (1096ª5–8). Whereas the discussion of the Laconians shows that the *EE* recognizes that there are people who systematically value wealth, health, and power above virtue; and the *EE* is even prepared to call such people good, provided their pursuit of wealth is within the bounds of virtuous behaviour.[18]

Secondly, the Laconian passage is the most explicit statement of an important theorem about Aristotelian value-systems, which is elsewhere left tacit. The theorem is this: every item in a person's hierarchy of choices takes its value from the highest point in the hierarchy. Thus, if in one person's system virtue is for the sake of wealth, virtue is only a useful good, not a noble one, because wealth is something merely useful. If, in another person's value-system, wealth is for the sake of virtue, then wealth too acquires the nobility which virtue has. Aristotle insists that in ordered choices the higher you go up the series of *hou heneka*, the greater the good must be (otherwise you fall into the category of Laconian).[19]

But what of the supreme point in the Aristotelian hierarchy, namely *eudaimonia*? To this we must return in the next chapter.

---

[18] The Laconian who pursues wealth is not the same as the miser who regards wealth as an ultimate end; unlike the miser, he makes money in order to spend it on other things, though, because he is a Laconian, these other things will not be manifestations of virtue. The sense in which, in the *EE*, the natural goods are things desirable in themselves is well explained by Broadie. '[T]he process of building up wealth, health or political power is not logically structured by any specific further purpose for which these results will be employed ... The practical skill of money making is the same whether one plans to use money for war, education, or pleasure ... This is why Aristotle classifies the natural goods as ends and as things desirable in themselves. This does not refer to motive, but to the logical form of effective practical seeking. Wealth is something which, in the very form of our seeking, we value as itself and not as a means to something else' (*Ethics with Aristotle*, 382).

[19] This is parallel to his insistence in the theoretical order that in a scientific syllogism the premisses must be better known than the conclusion.

2

PERFECTION AND HAPPINESS

In the hierarchy of choices in the specification of volition, happiness has a special place. It is not just an end, but a perfect end. In a familiar passage of the first book of the *NE* Aristotle has this to say:

Now something that is pursued for its own sake we call more perfect than what is pursued because of something else; and something that is never chosen because of something else we call more perfect than the things that are chosen both for their own sake and because of the other thing; and what we call unqualifiedly perfect is that which is always chosen for itself and never because of anything else.

Now happiness, more than anything else, seems to be a thing of this kind. (1097ª30–4)

There has been much discussion about the Greek word which is translated 'perfect'. The word means literally 'endy'. In some contexts the most appropriate English version may be 'complete'. Here the most appropriate translation is 'supreme'; and the sense has been well explained by Heinaman:

I take 1097ª30–ᵇ6 to be saying:

x is more *teleion* than *y* if
  (i) *x* is chosen for its own sake and *y* is always chosen for the sake of something else, or
  (ii) *x* is chosen for its own sake and never for the sake of anything else, and *y* is chosen for its own sake and for the sake of something else.

Aristotle gives wealth as an example of an end which is chosen for the sake of something else (1097ª27) and honour as an example of something chosen for its own sake (1097ᵇ24). So honour is more *teleion* than wealth on Aristotle's criterion.[1]

Happiness is the most perfect (*teleion*) of all things: it is chosen for its own sake and never for anything else; it is never chosen for the sake of honour, or pleasure, or understanding, or virtue. It is more perfect

---

[1] 'Eudaimonia and Self-sufficiency', 38.

than things like wealth which are always chosen for the sake of something else; and it is more perfect than things like honour which are chosen for their own sake, but also for the sake of something else (1097^b1-6).

Perfection is given by Aristotle as a formal property which happiness must possess. But he also makes use of the notion of perfection in giving his own definition of happiness after developing the argument from the function of man. The good for man, he says, turns out to be activity of soul in accordance with virtue, and if there are several virtues, according to the best and most perfect (1098^a16-18).

In this passage, is the most appropriate translation 'complete' or 'supreme'? This has been much controverted between supporters of the comprehensive and the dominant interpretation of Aristotle's eudaemonism, and the decision between the two versions plays a crucial role in the analysis of this key passage in the debate. Supporters of the comprehensive theory say that Aristotle is here talking about complete virtue, moral plus intellectual; supporters of the dominant theory say that Aristotle is talking about supreme, i.e. intellectual, virtue.

In favour of the translation 'complete', it may be said that in the very next line Aristotle goes on to speak of 'a perfect life', and his expression clearly means a complete life as opposed to a partial or interrupted one. But if we take it that *teleion* has the same meaning here as it had in the preamble to the function argument of 1097^b24-1098^a17, then it must mean 'final' or 'supreme'. According to that sense, as we have seen, honour is more perfect than wealth; but honour is not more complete or comprehensive than wealth.

Heinaman, who argues powerfully for this interpretation, concludes that in the second part of the sentence under discussion Aristotle is referring to perfect happiness (namely, contemplation), not just to happiness, and is therefore going on to make a further point, derived not just from the function argument but also from the notion of finality.

I would prefer to say that Aristotle is at this point leaving room for, rather than arguing for, the identification of contemplation with perfect happiness. It is only later that he goes on to distinguish between moral and intellectual virtues; and within intellectual virtues between wisdom and understanding. Only in book 10 are moral virtues, plus the intellectual virtue of wisdom, which is interlinked with them, eliminated as constituents of the supreme happiness. But

I would agree that the appropriate sense of 'most perfect virtue' here is 'supreme virtue'. It seems to me an error to say either that in this passage 'most perfect virtue' means total virtue, or that it means intellectual virtue.

John Cooper, when he first addressed this topic, took the expression in the latter sense, saying that it means a most final virtue, one that has its value entirely in itself; this he claimed, must be the virtue of the contemplative intellect.[2] Roche criticized Cooper in the following terms:

This interpretation must be wrong. For in the very same discussion which Cooper cites, Aristotle says that intelligence (*nous*) and *every virtue* are chosen both for themselves *and* for the sake of *eudaimonia*. Since *sophia* is a virtue, Aristotle cannot, without contradiction, assert that it is *teleiotate* in the sense insisted on by Cooper.[3]

Roche's criticism fails. All virtues are chosen for the sake of happiness (for the sake of their activities); but virtues other than understanding, according to Aristotle (1177ᵇ3), are ones where we pursue something other than their activity for its own sake. In the case of *sophia*, we do not seek anything other than the contemplation which is its exercise. So that understanding can be the most perfect virtue, in the sense defined, even though the virtue of understanding is not as perfect as happiness itself (which, on the intellectualist view, is not understanding but the contemplation which is the exercise of understanding).

None the less I agree with Roche that it is not correct to say that in this passage Aristotle is referring to understanding. Rather, he is giving a description which he will show only later, in book 10, to be uniquely satisfied by *sophia*. According to the traditional view, the clause 'if there are several virtues, in accordance with the best and most perfect' does no more than keep open a place for the eventual doctrine of *NE* 10 that happiness is the activity of the supreme virtue of understanding.

It is difficult to deny that in *NE* 10 the view of happiness which is adopted is a dominant one. Even Ackrill, the doyen of the inclusive interpreters, does not try to deny this. In book 10 the argument goes: If happiness is activity which is the exercise of virtue, it is reasonable that it should be activity which is the exercise of the most excellent virtue:

---

[2] Cooper, *Reason and Human Good*, 100 n. 10.
[3] Roche, 'ERGON and EUDAIMONIA in *Nicomachean Ethics* I', 186.

and this will be that of the best thing in us (1177^a12-13). This is either the understanding (*nous*) or something like it, so the activity of this in accordance with its proper virtue will be perfect happiness. In this passage, whichever sense we give to 'perfect' we are presented with a dominant, intellectualist interpretation.

Aristotle then goes on to show in book 10 that theoretic contemplation possesses all the qualities which, according to book 1, were properties of happiness. Thus: it is the best activity, most continuous and durable, the pleasantest; the most self-sufficient; it is loved for its own sake, and therefore perfect in the sense of final (1177^a19-^b24). If Aristotle underwent a spectacular change in his view of happiness between book 1 and book 10 he wrote book 10 in such a way as to cover up the change entirely.[4]

In the *EE* definition of happiness the word 'perfect' does not betray the same ambiguity as it does in the *NE*. In the second book of the *EE* we are told:

Since happiness was something perfect, and life is either perfect or imperfect, and virtue likewise (one being whole virtue, the other a part) and the activity of what is imperfect is imperfect, therefore happiness would be the activity of a perfect life in accordance with perfect virtue. (1219^a35-9)

Here 'perfect' must have the sense 'complete'. We are explicitly told that perfect virtue is whole virtue and imperfect virtue is partial virtue; similarly, perfect and imperfect life must be complete or incomplete life. Happiness therefore must be a complete whole: and indeed, a few lines later (1219^b7) we are explicitly told that nothing imperfect is happy, because it is not complete. The complete whole which is happiness is the activity of complete virtue in a complete life. So that when Aristotle goes on to list examples of moral and intellectual virtues, it is clear that the activities of these virtues are all supposed to be parts of happiness. The soul's virtue whose activity is the supreme good is a virtue which is constituted by the several virtues of the different parts of the soul. 'Just as good bodily condition is compounded of the partial virtues, so is the virtue of the soul considered as an end' (1220^a3-4). Given what has preceded (especially 1219^a31-3), 'considered as an end' must be shorthand for 'whose activity constitutes the end'.

This complete virtue, whose exercise in a complete life constituted *eudaimonia* according to *EE* II, is the sum total of the virtues discussed

[4] See p. 87 below.

in the central books of the *EE*, and is treated again as a unified whole
in the first part of the final chapter of *EE* VIII under the description
kalokagathia.

Aristotle says that anyone who deserves the description *kalos
kagathos* must have all the individual virtues, just as a body can only be
healthy if all, or at least the main parts of it, are healthy (1248ᵇ8-16).
The language of this passage echoes closely that of book II, and makes
clear that *kalokagathia* is the perfect or complete virtue whose activity
was there described as *eudaimonia*. Aristotle, as we have seen in the
previous chapter, goes on to make a distinction between natural and
noble goods, and on the basis of this to contrast two different kinds of
good people: the *kaloi kagathoi* who pursue the natural goods only for
the sake of the virtuous actions for which they are useful, and the
'Laconians', of a utilitarian cast, who value virtue for the sake of non-
moral goods.

The discussion of *kalokagathia* ends by saying that it is perfect virtue.
At this point, perhaps, the Eudemian use of 'perfect' combines the two
senses which we distinguished in the Nicomachean passages. For
while *kalokagathia* is undoubtedly perfect in the sense of complete,
since it is the amalgam of all the partial virtues, it is also defined—as
the immediately preceding passage has made clear—by being targeted
on a particular final or supreme end, namely *to kalon* or nobility.[5]

The *NE* insisted that *eudaimonia* was perfect in the sense of being
the one end which was sought always for itself and never for the sake
of anything else. Other things might be done for the sake of happiness,
but happiness was not for the sake of anything. It is not altogether
clear what is meant by 'choosing something for the sake of happiness',
despite Aristotle's own gloss that when we do this we judge that by
making the choice we shall be happy. Broadie has the following
comment on the passages where Aristotle says that holding happiness
to be the greatest good is being prepared to do everything else for the
sake of it (e.g. 1102ᵃ2, 1140ᵇ18-19):

This set of positions is difficult to assess, because Aristotle does not explain
how we are to take the crucial expression 'for the sake of (heneka) happiness'.
To make his claims plausible, we have to stretch this to mean 'having regard to
happiness'. Thus the central good functions sometimes as a constraint rather
than a goal in the ordinary sense of a positively aimed for objective. I would

[5] The sense of 'final' is perhaps also to be found already in one passage of book II,
1219ᵃ28.

stop doing what might adversely affect it, even if I was not doing that thing *in order to* obtain it. But even with this allowance, it may seem intolerably artificial to hold that, if we make one good central in our lives, then *every* other is viewed in relation to it.[6]

Whether or not this is a fair interpretation of the *NE*, there seems undoubtedly to be a difference between the Nicomachean notion of 'doing things for the sake of happiness' and the emphasis in the *EE* that the *kalos kagathos* does things 'because they are noble'. In the *EE*, as in the *NE*, happiness is an end; and we know from the book's first paragraph that happiness is the noblest thing there is (1214^a8). But the way in which happiness functions as an end seems to be not that the happy man does things in order to be happy, but rather that he does, for the sake of their own nobility, the noble things which in fact constitute the happiness which makes life worth while (cf. 1215^b30, 1216^a11-13).

For the ideally virtuous man, according to the *EE*, the concepts *good*, *pleasant*, and *noble* coincide in their application. We can bring this into relief by examining the cases where the concepts do not coincide.

Firstly, if what is pleasant for a man differs from what is good for him, then he is not yet perfectly good but incontinent. The road to virtue, Aristotle says, is through pleasure: 'What is noble must be pleasant; but when these two do not coincide a man cannot yet be perfectly good, for incontinence may arise; for incontinence is precisely the discrepancy between the good and the pleasant in the passions' (1237^a8-9).

Secondly, if what is good for him does not coincide with what is noble for him, then he is not yet *kalos kagathos* but merely good; for, as we have seen, for the noble person the natural goods of health and wealth and power are not only beneficial but noble, since they subserve his virtuous activity. So, for this ideal person, goodness and nobility coincide. What of pleasantness?

Pleasure has already been discussed: what kind of thing it is, and in what sense it is a good; and how things which are pleasant *simpliciter* are noble, and things which are good *simpliciter* are also pleasant. But there cannot be pleasure except in action: and so the truly happy man will also have the most pleasant life (1249^a18-21).

Whereas something can be noble or good whether it is a state or an activity, only an activity can be pleasant. States are not pleasant, but only the exercises of states. So it is in the noble activities of the noble and good man that the highest pleasure is to be found, and it is there that pleasure, goodness, and nobility meet. But the noble activities of the good man are the exercises of perfect virtue with which happiness was identified in book I. So the promise of book I has been fulfilled, to show how, *pace* the Delian inscription, goodness, nobility, and pleasure coincide in *eudaimonia*.

Among the noble activities of perfect virtue are the activities of the philosophic life. If *kalokagathia* is a synthesis of the virtues of the parts of the soul in the way that health is a synthesis of the health of various parts of the body, then it must include the virtues of the intellectual parts of the soul as well as of the passional part. But not only is it part of happiness, it also sets the standard to which the activities of the other virtues must conform if they are to remain within the realm of virtue and happiness ($1249^{a}21-^{b}15$).

Virtuous action consists in executing choices about the right amount of things—of the passions and external goods—which are the field of operation of the moral virtues. What particular behaviour in concrete circumstances counts as virtuous living cannot be settled, Aristotle tells us at the end of the *EE*, without consideration of the contemplation and service of God ($1249^{b}15-22$).

These difficult final passages of the *EE* will be the subject of a later chapter.[7] We can sum up the results of our present enquiry by contrasting the different notions of perfection in the two treatises. The word 'perfect' (*teleion*) in both treatises can bear either of the meanings 'complete' or 'final'. But in the definition of happiness the Nicomachean treatise places the emphasis on finality, while the Eudemian places the emphasis on comprehensiveness.

[7] See p. 86 below.

3

HAPPINESS AND SELF-SUFFICIENCY

PRIOR to elaborating the discussion of human function in the seventh chapter of book 1 of the *NE*, Aristotle lays down two conditions which happiness must fulfil. It must be perfect, and it must be self-sufficient. In the previous chapter we considered the perfection of happiness. The property which must now be considered is its self-sufficiency.

Aristotle, in making self-sufficiency a requirement of happiness, defines the self-sufficient (*to autarkes*) as 'that which on its own makes life worthy of choice and lacking in nothing' (1097^{b}14–15). Aristotle's requirement that happiness must be self-sufficient is used as a principal argument by those who wish to press an inclusive inter-pretation of the concept of happiness in *NE* 1. If perfect happiness on its own makes life desirable and lacking in nothing, then, so it is argued, it cannot be restricted solely to contemplation. For obviously there are all sorts of other goods which would be lacking in a life of pure contemplation.

Thus, for instance, T. Irwin has argued that 'A complete and self-sufficient good is one that all by itself makes life choiceworthy and lacking in nothing. If it really makes life lacking in nothing, a complete good must be comprehensive, nothing can be added to it to make a better good (1097^{b}8–21).'[1]

In considering self-sufficiency, we must distinguish two questions. Which of these two is Aristotle asking?

(1) Is the happy man self-sufficient?
(2) Is *x* by itself sufficient for happiness?

The two questions, though they may be connected, are in themselves quite distinct. Someone, for instance, who regarded love as the essence of happiness might answer the first question in the negative and the second in the affirmative. Aristotle does not maintain in the *NE* that a happy man is self-sufficient—he makes this plain when he discusses the question whether a happy man needs friends (1169^{b}2–1170^{b}19)—but

[1] Irwin, 'Permanent Happiness'.

he does think that contemplation alone (provided the conditions for realizing it have been fulfilled) is sufficient to make a man happy, and he gives as a reason for identifying happiness with contemplation that the contemplative approaches self-sufficiency more closely than the pursuer of the active life. The contemplative, no less than the just man, will need the necessities of life, but he will not need beneficiaries of his well-doing, and he will be able to theorize alone, even though he will do it better with colleagues (1177^a27-35; the point is made again in very similar terms at 1178^a22-^b7).

The discussion of self-sufficiency in *NE* 1 must be taken along with the passage which immediately follows. Aristotle says that when we are looking for happiness we are looking for something which, when not added to anything else, is most choice-worthy—though clearly, if so added, more choice-worthy with even the least additional good (1097^b16-20). This passage is most naturally taken as ruling out the comprehensive interpretation of *eudaimonia*.[2] If happiness were meant as an inclusive end, as the sum total of goods sought for their own sake, it would be absurd to speak of goods additional to happiness. Hence, Aristotle does not consider happiness as an inclusive end—unless he means the suggestion of addition to be absurd.

Some scholars, notably Ackrill, maintain that he does, saying that the condition 'if so added' is a *per impossibile* condition, because happiness already contains all goods which could possibly have been added to it.[3] John Cooper, too, regards this passage as establishing that happiness is an inclusive good. So let us look at the text more closely. It may be literally translated as follows:

> We think (happiness) most choice-worthy of all things, without being counted along with other things—but if so counted clearly made more choice-worthy by the addition of even the least of goods. (1097^b16-20)

There is an ambiguity in the Greek which my translation seeks to preserve. (1) By 'without being counted along with other things' Aristotle may mean 'if it is not counted along with everything else' and by 'if so counted' he will then mean 'if it is, as it might be, counted along with something else'. The sense would then be that happiness is that activity, or good, which if considered in itself and not conjoined with any other activity or good, is the most choice-worthy of all.

---

[2] See Kenny, 'Happiness', 101; Clark, *Aristotle's Man*, 153-4.
[3] Ackrill, *Aristotle on EUDAIMONIA*, 12. Irwin actually writes the counterfactuality into his translation, p. 15.

(2) The clause 'without being counted along with other things' may be not conditional, but explanatory: 'it is not, of course, the kind of thing that can be counted as one thing among others.' The 'if so counted' must then be read as an impossible counterfactual: 'If it were—*per impossibile*—counted along . . .'

In the abstract, these are both possible translations of the Greek. Like Eustratius and the Latin medieval commentators, and Zeller and Clark in modern times, I regard (1) as the more natural reading of the syntax of the text. Cooper points out that Aspasius, Alexander, and Heliodorus, followed by a host of modern commentators, read the text in the second way; he dismisses the Latin tradition as due to Christian bias; and he concludes that most interpreters take Aristotle to be setting down as an agreed premiss that happiness is the best comprehensive ordering of first-order goods.[4] But the matter, as he says, is not a simple one.

There are two quite different reasons which may be offered for saying that happiness cannot be counted along with other goods. One is that happiness includes other goods, so that to count it with one of them would involve counting something twice; the other is that happiness is a supreme end to which other things are means, and that means and ends are not commensurable. Some of the authors whose support Cooper claims take the one view, and some of them take the other. Alexander takes the first view (as does the author of the *Magna Moralia*, 1184ᵃ26); Heliodorus takes the second view; Aspasius, as is his wont, puts forward both views as if unconscious of the incompatibility between them.[5] A consensus in favour of the thesis that happiness cannot be counted along with other goods is not the same thing, therefore, as a consensus that happiness is a comprehensive ordering of the first-order goods.

But even if (2) is the correct reading, it does not follow that Aristotle is here viewing happiness as an ordering of first-order goods. Apart from syntax, there are two reasons why it is unlikely that Aristotle has in mind here a comprehensive good. First, he is listing agreed attributes of happiness: but the views of others so far discussed (e.g. 1095ᵃ18–28) have been views identifying happiness with some

---

[4] Cooper, review of Kenny, 384.

[5] If we have happiness we have all the other goods: *CAG* xix. 17. 8; happiness is incommensurable in the way that ends are incommensurable with productive means: *CAG* xix. 17. 4. 2; there is an allusion to *Topics* 3, 117ᵃ17, where the point is made that ends plus means are not more choice-worthy than ends alone.

particular highly valued good, not views regarding happiness as an inclusive goal. Secondly, if the reason why happiness cannot be numbered with other goods is that it includes them, it follows that it must include 'even the least of goods', such as the attractive hair mentioned by Eustratius; but this is surely absurd.

The most recent treatment of this passage is by Stephen White in his paper 'Aristotelian Happiness'. The expression 'counted together', he says, envisages a list of goods. Does the participle represent an indicative thesis, or a counterfactual thesis? And does 'counting together' entail treating happiness as a single item, such as honour or virtue or pleasure, or does it allow for some sort of composite of other items on the list?

If happiness is a composite, it would be absurd to count it together with its parts, and the thesis would be counterfactual. Many scholars[6] have argued in reverse that taking the counterfactual interpretation implies that happiness is a composite. On the other hand, White argues, taking the passage indicatively so as to allow for the possibility of counting happiness together with other goods does not entail that it is a single good. 'Happiness could consist of a subset of the goods on the list; and unless it includes *everything* good, counting it together with lesser goods does not entail counting its parts twice over.'[7]

White himself takes it as indicative: Aristotle's mention of 'the added good' implies a possible result, not a logically absurd hypothesis. The resulting greater good would be more than the minimum required for happiness. Happiness can be counted together with other good things; further goods can be added to it and it can be made better. 'But to use this procedure to construct the best good possible, and to look for something so good that nothing ever *could* be added to it, would be to mistake the kind of self-sufficiency possessed by happiness.'[8]

In support of this interpretation White cites passages from the *Rhetoric* (1363^b18–20) and *Topics* (117^a16–21). The *Topics* passage tells us that to count happiness together with anything that is simply a means to happiness would not yield a more choice-worthy whole; but that does not mean that happiness cannot be improved by the addition of some other goods not presupposed by it, and since the final end does not have to include all choice-worthy ends, there do exist other goods to be added. When Aristotle tells us, in *AE* C (1172^b23), that

---

[6] White cites Grant, Burnet, Gauthier-Jolif, Hardie, Ackrill, Cooper, and Irwin.
[7] 'Aristotelian Happiness', 120.
[8] Ibid. 120.

'the good does not become more choice-worthy when anything is added to it' he is not expressing his own view, but reporting Plato's, in reported speech.[9]

One reason why Aristotle rejects Plato's view is that happiness would be impossible to obtain. White explains why this would be so.

Ackrill illustrates the orthodox view with the example of a hearty breakfast of bacon, eggs, and tomatoes: self-sufficiency entails, he claims, that happiness is like a breakfast of all three, since that is better than any single item or pair on its own. But if nothing *could* be added to the best breakfast, it would have to include kippers, melon, muffins, potatoes, and so on *ad nauseam*; worse, it would have to include all the eggs and bacon in the world, and so on *ad maiorem nauseam*.[10]

White's own interpretation rests on a distinction between happiness as comprehensive, and happiness as inclusive. For the *NE*, he believes, happiness is inclusive in that it includes more than one component: contemplation all by itself cannot be identical with happiness, even happiness of the best sort. But while inclusive, it is not comprehensive: it does not contain all goods, and it can be improved by the addition of extra goods.

---

[9] This point was earlier made by Heinaman, 'Eudaimonia and Self-sufficiency', 43.

[10] 'Aristotelian Happiness', 123. In an appendix White considers the attitude of ancient commentators. Eustratius, he says, suggests an inclusive account of happiness when he lists a range of goods that he calls part of happiness. But he does not present an all-inclusive or comprehensive account, because he does not assert that all of these parts are necessary for happiness. Happiness is choice-worthy, but becomes more choice-worthy with an added good. Eustratius does not endorse either a single dominant end or an all-inclusive end: what his account characterizes is rather a dominant composite that still can be improved. White rejects Cooper's allegation that Eustratius' view is distorted by the Christian consideration that only God is a thing so good that it cannot be bettered. Aquinas had no difficulty in distinguishing the perfection of God from that of happiness. For Aquinas, though happiness can be improved, 'Still, the person's desire does not remain dissatisfied, since desire regulated by reason—such as the happy person's must be—has no dissatisfaction about things that are not necessary, even though they can be acquired' (Aquinas, *Summa contra Gentiles*, 1934 edn., 116).

After considering the relevant passages in Aspasius, Heliodorus, and Alexander on the *Topics*, White concludes that all the commentators interpret the passage as meaning that other goods can be added to happiness; the objection to counting together is that it is a ranking at the same level, and overlooks the special status of goals. 'Hence, Kenny is right when he claims that they understand [the passage] as indicative; and Cooper is right when he claims that they reject looking for the highest goal by "counting together". But both are wrong to equate the technical term "counting together" with the simple process of adding more goods. If Kenny is right that happiness is a dominant end, Cooper is also right that it is an inclusive end; but Kenny is wrong in thinking that it is a *single* dominant end, and the phrasing of orthodox interpreters is wrong in suggesting an *all*-inclusive end' ('Aristotelian Happiness', 143).

The distinction between comprehensive and inclusive goods is a sound one, and I agree with White that there is something absurd in the idea of a good which is so comprehensive that it includes all the goods that there are. When Aristotle says that a self-sufficient good makes life 'lacking in nothing' he does not mean that it contains everything, but that it is not deficient or needy. Nowhere does Aristotle say that happiness contains all possible goods, and the suggestion that it is a good which is inclusive without being comprehensive seems to me to be an accurate representation of his position in the *EE*. But for a number of reasons it seems to me wrong to regard the *NE* as presenting happiness as an inclusive, even if not comprehensive, good.

In trying to show this I will draw on the excellent treatment of the issue by Robert Heinaman. For Aristotle, according to Heinaman, the total life of a human being consists in a variety of types of activity, e.g. perceiving, growing, digesting, thinking. Each of these types of activity is called by Aristotle a 'life', and when he identifies happiness with a certain kind of life, it is 'life' in this sense that he means, not 'total life'. When he identifies happiness with the rational life, he is identifying it with intellectual activity, not with a certain kind of total life.

There are at least four different questions to be distinguished to which Aristotle gives different answers but which comprehensive interpreters tend to assimilate:

(1) What life is the highest kind of *eudaimonia*?
(2) What life counts as *eudaimonia*?
(3) What components will make up the total life of the happy man?
(4) What must a man have in order to be happy?[11]

Heinaman believes that the inclusive interpretation of the *NE* rests on a failure to distinguish between the first three questions. He offers his own answers to these questions, all of which I believe to be correct. The answer to (1) is that contemplation is the highest kind of *eudaimonia*. The answer to (2) is that both contemplation and moral action count as *eudaimonia*. The answer to (3) will include a variety of activities such as, for instance, perception and digestion. The answer to (4) will include friends, money, food, and drink.

Commentators' failure to distinguish these questions is the more understandable because in the *NE* Aristotle does not explicitly distinguish, as he does in the *EE*, between the constituents of good living and the necessary conditions of good living (1214^b10-25). As

---

[11] Heinaman, 'Eudaimonia and Self-sufficiency', 33.

Aristotle says in the *EE*, failure to make the distinction is the cause of controversy about happiness, because some take to be parts of happiness what are merely its indispensable conditions (1214^b24-7).

Items (3) and (4) above are clearly only indispensable conditions, and not parts of happiness; and this is true whether we consider the Nicomachean or the Eudemian treatment. What of (1) and (2)? Here, in my view, there is a difference between the two treatises. In the *EE*, contemplation and moral action are two parts of a single happiness; in the *NE*, there are two different kinds of happiness, contemplation the superior one, and moral action the inferior one. If there are parts of happiness (and the *NE* never uses this expression outside the disputed books),[12] then the parts of contemplative happiness would be the study of the different philosophical disciplines, and the parts of moral happiness would be the activities of the different moral virtues. Nowhere is it suggested in the *NE*, as it is in the *EE*, that contemplation and moral virtue are each constituent parts of a single overall happiness.

This view of the nature of Nicomachean happiness is, of course, based principally on the treatment of the topic in the seventh chapter of book 10. But it can be reinforced if we look again at the two most important passages from book 1.

At the end of the function argument we read:

If this is the case, human good turns out to be the activity of soul in accordance with virtue, and if there are more than one virtues, in the exercise of the best and most perfect. (1098^a16-18)

The first question to be settled is this. Is the second half of the quoted sentence a conclusion of the function argument, or something further added? It seems more natural to take it as part of the conclusion, and this is one of the strong points of the inclusive interpretation of book 1. Thus, Roche argues that there is nothing in the function argument which suggests that the human good should be confined to activities which are the exercise of contemplative virtue. To reach such an intellectualist conclusion, the argument should have concluded 'the function of man is activity of soul in accordance with theoretical reason'; but of course it says nothing of the kind.[13] It must be agreed, I think, that the second half of the sentence, if interpreted in the dominant sense, is not a conclusion of the function argument, but a separate, self-standing development.

---

[12] See Kenny, *The Aristotelian Ethics*, 66 n. 3.
[13] Roche, 'ERGON and EUDAIMONIA', 183.

The difficulties in taking the section in accordance with the inclusive view, however, are considerably greater. To do so, we have to translate the final part of the sentence not as most translators do, as 'the best and most perfect among them', but, with Ackrill, as 'the best and most complete virtue', that is to say, virtue which is the whole of which the individual virtues are parts.

There are several difficulties about this. It is true that the Greek word *aretē*, like the English word 'virtue', can be used as a mass-noun (as in 'a man of great virtue') or as a count-noun (as in 'a man of many virtues'), but on Ackrill's view Aristotle is made to switch from the mass-noun to the count-noun use and back again to the mass-noun use within a space of ten words.[14]

In the previous chapter I discussed the sense in which happiness in the *NE* is perfect, and argued that this did not mean 'complete' in the sense of inclusive, but 'final' in the sense of being the summit of the hierarchy of choice.

If the inclusive interpretation of this passage is strained, an even greater strain is put on the interpretation when we turn to the parallel passage in *NE* 1. 8 in the discussion of the Delian inscription. The properties severed by the inscription, Aristotle says, 'all belong to the best activities; and these, or one of them, namely the best, we identify with happiness' (1099ª30-1). The most an inclusive interpreter can claim here is that the inclusive view is offered here as one alternative. It is more natural—not only with hindsight from book 10 but also in the light of the function passage—to read the 'or' as epexegetic rather than disjunctive: 'These activities, or—to speak more precisely—one among them, the best, we identify with happiness.' It is certainly impossible for an inclusive interpreter to say that the dominant interpretation is *ruled out* by this passage.

---

[14] It is noteworthy that the commentators on whom Cooper relied to support the inclusive interpretation of 1097ᵇ16 ff. see the description in the present passage of 'the best and most perfect virtue' as a forward look to the theoretical life described in book 10. Thus explicitly Aspasius (*CAG* xix/1. 19. 2), despite Aspasius' own preference for the Eudemian ideal of *kalokagathia* which is there manifest; thus implicitly Heliodorus (*CAG* xix/2. 14. 19 compared with 221. 21). Gauthier and Jolif compare the passage with 1097ª23, 1097ª30, and 1099ª29, and remark excellently 'La réticence est calculée. Aristote pour l'instant va se contenter de conclure que le bien final, c'est le bonheur. Mais il se réserve de reprendre la question au livre X et de montrer cette fois que le bonheur final, c'est la contemplation (X, 7, 1177b24). Sans encore s'engager, il ne cesse tout au long de l'Éthique de préparer le terrain pour cette conclusion suprême' (*L'Éthique à Nicomaque*, ii/1. 51). This testimony is the more striking as Gauthier and Jolif have defended—implausibly, as Cooper has well argued (*Reason and Human Good*, 157-60)—a view of book 10 which represents a view of *eudaimonia* as a mixed life.

Those who wish to interpret book 1 in an inclusive way have two difficult options when they come to book 10. Either—like Ackrill—they accept the intellectualist interpretation of book 10, which seems plain on the face of it; or they must implausibly explain away the intellectualism of book 10. Thus Roche:

> The first book, as I have argued, presents a concept of the *ergon* and nature of man which involves practical (and moral) elements no less than theoretical ones. So if the tenth book identifies man with his theoretical intellect, we must attribute to Aristotle a contradiction so evident that he could not possibly have failed to see it.

> It appears that unless one is willing to accept the idea that *NE* 10. 7–8 is a textual anomaly, the traditional intellectualist interpretation of these passages must be abandoned. The rejection of this view will require the development of a plausible inclusive end interpretation of Aristotle's discussion of the good in these chapters of the Ethics.[15]

On the face of it, the concluding section of the *NE*, instead of offering, like the *EE*, a single life containing all the values sought by the promoters of the three traditional lives, offers us a first-class, perfect happiness, consisting of the exercise of understanding, and an alternative, second-class career, consisting in the exercise of wisdom and the moral virtues.

A later chapter will be devoted to this topic. In the present chapter, let us complete the treatment of the topic of self-sufficiency as a characteristic of happiness. Self-sufficiency is contrasted with vulnerability; and no one has discussed the vulnerability of Aristotle's happy man with such skill and sensitivity as Nussbaum.[16]

Nussbaum sets Aristotle's position in the context of the problem: What power has luck or fortune to influence the goodness or praiseworthiness of human life? One extreme position is that good living is a lucky gift of the gods. At the other extreme is the view that luck has no power at all and that the relevant causal factors are all within the agent's firm grasp. This extreme position can be reached by two different routes. On the one hand, one may identify the good life with good activity, but claim that only invulnerable activities are valuable; on the other hand, one may claim that good states are enough without good activities, and the good life can be lived on the rack. Aristotle wants to save the appearances in each of these views.

---

[15] Roche, 'ERGON and EUDAIMONIA', 194.
[16] Nussbaum, *The Fragility of Goodness*, 318–72.

The view that happiness is a matter entirely of luck is too much at odds with our evaluative beliefs. Human life, according to the *NE*, is worth living only if a good life can be secured by an effort which is within most people's capacity (1099^b18-25). In the *EE* we are told that life would not be worth living if there were only the things we do and suffer through luck (1215^b27 ff.). The belief that we choose, and the belief that choice counts for a lot, 'are beliefs that we use whenever we act; whenever we engage in ethical inquiry (for if it's all up to luck such inquiry has no point); whenever we argue about a practical decision. To deny them—especially inside an ethical inquiry—approaches the sort of self-refuting position of which Aristotle convicted the opponent of the principle of non-contradiction.'[17]

Against those who say that *eudaimonia* is invulnerable to luck because it is a state, Aristotle first argues that *eudaimonia* is not a state—everyone says it is good living and acting. Someone living all adult life asleep or in irreversible coma would not be living a good life, to be praised and congratulated. In a race it is those who run well, not those who are fittest, who are applauded. 'The opponent's very account of the case may be incoherent; for we do not know what it means to say of someone in irreversible coma that a virtuous condition is retained.'[18]

Without going so far as to claim that happiness consists merely in an unexercised state, a philosopher might claim that the important activities are the internal ones of the soul, and happiness is therefore compatible with prison, slavery, and other misfortunes which remove opportunities for external activities. One might cite the cheerfulness and creativity shown by some great and good men in prison. One might think of Sir Thomas More, answering his wife's laments about his captivity with the words 'Is not this house as nigh heaven as mine own?'; or of Bertrand Russell, who wrote his best philosophical monograph while imprisoned as a conscientious objector. Nussbaum counters this line of thought by asking: Cannot the inner activity of the prisoner be hampered by pain and deprivation? Certainly Aristotle said that those who say the person on the wheel, or victim of overturned fortune, is happy as long as he is good are saying nothing (*AE* C, 1153^b21). In sum: if only states are valuable, then the happiness of the virtuous is invulnerable but vegetable; if inner activity is valuable, then that too is vulnerable.

---

[17] Nussbaum, *The Fragility of Goodness*, 321–2.
[18] Ibid. 324.

How far do temporary or partial calamities diminish *eudaimonia*? Activities can be impeded by lack of resources, or cramped by lack of social position, family tragedy, sickness. Aristotle invites us to consider the case of the fall of King Priam: a virtuous man deprived of family friends and resources. Such a case shows that it is possible to be dislodged from living well. 'Aristotle's remarks about Priam and related cases go against a well-established tradition in moral philosophy, both ancient and modern, according to which moral goodness, that which is an appropriate object of ethical praise and blame, cannot be harmed or affected by external circumstances.'[19]

To acquit Aristotle of a view they see as immoral, Kantian commentators claim that in these passages a distinction is drawn between two ethical notions: between *eudaimonia* and *makariotēs*, living well and being happy. The former, they claim, consists in activity in accordance with virtue; the latter in this, plus the blessings of fortune. According to this view, the gifts and reversals of fortune can never diminish *eudaimonia*, i.e. that for which Priam can be praised or blamed; but because they can diminish his enjoyment of his good activity they do diminish contentment and good feeling. This is suspiciously like the Kantian distinction between moral worth and happiness.

Nussbaum maintains, against this position, that in Aristotle's vocabulary the words *eudaimōn* and *makarios* are interchangeable. For Aristotle the good condition of a virtuous person is not, by itself, sufficient for full goodness of living. Our deepest beliefs about value require that the good condition find its full expression in activity; and this activity takes the agent to the world, in such a way that he or she becomes vulnerable to reversals. Any conception of good living that we will consider rich enough to be worth going for will contain this element of risk; for certain central human values are available only in a context of risk. (A divine life would not contain these risky elements: the gods have no political life and no moral virtues.) The vulnerability of the good human being is not indeed unlimited, for even in diminished circumstances his practical wisdom will be flexible enough to show him a way to act well. But the vulnerability is real: and severe or prolonged deprivation and diminution can dislodge from *eudaimonia* itself.[20]

Nussbaum's discussion of Aristotle is imaginative and insightful, and much of it seems to me correct and enlightening. But I do not think it

[19] Ibid. 329.   [20] Ibid. 340.

is a totally accurate account of the relationship between luck and happiness in the *NE*. She is right to reject the attempt to import the Kantian distinction between moral worth and happiness into the Aristotelian context, but I think she is wrong to suggest that Aristotle never makes a technical distinction between *eudaimonia* and *makariotēs*. This pair of terms is, I believe, used to make an important distinction in the discussion of Priam.

In Chapter 10 of the first book of the *NE* Aristotle asks whether a man can be called 'happy' in his lifetime. Solon's dictum 'Wait to see the end' does not mean that it is the dead who are really happy: that is absurd, particularly when happiness is defined as the activity of the soul in accordance with virtue. Perhaps it means that it is not safe to call a man happy until he is dead and beyond the reach of misfortune: but this too seems open to objection. 'Is it not paradoxical that at a time when a man actually is happy this attribute, though true, cannot be applied to him?' (*NE* 1100ᵃ34–5).

The reason that we are reluctant to call a man happy during his life is that misfortune may befall him. But it is quite wrong, Aristotle says, to make our judgement depend on fortune. 'For fortune does not determine whether we fare well or ill, but is, as we said, merely an accessory to human life; activities in conformity with virtue control happiness' (1100ᵇ8–10). It is true that no state that is not durable deserves to be called happiness, but activities in accordance with virtue are the most durable and invulnerable of human activities (1100ᵇ12–14). Although fortune can impede the activities of virtue and thus mar supreme happiness, a happy man can never be made wretched by fortune:

The man who is truly good and wise will bear with dignity whatever fortune may bring, and will always act as nobly as circumstances permit, just as a good general makes the most strategic use of the troops at his disposal, and a good shoemaker makes the best shoe he can from the leather available, and so with experts in all other fields. If this is so, a happy man will never become miserable; but even so, blessedness will not be his if a fate such as Priam's befalls him. (1100ᵇ35–1101ᵃ8)

If a man is equipped with all that is necessary for the exercise of perfect virtue at the present time, then he is happy. But he is supremely happy only if this state of affairs is going to continue until death, which we do not know. It will be true, then, that the word for supreme happiness, *makarios* or blessed, cannot be safely applied until a life is complete.

Makarios, we might say, is a proleptic predicate. And even those who finally deserve the accolade will not be blessed as the gods are; their happiness, even if in the end it survives intact, being a merely human thing, will have been forever vulnerable throughout life (1101ª15-21).

Nussbaum can point to many places where Aristotle uses *makarios* and *eudaimōn* apparently as synonyms. Indeed, in this very passage, when he wants to make the point that the happy man, though he can fall from happiness, cannot fall as far as wretchedness, he does so once using the word *makarios* (1100ᵇ34) and once using the word *eudaimōn*. But as he seeks further precision and needs to introduce a distinction, he seizes on this pair of words to do so:

Why then should we not say that he is happy who is active in accordance with perfect virtue, and is sufficiently endowed with external goods, not for some chance period, but through a perfect life? Or must we add 'and who is destined to live thus and have a death to match his life'? Certainly the future is obscure to us, while happiness, we maintain, is an end and something perfect in every way. If so, we shall call blessed those among the living in whom these conditions are, and will continue to be, fulfilled—but blessed *humans*. (1101ª14-21)

If we do not take Aristotle to be making a distinction here between blessedness and happiness, we make nonsense of the points which he has just been making. For the passage comes after a long presentation of the thesis—so eloquently expounded by Nussbaum—that happiness is vulnerable and can be lost. But if 'blessed' meant the same as 'happy' in this passage, then Aristotle would be saying that someone is only really happy if he not only currently enjoys the conditions for happiness but will continue to enjoy them until death. But that would mean that happiness could not be lost; someone who fell into misfortunes like Priam would not be someone who had enjoyed a happy life and then lost it: he would be someone whose later career showed that he had never been happy at all.

There are therefore three degrees of fragility in human goodness. Virtue is a stable state: the good man on the rack may, because of his misfortune, cease to be happy (1096ª1-2), but there is no question of his ceasing to be virtuous (1100ᵇ22-3). Happiness is less tough: it can be lost, even though it will not turn into its opposite, the wretchedness of the wicked. The state that is most difficult to characterize is blessedness. It is an elusive state, in that even if someone possesses it, in his lifetime neither he nor anyone else can say with confidence that he has it. From another point of view it is the toughest state, in that if it is once possessed it will never be lost. But even if, *de facto*, it will never be lost, the happiness which constitutes it, in the case of human beings, is permanently fragile until death.

What Aristotle is looking for is a prescription for happiness that will make it as stable as it can possibly be, within the constraints of the intrinsic fragility of human nature. No human condition will achieve the goal of self-sufficiency; none the less, self-sufficiency provides an ideal norm by which to judge the merit of candidates for *eudaimonia*. In book 10 of the *NE* it is used as a criterion to discriminate between the claims of contemplation and the claims of the life of moral virtue to be the supreme happiness.

And the self-sufficiency that is spoken of must belong most to the contemplative activity. For while the *sophos*, as well as a just man and the rest, needs the necessaries of life, when they are sufficiently equipped with things of that sort the just man needs people towards whom and with whom he shall act justly, and the temperate man, the brave man, and each of the others is in the same case, but the *sophos*, even when by himself, can contemplate truth, and the better the more *sophos* he is. (1177^a28 ff.)

The fact that the contemplative is more self-sufficient, and less dependent on friends, than the practitioner of moral virtue is used by Aristotle as one of a series of arguments to show that the primary and perfect happiness consists in contemplation, while the activity of the moral virtues constitutes a life which is happy only in a secondary sense (1177^a12–1178^b10). The *EE* does not privilege the role of contemplation in the same way as *NE* 10; therefore, it does not use self-sufficiency as a criterion for prioritizing forms of happiness in the same way as the *NE* does. (*Autarkeia* is discussed only in the context of the relationship between *eudaimonia* and *philia*, 1238^a12 and 1244^b1–1245^b19). It is to be noted that the sense of self-sufficiency undergoes a shift between *NE* 1 and *NE* 10, in terms of the distinction which we made earlier:[21] whereas in the early book the dominant sense of *autarkes* was 'that which on its own makes a man happy', in the final book the dominant sense seems to be 'that which makes a man happy on his own'.

In the *EE* Aristotle makes a distinction between constituents and necessary or *sine qua non* conditions of happiness (1214^b24–7).[22] Using this terminology, one can bring out clearly the distinction between the two treatises. Whereas in both *Ethics* external goods are only

---

[21] p. 23 above. [22] ἐν τίνι vs. τίνων ἄνευ οὐκ. See p. 28 above.

necessary conditions, in the *EE* wisdom plus moral virtue is a constituent of the primary happiness, while in the *NE* it is at best a necessary condition of it. In the *EE* the best of what can be achieved by action is a state in which all the parts of the soul, *qua* human, are operating well.

That wisdom plus moral virtue is part of happiness, because of being the right functioning of one part of the soul, is stated most clearly not in an exclusively Eudemian book, but in the disputed book on the intellectual virtues, where we are told that wisdom and understanding are both productive of happiness 'not like medical skill in relation to health, but like health itself; it is thus that understanding is productive of happiness: for being a part of virtue entire by being possessed and by being operative it is productive of happiness' (1144^a3-6).[23] This passage spells out the contribution of understanding to happiness; the final book of the *EE* spells out in parallel terms the contribution of the life of virtue. The activity of wisdom plus moral virtues is itself part of the exercise of virtue which constitutes happiness; it has an efficient causal relationship to the contemplative happiness, but it is also itself a form of happiness, by being a form of service to God. It contributes to happiness by being part of it, in the way that good breathing contributes to good singing; not in the way that (say) eating certain foods rather than others may contribute to good singing.

This summary of the Eudemian account of happiness will be amplified later; but at this point it must be noted that the contrast between the two *Ethics* which I have just drawn would be contested by many scholars. Those who favour an inclusive interpretation of Nicomachean *eudaimonia* would argue that in *NE* 1, and perhaps even in *NE* 10, moral virtue is not just a necessary condition for, but an actual constituent of, supreme happiness. Their arguments in connection with *NE* 1 have already been rebutted,[24] and their arguments in connection with *NE* 10 will be rebutted later. At the other extreme, there are some who have argued that according to *NE* 10 moral virtue, so far from being a constituent of happiness, is not even a necessary condition of it: Aristotle's contemplative hero is free from all moral constraints in the pursuit of his theoretical goals. Thus Cooper at one time thought it important to note that

---

[23] In *The Aristotelian Ethics* I presented arguments, which I regard as decisive, for showing that this book properly belongs with the *EE*. See Appendix 1 below.
[24] See p. 30 above.

Aristotle in the *NE* consciously avoids saying that his theorizer will be a virtuous person ... He will not possess the social virtues or any other virtues, because he will lack the kind of commitment to this kind of activity that is an essential characteristic of the virtuous person.[25]

Devereux[26] has argued that on Cooper's interpretation there is nothing to prevent the contemplative from being quite ruthless in pursuing his goal, perhaps betraying his friends to secure the means for philosophical leisure. That is perhaps unfair: virtues, after all, are excellences, and in Aristotle's scheme someone may lack conspicuous virtue without falling into the opposite vice: the lack of virtue does not necessarily involve the performance of evil actions, as the case of the *enkratēs* or continent man shows.[27] The teaching of *NE* 10 is perhaps even compatible with the idea that the contemplative does possess the moral virtues, but does not possess them as forming part of his happiness. There will in that case be a difficulty in explaining how his performance of virtuous actions is compatible with the thesis that we all do everything for the sake of happiness (1102^a2), since, as Cooper points out, the contemplative is not committed to moral virtue as a constituent of happiness. But that thesis clashes in any case with other Nicomachean texts[28] and will not survive consideration of the case of incontinence.[29]

In 1985 two articles appeared which took up a position at the opposite extreme, claiming that Nicomachean happiness included as a constituent not only wisdom and moral virtue, but also external goods such as wealth, status, and power. T. Irwin argued that if happiness is comprehensive, and goods dependent on fortune are genuine goods, then happiness must include them. John Cooper, in a striking departure from his earlier position, saw the *NE* as being unique among the Aristotelian ethical treatises in requiring for *eudaimonia* a sufficient equipment of external goods (1099^a31 ff.). Unlike the *EE* and the *Magna Moralia*, Cooper argued, the *NE* actually writes the requirement of external goods into the definition of happiness itself as

---

[25] *Reason and Human Good*, 164.

[26] See Devereux, review of Cooper, and Kenny, *The Aristotelian Ethics*, 214.

[27] The full description of the continent man as the person who sticks with reason and refrains from evil deeds in spite of the presence of passion belongs, of course, to the disputed book C. But there are references in undoubted Nicomachean books to continence as a position between virtue and vice: e.g. 1128^b34.

[28] I have done my best to reconcile the clash at p. 20 above.

[29] According to *AE* C, 1146^b20-4, while both incontinent and intemperate pursue pleasure, the difference between them is that the incontinent does not pursue it as a constituent of the good life, while the intemperate does.

an important distinguishing feature (1101ª14–16). This, he claimed, is Aristotle's final and considered theory on the matter, and is reported as such in antiquity by authors such as Cicero.[30]

Cooper's article does a great service in bringing together the various ways in which Aristotle describes goods such as health, wealth, and friends, and the various texts in which he describes their relationship to happiness. But my own reading of these texts differs from his.

In the *NE* Aristotle often speaks of external goods (*ta ektos agatha*); half a dozen passages are listed in the index to Bywater's edition. The very first of these may give us pause in accepting Cooper's inter- pretation. In the eighth chapter of *NE* I Aristotle makes a series of attempts to show that his definition of soul as activity in accordance with virtue accords with commonly accepted dicta about the nature of happiness. His first essay in this genre is as follows:

Now goods are partitioned into three classes: some are called external and others are related to soul or to body; and we call those related to soul most truly and especially goods. But we are positing deeds and activities relating to soul. So our account should be sound, at least according to this opinion, which is traditional and an object of consensus among philosophers. It is correct also in defining the end as consisting in deeds and activities; for thus it belongs with the goods of the soul and not with external goods. (1098ᵇ12–20)

This is very strange language for Aristotle to hold, if Cooper is right in thinking that in his fully considered opinion the possession of external goods is actually part of happiness. On the face of it, Aristotle seems to be claiming it as a merit of his definition that it does *not* identify happiness in any way with the external goods, but rather with the goods of the soul.

But later in the same chapter there is a passage which gives more comfort to Cooper's interpretation.

[*Eudaimonia*] seems to be in need also of external goods; for it is impossible, or not easy, to perform noble deeds without the appropriate endowment. Many deeds are done using friends and wealth and political power as instruments; and there are some things whose lack takes off the gloss from blessedness, like noble birth, good children, and bodily beauty; for a man who is hideous, or ill- born, or solitary and childless is not the kind of person to be happy,[31] and even

---

[30] Cooper, 'Aristotle on the Goods of Fortune'.
[31] It is wrong to translate, as some translators do, as 'the man who is hideous . . . is not happy'; the Greek word is εὐδαιμονικός, not εὐδαίμων, and means, according to Liddell and Scott, 'likely to be happy'.

less so, perhaps, if he had worthless children or friends, or had lost good ones
by death. As we said, happiness seems to need in addition this sort of prosperity. This is why some people identify happiness with good fortune, just as
others identify it with virtue. (1099^a31-^b9)

But this passage falls far short of identifying external goods as a
constituent of happiness. They are necessary requirements of happiness: means of performing the noble deeds which really constitute
happiness, or conditions ensuring the absence of obstacles to the
enjoyment of happiness. This sort of prosperity is not happiness, but
something necessary in addition to it. In Aristotle's view the people
who identify happiness with good fortune are making a mistake, but an
understandable mistake. They are just like those who identify happiness with virtue (rather than with its exercise), to whose error Aristotle
has earlier in the chapter devoted a substantial paragraph ($1098^b30-
1099^a5$).

It is noteworthy that here beauty is listed as an external good. In the
passage considered earlier beauty would presumably have fallen into
the category of goods of the body. Unless, that is, Aristotle thought
that bodily beauty was in the eye of the beholder, as he thought that
honour, the greatest of the external goods (1123^b20),[32] was in the
people honouring rather than in the person honoured (1095^b26).
Cooper points out that *ta ektos agatha* may have a narrow sense, in
which it means goods external to the human being, and a broad sense,
in which it means goods external to the soul. Commonly, when
Aristotle says that *eudaimonia* needs external goods he means the
expression in the broad sense: wealth, position, friends, birth, children,
looks, health, etc. Indeed, according to Cooper, the external goods
include everything except a person's virtues, character, pleasure, and
knowledge. Another person's moral improvement will be an external
good.[33]

The way in which external goods are involved in happiness, according to Cooper, is not just by providing instruments for or removing
obstacles to virtue, but rather by providing the normal and expected
contexts for the exercise of the virtues. If you are ugly, for instance,

[32] In book 9, by contrast, friends are described as the greatest of external goods
(1169^b9-10); but that is in a dialectical passage, as Gauthier and Jolif point out (1959
edn., ii/2. 751).

[33] Cooper, 'Aristotle on the Goods of Fortune', 178. No warrant is cited from Aristotle
for the inclusion of health among the list of external goods. The list of internal goods
should perhaps include also perception, and such operations as digestion which are functions of the vegetative soul.

your opportunities for sex (and therefore for exercising temperance) will be limited. People will avoid you and take away opportunities for virtue.

The passage on which Cooper most relies for his contention that in the *NE* Aristotle recognizes external goods as a constituent of happiness is the section of chapter 10 which follows the discussion of Priam considered a little earlier:

Why then should we not say that he is happy who is active in accordance with perfect virtue, and is sufficiently endowed with external goods, not for some chance period, but through a perfect life? ($1101^{a}14$-17)

Here, Cooper claims, the endowment of external goods actually appears in a definition of happiness—a definition, moreover, which, coming at the end of the long discussion of *NE* 1, represents the most carefully considered of the formulations in that book.

But it is not correct to say that this is a definition of *happiness*. It is a thesis about the *happy person*. The happy person at any given time will be doing many other things besides the activities which constitute his happiness (e.g. digesting, breathing, seeing, and hearing). If he is to be happy many other things will have to be true of him besides the fact that he performs the activities in which happiness consists. As Aristotle himself made clear (but only explicitly in the *EE*), there is a great difference between the things in which happiness is to be found, and the things without which happiness is not possible ($1214^{b}16$, 26). Aristotle compares this with the difference between the constituents of bodily health and its necessary conditions. A good climate is essential for health, but living in a certain place is not what being healthy consists in. Cooper is right that the external goods provide not just a chance occasion for virtue, but the normal and natural context for it. Similarly, a golf course is the normal and natural context for a game of golf; but a golf course is not part of playing golf, and when we ask whether someone plays a good game we are not asking whether he only plays on the best courses.

If the mention of external goods was meant to be the adding of a final and essential ingredient to the definition of happiness, it would be difficult to explain the further course of the *NE*. After two brief interludes, devoted to the questions 'Is there good and evil after death?', 'Is happiness to be praised or prized?', Aristotle takes up his main theme with the words

Since happiness is an activity of soul in accordance with perfect virtue, we must consider the nature of virtue; for perhaps thus we shall see better the nature of happiness . . . By human virtue we mean not that of the body but that of the soul; and happiness also we call an activity of soul. But if this is so, clearly the student of politics must have some knowledge about the soul. (1102ᵃ5-19)

The mention of external goods does not appear in these reprises of the definition of happiness, and after the brief treatment of the nature of the soul in *NE* 1. 13 the next books of the *NE* are devoted not to the nature of external goods, but to the nature of virtue in general and in particular.

To this generalization, however, there is one great and important exception: two books of the *NE* are devoted to the most interesting and profound of the topics which come under the rubric 'external goods': namely friends and friendship. In the next chapter we will consider how these goods are related to Aristotelian happiness.

4

FRIENDSHIP AND SELF-LOVE

In both the *EE* and the *NE* Aristotle poses the question: Will the *eudaimōn* be so self-sufficient that he will not need friends?

The question is seen by Nussbaum as a particular instance of the general question of the relationship between happiness and relational goods. Love and friendship differ from the virtues in being relationships: the other person enters in not just as an object who receives the good activity, but as an intrinsic part of love itself. Political attachment, likewise, consists in a relationship to a structured social context. So these components of the good life are minimally self-sufficient, vulnerable in an especially deep and dangerous way. On the other hand, friendship, love, and politics seem dispensable: human beings can do without them in a way that they cannot escape the contexts of the virtues. Hence, some say that the pursuit of self-sufficiency demands the cultivation of a solitary life; but not Aristotle.

Political goods are outstandingly vulnerable, as Aristotle's own life showed. Yet the political community is necessary for the formation of good character by public education under a good system of laws. Moreover, favourable political conditions are needed for acting well: a slave cannot be *eudaimōn*. According to Nussbaum, Aristotle believes that to lack the chance of office is a diminution of good living; a life lacking the political element is seriously frustrated or incomplete. 'Surely it is peculiar to make the *makarios* a solitary: for nobody would choose to have all the good things in the world all by himself. For the human being is a political creature and naturally disposed to living-with' (*NE* 1169^{b}16–19).[1]

The most emphatic link between happiness and relational goods is made in Aristotle's treatise on justice. There Aristotle seems to claim that with only solitary concerns, without the excellence that consists in having an appropriate regard for the good of others, a human being will lack not just one important human end, he will lack all of the excellences—for each is, as he says, a thing 'in relation to others' (*pros*

---

[1] See Nussbaum, *The Fragility of Goodness*, 350.

heteron) as well as in relation to oneself (*pros hauton*)'. One cannot choose the excellent activities of moderation, courage, generosity as ends in themselves without also choosing the good of others as an end.[2]

However, the book which in our manuscripts appears as *NE* 5 is also the fourth book of the *EE*; and Nussbaum can make her account of non-self-sufficiency fit the strictly Nicomachean evidence only at the cost of discounting book 10, as we shall see in a later context. But the difficulty of extracting a systematic account of the relationship between friendship and happiness in the *NE* is not simply a matter of the overall coherence of the relevant texts. The section most explicitly devoted to the topic, the ninth chapter of *NE* 9, is itself one of the most obscure passages in the book. Let us try to tease out its meaning, and compare it with the parallel passage in the *EE* (VII. 12).

Briefly summarized, *NE* 9. 9 proceeds as follows. Does the happy man need friends? No, we might say, for he is self-sufficient and needs nothing. On the other hand we might say yes, he does, and that for three reasons. (1) Friends are the greatest of external goods; so if the happy man has all goods he must have friends. (2) Friends do each other good turns: so a good man, if he is unfortunate, will need friends to assist him; if he is fortunate, he will need friends to be recipients of his benefaction. (3) The solitary enjoyment of goods is insufficient for happiness: humans as social animals need company, and the company of friends is better than that of strangers. (1169^b3-21)

Having set up popular arguments on both sides, Aristotle gives his own account. Those who argue for the negative are to this extent right, that the happy man does not need friends for utility or pleasure. But the very fact that happiness consists in virtuous activity means that he needs the third kind of friend, friends in virtue (cf. *NE* 8. 3, 1156^a6-^b8).

(1) A virtuous person will enjoy the virtuous acts of his friends, just as a musical person will like hearing his friends singing well. He will take pleasure in contemplating them both because they are virtuous deeds, and because it is *his* friends who are doing them. ($1169^b30-1170^a4$)

(2) The virtuous person's own virtuous deeds are easier, and therefore pleasanter, to perform in company with others and for the benefit of others. (If Aristotle had pursued the musical analogy, he would no doubt have said that it is easier and pleasanter to sing in concert and with an audience than to sing unaccompanied in solitude.) (1170^a4-10)

---

[2] Nussbaum, *The Fragility of Goodness*, 335–42.

(3) The virtuous person will himself acquire training in virtue from the company of others. (1170^a11-13)

So far the arguments presented by Aristotle, while they may seem rather self-regarding reasons for having friends, are reasonably intelligible. There follows a further argument which is described by Aristotle as probing deeper into the nature of things, but which commentators have found quite unnecessarily complex and obscure. The argument and its conclusion are summarized thus by Aristotle:

> If, then, existence is in itself desirable for the blessed person (since it is by its nature good and pleasant), and that of his friend is something similar to his own, a friend will be one of the things that is desirable. And what is desirable for him he should have, or he will be lacking in this respect. Therefore the man who is to be happy will need good friends. (1170^b14-16)

The puzzling feature of the argument is that in order to establish the uncontentious proposition that existence is desirable for the blessed man Aristotle piles up axioms and lemmata in apparently haphazard order. Pairs of propositions appear more than once in such a way that sometimes A seems to be the premiss on which B is based, and sometimes B seems to be the premiss on which A is based. Moreover, in the course of the argument special weight is laid on the fact of self-consciousness (1170^a29-32). But when the conclusion comes to be drawn, self-consciousness seems to have disappeared from the premisses on which it rests. The following attempt to solve the puzzle and set out the logical structure of the argument cannot be more than conjectural.

(1) Human existence, or life, is, of itself and by nature, a good. This is stated at 1170^a20, 1170^a26, and 1170^b2. Two reasons are offered in support: life is determinate (1170^a20), and all men desire life (1170^a26).

(2) The existence or life of a good and blessed man is especially good. This is stated at 1170^a28, 1170^b2, and 1170^b14. Two reasons are offered in support: what is good by nature is good for a good man (1170^a22), and good and blessed men specially desire life (1170^a26).

(3) Human existence is a life of self-consciousness, because human life consists of perception and thought, and both of these are self-conscious activities. A perceiver is conscious that he perceives and a thinker is conscious that he thinks, and therefore everyone who is alive is conscious that he is alive. (1170^a29-32)

(4) Because of self-consciousness, life is not just good but pleasant. For the consciousness of the possession of a good is pleasant; and the

consciousness that one is alive is the consciousness that one possesses a good. (1170^b1-3, 8–10) Moreover, the life of the good man will be specially pleasant, because the life of whose possession he is conscious is an especial good, as established in (2) above.

(5) A friend is another self or *alter ego* (1170^b6). Hence the consciousness of a friend's life will be a kind of self-consciousness; and if the friend is a good person this consciousness will be a pleasure like the good man's self-consciousness of his own life.

So [the happy man] needs to be conscious of the existence of his friend as well; and this will come about in their living together and sharing in speech and thought; for this is what living together would seem to mean in the case of humans, not just browsing side by side like cattle. (1170^b10-14)

There is no doubt that the passage is cramped and confusing; but if our interpretation is correct it is at least clear why Aristotle feels he has to go to such lengths to show that life is desirable. The reason is to be sought in the *way* in which life is desirable—namely, because of the role of self-consciousness. It is only because of this that there is an argument from the desirability of one's own life to the desirability of a friend's life. (If it was the *ownership*, rather than the consciousness, of goodness which made life pleasant, then there would be no argument to the benefits of friendship; because one cannot in the same way *own* one's friends' goodness.) And we can also see why in the final summary of the argument and its conclusion at the end of the chapter self-consciousness disappears: for the consciousness which is the good to be ascribed to the happy man really is the consciousness of his friends and not of himself.[3]

But if this is the structure of the argument it is also clear that despite its length and laboriousness it does not add anything to the very first argument of the chapter, other than the introduction of the dictum that a friend is another self—a dictum which cannot explain, but must be explained by, an account of how one's friend's good is one's own good. The earlier argument indeed takes a further step which the lengthy argument omits. 'We can contemplate our neighbours better than ourselves,' Aristotle says 'and their actions better than our own' (1169^b34); and this is what makes the contemplation of our friends' virtuous activity especially pleasant. Presumably Aristotle means that

[3] The argument is quite different from that in the *Magna Moralia* to the effect that the happy man will need friends as a mirror in which to know himself. Here I agree with Kraut, *Aristotle on the Human Good*, 140 and 144, against Cooper, 'Aristotle on Friendship', 320–4.

reflection on our own activity is likely to have a disruptive effect on the activity itself. If so, then it is not so much our self-consciousness as the imperfection of our mode of self-consciousness which makes the need for friends so crucial in human life.[4]

Let us now compare the Nicomachean account with the Eudemian one. *EE* VII. 12, like *NE* 9. 9, is devoted to the question whether the happy person needs friends. It begins with a *videtur quod non*, which is more fully developed than its Nicomachean counterpart:

One might doubt whether, if a man be in all respects self-sufficient, he will have a friend, if one seeks a friend from want and the good man is perfectly self-sufficient. If the virtuous man is happy, why should he need a friend? For the self-sufficient person neither needs useful people, nor people to cheer him, nor society. His own society is sufficient for him. This is most clear in the case of a god; for it is clear, that needing nothing he will not need a friend, nor have one, supposing that he does not need one. (1244^b2-10)

The rest of this chapter makes clear that this is not Aristotle's own view; but the position criticized here has affinities with the description of the godlike intellectual in *NE* 10. 7 (1177^a32-$^b1$, $^b26$-31). Here in the *EE* Aristotle at once proceeds to dissociate himself from the position.

First, Aristotle argues that it is a mistake to think that friends are only for the sake of need. 'For when we need nothing, then we all seek others to share our enjoyment, those whom we may benefit rather than those who will benefit us' (1244^b17-19) 'All of us find greater pleasure in sharing with friends the good things that come to each and the greatest good one can share; but to some it falls to share in bodily delights, to others in artistic contemplation, to others in philosophy' (1245^a19-22).

NE and *EE* both accept a tripartite classification of friends, and both agree that the happy man will not need friends for use or help (*NE* 1169^b24-5; *EE* 1244^b14-16). *NE* adds that the happy man will not need friends for pleasure (1169^b25-8); *EE* does not say this, and the omission is probably deliberate. Certainly, in *EE* as in *NE*, true

[4] This point is well brought out by Gauthier and Jolif, ii/2. 761: 'Si nous avons besoin d'amis, ce n'est pas parce que nous possédons la conscience, c'est parce que nous ne la possédons que dans un état imparfait, voilà ce que montrait le premier argument (1169^b30-1170^a4): nous sentons mieux le bien d'autrui que le notre propre, et donc nous en éprouvons plus de joie, fût-il moindre. Voilà un des fondements de notre besoin d'amitié et une des raisons pour lesquelles Dieu, lui, n'a pas besoin d'amis: il possède la conscience à l'état parfait, ou plutôt, il *est* conscience pure (Met, Lambda, 9, 1074^b33-1075^a5).'

friendships are not those between people brought together merely by a common love of pleasure; none the less, in the *EE* one of the things in which a good man can share with his good friends is the enjoyment of bodily delight.

Both treatises place the emphasis on the third kind of friendship, friendship through virtue.[5] Both want to say that the virtuous man's friendships are expressed more in the good he does than in the good he receives, and therefore the link between friendship and need can be severed. The *NE* puts the point by saying that doing good is more proper to a friend than receiving good, the *EE* says that our best judgement in the choice of friends is made when we are not in need but are looking for those to share the enjoyment of our good life (*NE* 1169^{b}10–12; *EE* 1244^{b}16–21).

Secondly, Aristotle wants to show that in a higher sense of 'need' the happy man does need friends. The argument turns on an account of knowledge and self-knowledge which, though less sprawling, is hardly less obscure than the discussion in the *NE* which we have already considered. The obscurity is compounded because the argument, from time to time, is presented as if it took the form of a commentary upon another, unidentified, written text (the *logos* referred to in 1244^{b}31, 35, 1245^{a}27).[6]

The starting-point of the argument in the *EE* is very similar to that in the *NE*. Life is perception and knowledge, and it is because perception and knowledge are most desirable for everyone that the desire for living is natural to all (1244^{b}24–9). But whereas the *NE* immediately goes on to develop the theme that self-perception and self-knowledge are desirable, the main line of argument in the *EE* will be rather that perception involves shared perception and knowledge involves shared knowledge. The direction the argument will take is hinted at right at the beginning of the passage: 'Life in common is perception in common and knowledge in common' (1244^{b}25).[7]

---

[5] This emphasis is more explicit in the *EE*, if we accept, with most editions but not the OCT, the text supported among the MSS only by Oxon. at 1244^{b}17: ἀλλ' ο' δι' ἀρετὴν φίλος μόνον 'the friend through virtue is the only friend'.

[6] Most commentators take this to be an earlier work of Aristotle. Gaiser, 'Zwei Protreptikos-Zitate', 314 ff., and von Fragstein, *Studien*, 345–7, think that the *logos* referred to is the *Protrepticus*. In *The Aristotelian Ethics*, 226–9, I conjectured that the work referred to might be the parallel passage in the *NE*; but as will be seen from my exposition of the text, I do not now think that this conjecture is defensible.

[7] Most editors since Bonitz (anticipated by a late hand in the Marcianus), under the influence of the *NE*, have introduced the topic of self-reflection at this point by emending τὸ αὐτὸ αἰσθάνεσθαι καὶ τὸ αὐτὸ γνωρίζειν to τὸ αὐτοῦ αἰσθάνεσθαι καὶ τὸ αὐτοῦ

It is because life is knowledge that people desire to live (1244^b28). But the desire for life is not simply the desire for knowledge, if that is the desire that there should be knowledge. If that was all it was, the desire would be satisfied by the mere existence of knowledge, no matter who the knower was! For that matter, the desire for life would be satisfied by the existence of life, no matter whose life it was. 'If one were to cut off and take knowledge by itself and not together[8] ... it would make no difference whether another person knew instead of oneself, and that would be like another person living instead of oneself. But obviously one's own perception and knowledge is more desirable' (1244^b28-34).

What is it that knowledge should be taken together with? From the context the answer seems to be that it should be taken together with the conditions which characterize its presence in human beings as opposed to gods. The details of the answer, however, are extremely obscure because they are presented by way of allusion to the mysterious lost text, and to a table which it appears to have contained of columns of opposites (1244^b34-1245^a2).

Detached, so far as is possible, from these encumbrances, the argument seems to go as follows. Perception and knowledge are only possible if the object perceived and the object known share in a certain determinate nature with the perceiver and the knower (1245^a2-3). To want to be oneself a perceiver[9] is therefore to want to share in such a determinate nature (1245^a4-5). But this is itself a form of goodness (1244^a36-1245^b1), and that explains why I want not just that there should be knowledge, but that *I* should have it.

The determinate form of goodness, which is the condition of perception and knowledge, is not something which we, as opposed to a god, possess all by ourselves; it is something which we acquire 'by partaking of potentialities in perceiving and knowing'. It is characteristic of human life that a perceiver becomes perceived in the same way and respect in which he perceives, and that a knower becomes known.

γνωρίζειν. But the MSS reading is rightly defended by von Fragstein, *Studien*, 345, who also shows that ἑαυτοῦ in 1244^b33 should be taken as subjective, not objective, genitive.

[8] I follow Dirlmeier, *Eudemische Ethik*, 460, in supposing that after μή, ἅμα has dropped out by haplography.

[9] I take this to be the sense, whether the correct reading is τὸ αὑτὸν ... αἰσθάνεσθαι (Fritzsche) or τὸ αὑτοῦ ... αἰσθάνεσθαι (OCT) as subjective genitive. Surprisingly, von Fragstein takes this to be a reference to self-knowledge (*Studien*, 346), after having convincingly argued that 1244^b33, which it is clearly echoing, contains no such reference.

We wish to go on living because we wish to go on knowing; and that amounts to wishing that one should be in some sense identical with the object of knowledge ($1245^{a}5$-10).

Difficult though this passage is, it becomes intelligible if we take the underlying theory to be something like that expressed in *De Anima*, that perception consists in a sentient subject's passing from a state of potentiality in which it is unlike its object to a state of actuality in which it is like it ($418^{a}13$-6); the actualization, indeed, of the sensible object and of the sense-faculty is one and the same thing, which is simultaneously an actualization of the potentiality of the object and an actualization of the potentiality of the subject ($425^{b}27$-8) and can thus be described as a commingling or 'partaking of potentialities'. In both sensation and thought, in different ways, knowledge involves an identity of some kind of the knower with the object known.[10]

So far, so good: but what has all this to do with friendship? The answer seems to be that Aristotle is preparing the ground for the proof that the good man needs friends by showing that the good involved in perceiving and knowing is essentially a *shared* good, something which belongs to both perceiver and perceived, to both knower and known. If this is so, then the perception and knowledge of other human beings is essentially a good shared with them.

The topic of shared life is explicitly reintroduced at $1245^{a}11$, after the long excursus on the nature of knowledge, sensation, and thought.

Choosing to live with others might seem, from one point of view, futile. First of all, in the case of the things common to other animals too, such as eating together and drinking together, what is the difference whether you do this next to someone else, or at a distance from them—if you take away speech? ($1245^{a}11$-15)

Aristotle is not denying that commensality is an important part of friendship ($1245^{b}4$), but emphasizing that in the case of human beings it is the conversation that is the most important feature of the common table. But not every kind of conversation will reach the appropriate standard: the conversation must not be on trivial matters, and it must be conversation on equal terms. Teaching and learning are

---

[10] In the *De Anima*, as in the *EE*, there is said to be a parallel between the relation of sense to the objects of sense and the relation of thought to the objects of thought ($429^{a}17$-18). But in the *EE* I find no trace of the doctrine that thought is actualized by the mind's becoming identical with forms stripped of matter ($429^{a}20$-$430^{a}25$). Instead the theorem that the knower must also be the known seems to be supported by a consideration of the nature of language ($1245^{a}14$ ff.).

important functions of speech, but the relation of teacher and pupil, which implies a deficiency on one side of the relationship, is not the same as that between friend and friend (1245^{a}15-18). But provided that the friendship is one which finds expression in discourse upon equal terms, then

all of us find greater pleasure in sharing good things with friends to the extent that these fall to each of us, and sharing the best that is according to one's ability; to some it falls to share in bodily delights, to others in artistic contemplation, to others in philosophy. (1245^{a}8-22)

Two contrasts can be made between the rationale of friendship given in this passage and that which was dominant in the *NE* treatment of the subject. First, whereas in the *NE* the friend contributes to the life of a happy person as an assistant (1170^{a}4-13) or as an object of comparatively detached contemplation (1169^{b}30-1170^{a}4), in this passage of the *EE* the emphasis is on sharing the joyous activities of life on equal terms. Secondly, in the *NE* the domain of the good man's friendship is described in general terms as the exercise of virtue; in the *EE* the list of activities in which friends will share is both wider and more specific, and includes not only the exercise of intellectual virtue in philosophical activity but also the common enjoyment of the pleasures of the body. Of course, the good friends' pursuit of physical pleasures will be within the bounds of temperance—unlike the erotic activity of the sensual lover denounced in 1245^{a}25-7—and therefore will itself constitute an exercise of a moral virtue. But in listing 'artistic contemplation' as one of the domains of friendship the *EE* makes room for an important feature of the good life which elsewhere seems to be neglected in the Aristotelian ethical system.

At 1245^{a}7 the Eudemian treatment rejoins the Nicomachean one, presenting the argument that friendship makes an indispensable contribution to self-knowledge. According to the proverb, a friend is a second self: this does not mean that your friend will resemble you in all respects, but rather your friend will resemble you either in body (i.e. in the bodily activities she enjoys) or in soul (i.e. in the spiritual activities which she enjoys) or in some other particular characteristic. However it may be,

A friend wishes to be as it were a separate self. Therefore, to perceive a friend must be in a way to perceive one's self and to know one's self. So that even the vulgar forms of pleasure and life in the society of a friend are naturally pleasant (for perception of the friend[11] always accompanies them) but still more the sharing of diviner pleasures, and the reason is that it is always more pleasant to see one's self enjoying the superior good, and this is sometimes a passion, sometimes an action, sometimes something else.[12] But if it is pleasant for a man himself to live well and also his friend, and in their common life to engage in mutually helpful activity, it is surely especially appropriate to include such partnership in the end. Therefore men should contemplate in common and feast in common . . . Thus it is clear that friends ought to live together, that all wish this above all things, and that the happiest and best man tends especially to do so. (1245ª29–ᵇ11)

The opposite conclusion was the result of a misleading comparison between man and God:

Because God is not such as to need a friend, we claim the same of the man who resembles a god. But by this reasoning the virtuous man will not even think; for God's perfection does not consist in this, but in being superior to thinking of anything beside himself. The reason is that with us welfare involves a something other than ourselves, but the deity is his own well-being. (1245ᵇ14–19)

Even in the passage where the *EE* resembles the *NE* in linking friendship with self-knowledge, the emphasis quickly shifts from self-knowledge back to partnership and common activity. Altogether, the treatment of friendship in the *EE* appears more altruistic, less self-absorbed than that in the *NE*. It may well be that the allegation of egoism, which is often made against the *NE*, is ill founded;[13] but even the prima-facie appearance of egoism is much less in the *EE*. In both *Ethics*, however, the contorted and obscure nature of the writing seems to betray that Aristotle felt uncomfortable in the attempt to find room within his eudaemonistic system for the manifest importance of friendship.

In the *NE*, but not the *EE*, there is a treatment of the topic of self-love. Here Aristotle seems much more at ease, and in command of his theory. At 1168ª28 he begins to develop an *aporia*. Should one love oneself most of all? For the answer No, there is the argument that self-love is a term of reproach, and that nobility, not self, should be the thing most loved. For the positive answer, there is the argument that a man's best friend is himself; blood is thicker than water and one's own blood is thickest of all.

---

[11] OCT is at fault in accepting Robinson's emendation of ἐκείνου to αὑτοῦ in line 38.
[12] Once again the domain of friendship is drawn broadly, and not restricted to co-operation in virtuous action.
[13] This has recently been ably argued in Kraut, *Aristotle on the Human Good*, 78–154.

The answer to the *aporia* is to be found, as ever, by making distinctions (1168^{b}13 ff.). It all depends what kind of goods a person is seeking for himself; and what self they are being sought for. If the goods are competitive goods, like money, honour, sex, etc., then the self that is being cosseted is the unreasoning passional self, and self-love is bad (1168^{b}15 ff.). If the goods are just and temperate deeds, then the self that is being obliged is the controlling element, the *nous*, which is his real self (1168^{b}25 ff.).[14] Self-love in this case is a good thing, and a person like this, allotting the noblest and best goods to the supreme part of himself, is the most genuine self-lover.

In final response, then, we should say that a good man should love himself (that will be good for himself and for others) and a bad man should not love himself (that will be bad for himself and for others).

Aristotle goes on to apply this conclusion to the crucial case of self-sacrifice (1169^{a}18 ff.). The good man will throw away all the competitive goods, and even life itself, for the sake of friends and country: but of course even in doing so he is competing to win for himself the palm of nobility. The good man will let his friends have his money, but will seize the noble deeds for himself. Or will he? May there not be a supreme degree of altruism in which, when an opportunity for a noble deed arises you let your friend take it instead of yourself? But even in this case the good man ends up better off, in terms of true nobility, than his friend: for it is a nobler thing to cause a friend to do a noble action than to do it oneself.

In the discussion of altruism vs. self-love, as in the discussion of friendship vs. self-sufficiency, there is in the *NE* an effort to make the virtuous man's friends subordinate, in one way or another, to his own good. In the *EE*, as we have seen, the end of the virtuous person's life is rather an end which is shareable and is enhanced by the sharing. But it is important not to overemphasize the difference between the two treatises. There is a clear contrast between the happy man of the *EE*, in whose happiness friendship is a major constituent, and the contemplative of *NE* 10, who can perhaps contemplate truth better if he has fellow workers, but still is the most self-sufficient. But within the *NE* itself there is a tension between what is said of the relation between self-sufficiency and friendship in book 9 and what is said of the relation between self-sufficiency and perfect happiness in book 10.

---

[14] It is noteworthy that νοῦς here, in *NE* 9, is νοῦς in the broad sense: the rational part of the soul, controlling the irrational part in consort with the moral virtues; it is not the purely contemplative νοῦς of *NE* 10.

Moreover, it cannot really be said that in the *EE* any more than in the *NE* Aristotle totally resolves the tension between the self-sufficiency of happiness and the mutual dependence of friends.

Whichever *Ethics* we take as our text, we are left with the same question to pose to Aristotle. If the happy man needs friends in order to benefit them rather than himself, then surely his ultimate goal is not, as the systematic development of the treatises leads us to believe, his own supreme good. If, on the other hand, he needs friends to promote his own self-knowledge and self-satisfaction, then surely his friendship is not a genuine love of his friends for their own sake.

The difficulty continued through the centuries to haunt the Aristotelian tradition; and it took on renewed intensity in a Judaeo-Christian context. For according to both the Old and the New Testament friendship and mutual love are possible not just between human beings, but also between man and God. Theologians disagreed about the degree of self-love which was permissible, or necessary, in the love of God above all things which was essential for salvation.[15]

In whatever way friendship is to be related to the overarching eudaemonism of the Aristotelian ethics, its inclusion among the goods which constitute the ends of life increases the fragility of happiness. This has been well brought out by Nussbaum in one of her most eloquent chapters.

The best sort of love between persons, she emphasizes, is highly vulnerable to happenings in the world. First, there is the luck of finding, in the first place, a loved one to value. Then there is the necessity that the two should be able to trust each other. The basis of love must remain constant: so for love to persist it must survive many risks—the risk of changes in character, or of relationships with third

---

[15] The high point of the theological argument was reached in the reign of Louis XIV, in the conflict, famous in the annals of French literature, between Bossuet and Fénelon. Fénelon took the view, known as 'Quietist', that the highest grade of love of God deliberately and permanently excluded all consideration of self-interest, such as the thought of winning heaven and avoiding hell. Indeed, a soul could love God so much that it could acquiesce in the prospect of its own eternal damnation. Bossuet, on the other hand, saw happiness as the end of every human action, and obtained from Rome a condemnation of the Quietist proposition that there is a habitual state of love of God which is pure charity without any admixture of the motive of self-interest, in which the fear of punishments, and the desire for reward, has no part, and in which God is not loved for any happiness to be found in loving him. Thus, in condemning this proposition, Pope Innocent XII placed the official Church, against a powerful mystical tradition, on the side of Aristotelian eudaemonism: even the highest form of altruistic love must have a motive of self-interest. For a lively account of the controversy see Knox, *Enthusiasm*, 339 ff.

parties. Even if love should survive life's changes, there is always death, which comes to one before another.

By ascribing value to *philia* in a conception of the good life, we make ourselves more vulnerable to loss. And we can add one further point: we also, through our attachments make ourselves susceptible to losses that are not, properly speaking, our own. A person with no strong attachments has only his or her own health, virtue, and success to worry about. A person who loves another will be grieved or made anxious by a double number of events and becomes doubly susceptible to luck.[16]

Happiness, for Aristotle, both in the *NE* and in the *EE*, retains an essential vulnerability, which was to prove a scandal for some later philosophers in antiquity. The attempt to eliminate the role of luck in happiness was carried to the extreme in Stoicism. The Stoic refusal to come to terms with the fragility of goodness mirrors a tendency which was a constant feature of Greek epistemology: the refusal to come to terms with the fallibility of judgement.

The epistemological temptation is embodied in the fallacious argument from

> Necessarily, if I know that *p*, then *p*

to

> If I know that *p*, then necessarily *p*

an argument which, if successful, denies knowledge of the contingent.

The parallel ethical temptation is embodied in the fallacious argument from

> Necessarily, if I am happy, then I have goods *x* and *y*

to

> If I am happy, then I have goods *x* and *y* necessarily

an argument which, if successful, denies that happiness can be constituted by any contingent good, any good which can be lost. Given the frail, contingent natures of human beings as we know ourselves to be, the denial that contingent goods can constitute happiness is tantamount to the claim that only gods can be happy.

---

[16] Nussbaum, *The Fragility of Goodness*, 361.

5

FORTUNE AND VIRTUE

THE frailty of human life and the vulnerability of human goods mean that in the pursuit and retention of happiness there is great scope for good and bad luck. In all his ethical treatises Aristotle rebukes those who identify happiness with good fortune; but he is always ready to recognize the role of luck in the acquisition and operation of the virtues whose exercise constitutes the happy life.

The fullest treatment of the relation between luck, virtue, and happiness is to be found in the penultimate chapter of the *EE*, which is devoted to the topic of good fortune. This chapter, historically, has been the most influential passage in the entire *EE*. It circulated apart from the rest of the treatise (but along with the corresponding chapter of the *Magna Moralia*, 2. 8) in a Latin version under the title *De Bona Fortuna*, which was popular enough to survive in 150 manuscripts (compared with 55 of the *Magna Moralia* and none of the *EE* in Latin).

The present chapter will be devoted to an examination of the Eudemian teaching on good fortune. Because the Greek text is in a poor condition, and has often to be reconstructed with the aid of the Latin translation, I have printed in appendices both the Greek text which I take to be the closest approximation to the original and my own translation of that text. The paraphrase which follows should be read in conjunction with that text and translation.

Aristotle sets out the topic of his enquiry in these terms:

Since not only wisdom and virtue bring about well-doing, but we say also that the fortunate do well, on the assumption that fortune produces well-doing and the same results as knowledge, we must enquire whether it is by nature, or otherwise, that one man is fortunate and another unfortunate, and how matters stand on this topic. (1246ᵇ37–1247ᵃ3)

Right at the beginning we meet a textual difficulty. However the text is read, it is clear that the point is being made that *eupragia* (well-doing) is caused not only by *phronēsis* (wisdom) but also by *eutukhia* (good fortune). What is doubtful, given the textual tradition, is whether we say not only that both *phronēsis* and *eutukhia* can cause well-doing, or also that both these two sources can give rise to virtue or *aretē*.[1] But the most likely sense of the passage is this: virtue and wisdom, in the normal case, are the causes of good action; but good action can be caused not only by virtue and wisdom, but also by good fortune.

In the previous paragraphs I have translated *eupragia* as 'well-doing'. I take the word to mean the actions which a virtuous person does. It is common ground, in both the *NE* (1105^b5-9) and in the *EE*,[2] that one can do the acts of a virtuous person without being virtuous. Despite a weight of scholarly opinion, I do not think that *eupragia* in this context can mean anything like *eudaimonia*.[3] Neither in the *NE* nor in the *EE* would Aristotle have agreed that true happiness could come about by mere luck.[4]

When Aristotle says that fortune produces the same results as knowledge (*epistēmē*), should the word here be taken as a synonym for *phronēsis*? Though the two states of mind are sharply distinguished in

---

[1] This turns on whether we read, at the end of 1246^b38, ἀρετή or ἀρετήν. With the first reading, the sense is that it is not only wisdom and virtue that can cause well-doing, but also good fortune; with the second reading, the sense is that not only wisdom, but also good fortune, can cause virtue. The second reading is better supported by the MS tradition (PL) than the first (C); but the second reading goes very much against the Aristotelian doctrine, to be found equally in the *NE* and the *EE*, that φρόνησις is necessary for there to be ἀρετή. According to that general teaching, mere luck might cause correct action (εὐπραγία), but not ἀρετή or πρᾶξις κατ' ἀρετήν. The reading ἀρετή, though less well attested, is preferred, surely with reason, by the new Oxford edition.

[2] See p. 10 above on the Laconian person and the continent man.

[3] I disagree, therefore, with the translations of Woods ('welfare') and of Décarie ('bonheur'). Cooper, 'Aristotle on the Goods of Fortune', 192-4, seems to me much better inspired when he says that the fortunate person mimics the virtuous person in action. However, I think he overstates the similarity when he says 'The good fortune of the fortunate person consists primarily in his regularly achieving by his actions the more particular goals that the virtuous man would aim at were he in the same situation.' This seems to confuse the πρᾶξις which marks the virtuous man with the ποίησις which consists in the achievement of particular desirable goals.

[4] There are other textual problems in this section. In line 1247^a1 should we prefer εὐτυχίας εὖ ποιούσης (L), or εὐτυχείας εὐποιούσης (PC) or ἐμποιούσης, as Fritzsche conjectured? Or should we simply leave out the εὖ with Spengel and the Oxford text)? Again, in the same line, should we read τὰ αὐτὰ τῆς ἐπιστήμης, as the MSS say, or τὰ αὐτὰ τῇ ἐπιστήμῃ, as Spengel conjectured, followed by the Oxford text? These are matters which affect the concinnity of the Greek, but not much the sense of the text. For my part, I would prefer to accept Fritzsche's conjecture (the emendation being very simple, and the word ἐμποιεῖν of frequent occurrence in Aristotle in similar contexts, such as *NE* 4, 1126^a22); and to preserve the MS reading τῆς ἐπιστήμης as an abbreviation for something like τοῖς ἔργοις τῆς ἐπιστήμης, which makes the text read more smoothly than Spengel's emendation, accepted by the OCT.

the common book B, *epistēmē* and its verb seem to be used to refer to practical wisdom in passages in the common book C (1146ᵇ7 etc.) and in *EE* II (where the mean is said to be as *epistēmē* orders). However, in this very book of the *EE* wisdom and knowledge have been distinguished just four lines back (1246ᵇ36). If the two words are, none the less, used synonymously here, the sense is that good fortune can engender good action, and produce the same effects as (practical) knowledge. If the distinction is being preserved, then Aristotle is making the further point that luck can mimic not only the effects of wisdom, but the effects of science. Even on this second account, *epistēmē* must be being used in a broad sense, to cover *tekhnē* if not *phronēsis*; for there is no external product of strict knowledge as there is of skill and wisdom.

The next question which arises is whether this good fortune, which can rival the effects of wisdom and knowledge, is something that is inborn or not. According to the theory which occurs both in the *EE* (1234ᵃ28) and in the common book B (1144ᵇ1-16), neither wisdom nor virtue, strictly so called, is inborn; so from these two causes no one could be a good agent by nature. But if good action can be caused by good fortune, and good fortune is something inborn, then perhaps someone could, after all, be a naturally good agent. But are good fortune and bad fortune inborn?

Before answering this question, Aristotle takes a step backward to ask whether fortunate people exist at all. For if there is no such thing as a fortunate person, it is futile to ask whether such a person owes his good fortune to nature or to something else. His answer appears to be a definite affirmative: that there are fortunate men is just something we see (1247ᵃ4).

There are people—stupid people—who get things right, often, in two different cases: first, in areas where luck rules; and secondly, in cases where, while there is an appropriate skill, there is plenty of room also for luck. Games of chance are the paradigm of the former case; Aristotle gives strategy and navigation as examples of the second. So, we have lucky gamblers, lucky generals, and lucky helmsmen. The question is: what kind of thing is this good fortune of theirs, their being fortunate or lucky? Is being fortunate an inborn or an acquired characteristic?

The question which I have just put could easily be put into Aristotelian terms. Is this quality (*poiotēs*) one that is natural (*phusikē*) or is it an acquired disposition (*hexis*)? But this does not appear to be how Aristotle here puts the question, with his usual irritating nonchalance about the helpful distinctions which he himself has introduced. He asks 'Are these people [such] through some disposition (*hexis*), or is it not through their possessing some quality (*poiotēs*) that they are capable of lucky action?'—a form of question which suggests that he is here using 'quality' (being *poios*) as a synonym for acquired disposition.[5] He gives a provisional answer: as things are, people think that there are some who are by nature thus; for it is nature which gives people their qualities (*poious tinas poiei*), so that they differ right from birth. This suggests that he is here using 'quality' (being *poios*) as a synonym for an inborn characteristic. We have to look to the example he gives in order to seek clarification.

Put in concrete terms, Aristotle asks whether being fortunate or unfortunate is like being black-eyed or blue-eyed. Clearly, he thinks of this as a feature which is inborn, not acquired.[6] So the sense of the passage is that people think fortune is something inborn: just as people are blue- or black-eyed, through the necessity of their being, so—on this view—are the fortunate and the unfortunate. From a later passage (1247[a]37) it is clear that Aristotle thought that blue- and black-eyed people saw differently: blue-eyed people do not see as clearly as black-eyed. So the thesis being considered here is that there is a hidden natural quality related to luck as visible eye-colour is to sharpness of vision.[7]

The argument for this thesis proceeds by ruling out the possible acquired *hexeis* which might be thought to make people fortunate or unfortunate. It is not by *phronēsis* that people succeed,[8] because

[5] Dirlmeier suggests, perhaps rightly, that one does not have to read this text in the natural way as offering a choice of the form 'Is it *p* or not-*p*' but rather as running 'Is it *p*? Or is it not rather *q*?' If the text can be read in this way, then ποιότης is a natural disposition after all.

[6] The terminology to express this is here made obscure, once again, by textual difficulty. The MSS at 1247[a]11–12 say τῷ τὸ δεῖν τοιονδὶ ἔχειν (L) or τῷ τὸ δεῖν τοιὸν δεῖ ἔχειν (PC). The Latin version reads 'eo quod tale secundum esse tale opportet et habere'. From the Latin Susemihl constructed a text which is accepted by the OCT: τῷ {τὸ} δεῖν τοιονδὶ ⟨κατὰ τὸ εἶναι τοιονδὶ⟩ ἔχειν. Susemihl's version presumably means that something which is of a certain kind ought to have a ἕξις of a certain kind. Ποιότης is the variable for which τοιοσδὶ is the substitution instance, and the contrast is between ποιότης as a genus, and two species of this genus: κατὰ τὸ εἶναι and κατὰ τὴν ἕξιν. The point appears to be that there is a natural ποιότης, a ἕξις which you have as necessary for the kind of thing you are—and a ἕξις strictly so called, which is something you acquire. Essentially we are being presented with a definition of natural ποιότης.

[7] In terms of the distinction drawn in the previous footnote, the good and bad eyesight would be the different ἕξις related to the eye-colour as the εἶναι.

[8] 1247[a]13 κατορθοῦσι = εὖ πράττουσι. Or perhaps the word is meant more generally, to cover success in the realms of both skill and wisdom.

wisdom is not inarticulate, but gives reasons for action; but the fortunate people could not explain how it is they succeed. Then comes a puzzling remark: 'for [if they could] it would be *tekhnē*'.[9] One might have expected 'for it would be *phronēsis*'. For if fortune is supposed to be like wisdom except that it lacks reasoning, then it would be expected that if you added reasoning it would turn into wisdom. Why should it turn into something different, namely skill?

Possibly Aristotle's meaning is as follows. If those who do morally well could give an account, it would not be a matter of luck that they do well, but wisdom; just as if those who do technically well could give an account it would be skill and not luck. If this seems excessively compressed, then perhaps he should be taken to be saying: it isn't articulate, and that is enough to prove that it isn't wisdom; but even if it were articulate it would not be wisdom but skill. The whole section, it is true, began with *eupragia* as the product of good fortune; however, the more recent examples discussed have been things like strategy and seamanship, which are skills. Aristotle is basically interested in the case where luck replaces *phronēsis*, and not when it replaces *tekhnē*; but he is following his usual method of using technical illustrations to make ethical points.[10]

It is obvious, Aristotle says, that some people do succeed in areas where they lack wisdom.[11] What is obvious is not that some who are foolish in A succeed in B but that some who are foolish in B succeed in B. To illustrate the first case, Aristotle tells the story of a clever geometer who was cheated by the customs in Byzantium. This seems a little off the mark: it appears to be a case of someone clever in A failing in B (clever in geometry, failing to be streetwise). It illustrates only the general point that one can be skilled at one thing (geometry is presumably a *tekhnē*) and unskilled at another. What Aristotle wants is a case of someone succeeding in the area of the very skill which he lacks.[12] The case he offers of those foolish in B succeeding in B is that of not very clever steersmen who sail well. These are compared with people

---

[9] Walzer's emendation (OCT) into the dative is ingenious but not necessary; the sense is not substantially affected either way.

[10] See Kenny, *Aristotle's Theory of the Will*, 125, 148.

[11] The MSS at 1247[a]15–16 read ἔτι δὲ φανερὸν (PC) or ἔστι δὲ φανερὸν (L). Susemihl emended to ἔτι δὲ φανερὸν ὅτι. The same purpose, at less cost in emendation, is achieved by Jackson's reading ὅτι δέ, φανερόν. The sense is: how people succeed, we still wonder, but *that* they do is clear. The OCT accepts an ill-inspired emendation of Allan's.

[12] There is no need to delete ὅτι in line 20 with the OCT. It picks up ὅτι [κατορθοῦσι] from line 15 as emended by Jackson; the correspondence can be taken as a further argument in favour of the emendation.

who throw sixes as being by nature luckier than those who throw blank ($1247^a22\text{-}3$).[13]

What is being assumed here? Is Aristotle accepting that there is natural gambler's luck, and extending the naturalness of this to technical luck? If so, there seems to be an argument in a circle. Aristotle wants to show that there is natural luck by eliminating the other alternatives; but here he assumes the existence of natural luck in the course of eliminating skill. It is clear, at all events, that dicing is not a matter of skill or wisdom; and perhaps all he needs is to make a comparison with the alleged case of a naturally lucky gambler, whether or not such a person genuinely exists.

'Or is it through being favoured, as they say, by a god?' (1247^a23). A new sentence begins here,[14] and indeed we are turning to a different argument. Aristotle wants to exclude a second alternative to the possibility of natural fortune, namely that there is some source of good fortune external to the agent. Aristotle makes the comparison 'A ship badly constructed often sails better, though not because of itself but because it has a good steersman.' Here it is no longer the steersman who is the possessor of the luck: it is the ship which is lucky in its steersman. Decoding the analogy, the fortunate person would be like a lucky ship, because he has a divine being to steer him through life, or perhaps like a steersman who takes on a divine pilot. But this is rejected on the principle—later defended in the Christian era by the Pelagian heretics in controversy with St Augustine—that divine favour depends on human merit. 'It is strange that a god or divine being should favour such a man, rather than the best or the wisest.' Gods or guardian angels would need reason to love a human being, and this would be either virtue or wisdom ($1247^a28\text{-}9$).

This whole section has been exploring three possible causes of the successful activity of the fortunate. One—intelligence (*nous*)—is ruled out, because *phronēsis* and *tekhnē*, the two relevant kinds of intelligence, are articulate, and the fortunate person is not. Another—guidance (*epitropia*)—has been ruled out on the Pelagian principle. That leaves the third possibility: nature. 'So if success must come about either by nature or intelligence or some guidance, and it is not two of these, the fortunate must be so by nature' ($1247^a29\text{-}31$).

---

[13] Unlike the OCT, I accept the brilliant emendation of Jackson, ἄλλος δὲ βάλλει ἔξ, corresponding to Bf 'alius autem iacit ex'.

[14] Here I am agreeing with Woods, *Aristotle's Eudemian Ethics*, 40, against the punctuation of the OCT and other commentators.

Aristotle now turns to build up the other side of the *aporia*, by arguing against the view that good fortune is a gift of nature.

First, nature acts uniformly, or at least with a degree of regularity, while luck is irregular and unexpected. 'Now if prosperity contrary to expectation seems to belong to luck—but if someone is fortunate he is so by luck—the cause would not seem to be the kind of thing that is universally or generally the same' (1247^a32–6).[15]

Secondly, if someone prospers or fails to prosper because of being of a certain kind, that is, having a certain *poiotēs*, in the way that someone sees poorly because he has eyes of a certain colour, then not luck but nature would be the cause of his prosperity or lack of it.[16] Such a person should not be called fortunate, or blessed by luck (*eutukhēs*), but blessed by nature (*euphuēs*). But this leads to an absurd conclusion. For fortunate people are those whose goods are caused by good luck.[17] But on this account we would have to say that the people we call fortunate do not owe their fortune to luck, since their goods are caused not by luck, but by nature. Therefore the fortunate are not fortunate, which is absurd.

We have met a difficulty, then, in each of the hypotheses we have explored: that fortune is a form of intelligence, or a divine guidance, or a natural endowment. This *aporia* is finally to be resolved when different kinds of fortune are distinguished. There is one kind of fortune which is the possession of natural good desires: this is indeed regular, and so there is no objection to saying that it is natural, but it is not a matter of luck. 'Not all who seem to have good fortune prosper by luck, and not through nature' (1248^a12 ff.). And there is one kind of fortune which is indeed due to divine guidance (1248^b4). Every kind of fortune is inarticulate (1248^b6), and that makes it different from

---

[15] I follow Jackson in inserting δόξειε before εἶναι corresponding to B^f 'videbitur . . . esse'. Just possibly one could defend the MSS reading with εἶναι alone, understanding δοκεῖ as carried over from the first part of the sentence before the parenthesis. The matter does not affect the sense.

[16] The OCT here makes an excellent job of a difficult textual situation, with its reading ἔτι εἰ, ⟨ἤ⟩ τοιοσδί, ἐπιτυγχάνει ἢ ἀποτυγχάνει, ὥσπερ, ὅτι {ὁ} γλαυκός. This follows Mb (and B^f) in reading ἔτι εἰ; Langerbeck's conjecture in reading ἤ; PCL in reading both verbs instead of the single one read by Bekker—you need them both to match the example of misfortune in the case of the short-sighted; and finally Mb (and B^f) in reading ὥσπερ, ὅτι γλαυκός.

[17] Unlike the OCT, I read εὐτυχεῖς at 1247^b1 with Jackson, after 'fortunati' in B^f. There is no need to emend ὅσων into ὅσοις with Jackson and Woods. The text can be construed: 'those of whose goods good luck is cause', taking ὅσων as the possessive with ἀγαθῶν.

wisdom and skill; but there is a role in it for intelligence or *nous* (1248ª29).

This is not made fully clear until later on. At this point, having reached *aporia* about the nature of good fortune (*eutukhia*), Aristotle now raises the more fundamental question: Is there any such thing as luck (*tykhē*) at all? He mentions the possibility that there is no such thing as luck, but rejects it, without any general argument. The existence of luck belongs to non-ethical treatises: it is its effect on good and bad which matters here.

'Will luck not exist at all, or will it exist, but not be a cause?' Aristotle answers: it must exist, and it must be a cause. And if it is a cause, it will cause good and bad things to people—and therefore, we are left to conclude, there will be fortunate and unfortunate people (1247ᵇ2-4).

The passage which follows (1247ᵇ5-9) is puzzling.[18] It can be read as meaning that Aristotle is not enquiring whether the notion of luck is a cloak for ignorance of causes, because that is something that belongs to another enquiry. The difficulty with this reading is that he then goes on to present the argument that if there was a hidden cause of luck, then lucky breaks would be a regular occurrence. So he is in fact undertaking the enquiry.

It seems preferable, therefore, to take the argument to run as follows: If we took the line that luck is a cloak for hidden causes, we would meet the following further problem—the problem which is then spelt out in the following lines, and which provides reinforcement for the view earlier stated brusquely, that luck does exist and is a cause.[19]

In 1247ᵇ9-18 the rejection of the suggestion that there is no luck, but only hidden causes, is presented in two parts. First, suppose that there is a single cause, which is unknown to us. In that case, we would expect not a single stroke of fortune, but repeated success:[20] for if there is the same cause we would expect the same effect. But of course, 'same cause, same effect' does not imply 'same effect, same cause'. Suppose then that the same outcome is the result of multiple and

---

[18] At 1247ᵇ7 I read ἄλογον, rather than ἀνάλογον with PC against L (Bᶠ 'sine ratione'). OCT's ἄδηλον is unsupported, but does of course represent the sense.

[19] This interpretation is facilitated if we emend εἰ δ' in line 4 to ἤ, and place a mark of interrogation after αἰτίαν.

[20] At 1247ᵇ10 the MSS read διὰ τὸ ἀποκατορθῶσαι. The correction from ἀπο to αὐτὸ seems justified by BF ('propter idem'). But the further emendation κατορθώσαιεν (Jackson, OCT) seems unnecessary; κατορθῶσαι can surely be infinitive after ὁρῶμεν, understood, which fits Bᶠ 'dirigere'.

undefined causes[21]—it will be good or bad[22] but there will be no empirical science of it. If there were such a science, some of the fortunate would have learnt it (and would therefore be able to give an account of it and pass it on to others).

The direction of Aristotle's argument is here uncertain: is he arguing from the fact that there is no science to the lack of cause; or is he arguing from the hypothesis of multiplicity of causes to the consequential lack of a science? It is not obvious what is premiss and what conclusion here. Do we conclude that there is no science (1) because if there were someone would know it, or (2) because the causes are indeterminate? Is the non-existence of a science a fact appealed to, or the consequence of a supposition? To answer this we have to emphasize the distinction between theoretical science and inductive or empirical science (1247^a14). That there is no theoretical science is part of the initial hypothesis being explored (1247^b8). That there is no empirical science is established by the fact that the fortunate have not acquired it.

'Or would all the sciences, as Socrates says, be types of good fortune?' (1247^b15). The reference to Socrates is presumably to Plato's *Euthydemus*, 279 D—a passage in which, like the present context, use is made of the example of lucky steersmanship. The reference is puzzling, because Plato's Socrates seems to say not that all sciences are pieces of luck, but that all pieces of luck are really science. The allusion is perhaps best taken as a loose and light-hearted one: 'We might as well say that Socrates was right, after all, to regard science and luck as coextensive!'

What, then, prevents such things from happening to somebody often in succession, not because that is what is appropriate for the kind of person he is, but like a permanent run of success in throwing dice? (1247^b15-18)[23]

This passage is puzzling. The argument hitherto seemed to be that there cannot be a cause of lucky phenomena, because they are irregular. If so, what is the relevance of saying that you might go on and on throwing sixes? It seems that the passage must be taken, not as a statement of Aristotle's own position, but as a further exploration of

---

[21] At 1247^b12 I read ἀπ' ἀπείρων with Jackson (B^f 'ab infinitis'), against all MSS.

[22] At 1247^b13 all MSS read ἔσται μὲν τὸ ἀγαθὸν (BF 'erit quidem quod bonum'). Jackson, followed by OCT, emends to τῳ, Dirlmeier to ὅ. Neither is necessary.

[23] At 1247^b17 the MSS read ὅτι τοῖς δεῖ. Jackson, followed by the OCT, emends to ὅτι τοιοσδί. I suggest ὅτι τοιούτοις δεῖ (picking up the dative of τινι). This achieves the same sense, but with a text which is closer to the 'hos oportet' of B^f.

the Socratic suggestion. If there was no difference between science and luck, then every single case of scientific regularity would be no different from a dicer's run of sixes.

We can now look back and try—with only very limited confidence—to outline the general course of the argument. We start from the hypothesis that luck is a cloak for hidden causes, causes of which there is no theoretical science. Now either there is a single hidden cause or there are multiple, indeterminate causes. If there was a single hidden cause, there would be regularity in the effect (which is inconsistent with the outcome being a matter of luck), and there would be a theoretical science of the cause–effect relationship (which is inconsistent with the hypothesis that the cause is opaque to reason). If lucky outcomes are the effects of multiple indeterminate causes, then indeed there could be no theoretical science; but there could be an empirical science. But there is no such science; for if there were, fortunate people would have learnt it. But they don't seem to have done so: unless we accept the Socratic view that every lucky stroke is in fact an exercise of science. But if we take that view, then the difference between science and luck vanishes altogether, and there is neither luck nor science.

Aristotle has not yet finished piling up problems, and is not yet ready to take his own stand and outline the necessary elements for a solution. His final contribution to the *aporia* starts from a surprising point: an analysis of the nature of *hormē* or impulse in the soul.

At 1247ᵇ18 ff. we are told that there are two kinds of impulse in the soul: those from reasoning and those from unreasoned appetite (*orexis*). An impulse from reasoning would be a *proairesis* or purposive choice. An unreasoned impulse could be either an animal desire for pleasure (*epithumia*) or a general, undifferentiated appetite for goodness (*boulēsis* or volition).[24] The unreasoned ones are prior: for the impulse which comes from the desire for pleasure is natural, and the undifferentiated natural appetite for good is prior to its specification by reason into particular choices. This means that everything has a natural tendency to goodness.[25]

If then there are some people well endowed by nature (as musical people without professional knowledge of singing are well endowed in that respect)

---

[24] See Kenny, *Aristotle's Theory of the Will*, chs. 2 and 6.

[25] This is preferable to the alternative punctuation and translation: 'And these are prior, if the impulse which comes from the desire of the pleasant is by nature, and appetite by nature tends towards good of every kind.' But there is no need to reinforce the preferred interpretation by emending πάν to πᾶσα with Allan and the OCT at line 21.

and who without reasoning are impelled in accord with nature, and desire what they ought and when they ought, these persons will succeed even though they lack wisdom and reasoning, just as men will sing well who are incapable of teaching singing. (1247^{b}21-6)

People like this, Aristotle concludes, will be fortunate—that is to say, people who succeed for the most part without reason or *logos*. So fortunate people would be thus by nature. This is the antithesis to the thesis argued for up to 1247^{a}39. Which of the two positions does Aristotle really support? Does he believe there really are people of this kind? If so, does he regard them as genuinely fortunate? Before finding out the answer to this question we have to follow Aristotle through a number of distinctions. For at last, having built up the *videtur quod sic* and the *videtur quod non*, he now turns to solve the *aporia* by distinguishing between kinds of *eutukhia*.

The two kinds of good fortune are distinguished on the basis of two kinds of action: action in accordance with impulse, and action of the opposite kind. The distinction made here at 1247^{b}29-30 is later echoed at 1248^{b}5-6,[26] where we are told that there are in the end only two forms of good fortune, one in accordance with impulse and one contrary to impulse. One of these two kinds of good fortune is divine (but it is not immediately clear which of the two) and one of them is continuous (but again it is not clear which).[27] The important point is that the parallel text at the closure indicates that from this point onwards Aristotle is presenting his own account of the two genuine cases of good fortune.

What is meant here by impulse (*hormē*)? We saw a little earlier that there are three kinds of impulse: choice, desire, and volition.[28] One kind of impulse in which Aristotle is especially interested is pre-reflective wanting, whether sensual desire or the imprecise wanting of the good typical of naturally good people. For instance, in the discussion of natural virtue in the common books, at B 1144^{b}3 ff. we are told that each ethical characteristic is present in a manner naturally; as children and from birth we have natural qualities resembling courage and justice, but we seek to have the real virtues in a different form, because without intelligence the natural virtues can be harmful. It is *phronēsis* or wisdom that makes the difference between natural virtue and genuine virtue.[29]

---

[26] οὗτος δέ ἐστιν ὁ κατὰ τὴν ὁρμὴν διορθωτικός.
[27] For my own conjecture as to which is which, see below, p. 74.
[28] See above, p. 65.
[29] This passage goes on to make a reference to Socrates' idea that all the virtues were

Frequently, when Aristotle uses the word *hormē* he uses it as a genus to cover the contrasting impulses of sensual desire and rational choice (e.g. *NE* 1102^{b}21; *EE* 1224^{b}9). In this passage the one kind of good fortune is said to be connected with the things 'that come from impulse and from people who choose to act'. Is Aristotle thinking here of a single case, the 'and' being epexegetic, so that what he has in mind is action on impulse, that is to say in accordance with choice? Or are there (at least) two cases: one from an impulse such as desire (case 1), and the other from choice (case 2)? Correspondingly: what is the opposite? Is it: not from choice; or not from *epithumia*; or not from either of the two?

From what follows it seems that what Aristotle has in mind is the case of an agent who has not just a general volition for the good, but a volition which has, through reasoning, become a specific choice; only, the reasoning has been faulty, and so the choice is only of an apparent and not a real good. 'In those cases if people succeed in things in which they seem to have reasoned badly,[30] we say that they have also been fortunate.'[31]

What are the cases which Aristotle is calling 'those cases'? Are they the cases of action in accordance with impulse, or the cases of action against impulse? The cases in accordance have been mentioned more distantly, and there is reasoning where there is choice, whereas if there was no reasoning at all there could not be bad reasoning. So it must be the case in accordance with *hormē* that Aristotle has in mind.

'So again in these cases, if they wanted a different, or a lesser good than they have received' (1247^{b}33-4). 'These cases' are the cases of action contrary to *hormē*. The point to be made is, crudely, that one way of being fortunate is to achieve good when what you want is evil. But as all wanting must be for a good of some kind, bad desire must be desire for a lesser good. So there is a class of *eutukheis* who want an inferior good and get a greater good against their wishes (against *hormē*).

forms of wisdom; this parallels the reference above in 1247^{b}15 to his idea that all the sciences were pieces of good fortune.

[30] The MSS at 1247^{b}30-1 read ἐν ἐκείνοις κακῶς λογίσασθαι; B^f 'in illis in quibus male ratiocinasse'. Fritzsche, followed by the OCT, introduced ἐν οἷς after ἐκείνοις to match B^f. In addition Woods inserted εἰ before ἐν οἷς (wrongly claiming the authority of B^f). This is attractive, for εἰ ἐν οἷς in the Greek text could drop out by haplography from ἐκείνοις, and similarly in a Latin ILLISSIIN the second 's' and the following 'i' could drop out.

[31] I see no reason for following the OCT in emending the MSS reading κατορθοῦνται καὶ.

If we presume that in this second case of good fortune there is nothing wrong with the reasoning—the agent reasons correctly how to satisfy his bad desire, but fails to carry out his plan—we can compare the elements of the two cases in the following way:

> In the first case there is good volition; bad reasoning; unsuccessful choice; successful action.

> In the second case there is substandard volition; good reasoning; unsuccessful choice; successful action.

In each case the action finally performed is contrary to *prohairesis* or choice: that is where the luck comes in. But only in the second case is the action performed contrary to the initial *hormē* or underlying desire for good. Later, in his final description of the two kinds of *eutukhia*, Aristotle says they are both unreasoning (1248^{b}6). But this does not mean that no reasoning takes place in the agent; it means that the action actually performed is not an action in accord with the agent's reasoning, an action which he could justify by pointing to his reasons for acting.

The first class, Aristotle goes on to say, are fortunate by nature, because their appetite (*orexis*) and impulse (*hormē*) were for the right thing, even though their reasoning was naïve. Are appetite and impulse the same here? Or is one initial undifferentiated desire, and the other the choice which is the result of the faulty reasoning? If so, which is which?

It is not easy to answer these questions with confidence. Instead, let us sketch out the kind of concrete case which Aristotle may have had in mind. Let us suppose that the administrator of a city has a firm basic desire for justice. He believes—wrongly, according to Aristotle—that justice involves distributing to each according to his need. He then calculates the distribution of the goods at his disposal on this principle, but confuses the calculation and comes out with a result which reflects not the needs, but the deserts, of the original citizens. When he makes his distribution on this basis, he performs an act of justice (according to Aristotle), but he does so by luck and not because of good reasoning. But his final intention to give X ten drachmas, Y five drachmas, and so on, as well as his initial volition for justice, are good desires.

It is cases such as these which Aristotle has in mind when he goes on to say: 'In the case of these people, when reasoning seems not to be correct, but desire happens to be present as a cause, the desire being rightly directed comes to the rescue.'[32] Of course, Aristotle adds, in other cases reasoning on the basis of *epithumia* could lead to misfortune. He must have in mind bad reasoning on the basis of good desire. If it was good reasoning on the basis of good desire, it could not lead one astray. If it was good reasoning on the basis of bad desire, then it would be worse than misfortune. As Aristotle pointed out in the common book C at $1142^{b}18$: the incontinent man gets what he wants by his reasoning, but acquires a big evil. The case which Aristotle has in mind here is different: it is the case of a bad outcome turning out against one's impulse.

What of the case where the desire is bad and the reasoning is erroneous? If, despite all that, the action performed is not a bad one, then we have the other case of good fortune. If we look for a concrete case here, we do not need to invent one: Mozart and Da Ponte have done so for us. In *The Marriage of Figaro* the unfaithful Count Almaviva desires to seduce his wife's maid Susanna. But when he goes to keep his assignation with her, the woman he meets is in fact the Countess in disguise. Despite his evil desire, because of the foiling of his plot he fails to commit adultery. This is a case of good fortune contrary to impulse—contrary to the Count's lecherous impulse. It is of cases such as this that Aristotle raises the question in $1247^{b}39$ 'In the other cases how can there be good fortune in accordance with a good endowment of appetite and desire?' So the Almaviva case must be the other, non-natural kind of good fortune.

The section ends with the question 'But then if on this side there are two kinds of luck and good fortune, is the good fortune on the other side one and the same, or are there more than one?'[33] This question itself raises many questions. What is 'this side' and what is 'the other side' (literally 'here' and 'there')? Are we being invited to consider a

---

[32] At $1247^{b}36$ the MSS read εἶναι τύχη δ' αὐτοῦ αἰτία οὖσα, αὐτὴ δ' ὀρθή, and B^f reads 'esse fortuna autem ipsius cause existens concupiscentia ipsa recta'. The OCT retains the MS reading but places οὖσα and δ' in curly braces, and marks the whole sentence with an obelus. Dirlmeier, on the basis of B^f, inserts ἐπιθυμία after οὖσα. This seems sound; one then has to correct the noun τύχη to the verb τύχῃ. But to make the passage render an acceptable sense, one has to take ἐπιθυμία here to have a broader application than to mere sensual desire; it must cover the initial appetition of good.

[33] In the MSS this sentence reads: ἀλλὰ μὴν ἡ ἐνταῦθα εὐτυχία καὶ τύχη διττὴ κἀκείνη ἢ αὐτή, ἢ πλείους αἱ εὐτυχίαι B^f 'at vero si hic bona fortuna et fortuna duplex et ibi eadem aut plures bona fortune'. The passage has puzzled commentators and has inspired elaborate emendations, as in the OCT. But the key to understanding it is to read it as a question. The only emendations necessary are εἰ for the first ἡ (Fritzsche, after 'si' in B^f), and κἀκεῖ for κἀκείνη (Susemihl, after 'et ibi' in B^f).

fourfold kind of *eutukhia*, with two subdivisions of the two kinds of good fortune?

The answers seem to be as follows. 'On this side' refers to the case of the natural good fortune; it looks back to the immediately preceding words 'in accordance with a good endowment of appetite and desire'. On this side there are two kinds of luck, and there is good fortune. This does not mean that there are two kinds of good fortune: there is good and bad luck, but only one kind of natural good fortune. The two kinds of luck are good and bad luck arising from bad reasoning with good desire (1247^b37-8). On the other side, there is the non-natural good fortune such as Almaviva enjoyed. The answer to the rhetorical question is that it is not the same kind of good fortune as the good fortune 'on this side', but that good fortune does indeed come in more than one kind. But we have so far only two, not four, kinds of good fortune. However, Aristotle now goes on to take a closer look at natural good fortune, and to make some further distinctions.

We see some people, he says, having good fortune contrary to every sort of knowledge and correct reasoning. These appear to be the people whom we have already met in the section on natural good fortune (1247^a16, 1247^b25-7). In such a case Aristotle says it is clear that something else (i.e. something other than reasoning) is the cause of their fortune. But now a new question is put: is this really good fortune at all?

Aristotle's answer, on reflection, seems to be: No, it is not; it is the result partially of natural good desire and partially of distorted reason; but it is not something which is caused by luck. Unless, that is, natural good desire is itself caused by luck. But if it is, then even good deliberate action will be caused by luck (for this first appetite is what starts the whole deliberative process). But natural good desire is not from luck, but from God.

It is difficult to spell out the detailed steps of this argument in the text. Of the section 1248^a7-16, Woods says 'This passage raises perhaps the worst textual problems in the chapter; and it is not possible to reconstruct more than the general sense.'[34] The conclusion, however, seems to be clear enough: not all those who seem to be fortunate succeed through fortune; some of them succeed through

---

[34] *Aristotle's* Eudemian Ethics, 181. Accordingly my translation, in Appendix 4, is very tentative. It presupposes the following readings, other than those in the OCT: at line 6 ᾧ for τὸ, after Jackson; at line 7 εἴη αἴτιον for εἴη, after Bᶠ 'erit causa'; at line 8 οὔ γε for οὐδὲ, after Jackson; in line 15 insert οὐδ' before αἰτία as a more economic way of achieving the goal of Jackson's supplement οὐδ' ὅτι οὐκ ἔστι τύχη.

nature. The argument does not show that luck is in no way a cause of anything, but only that it is not the cause of everything it seems to be the cause of. So here we seem to have two kinds of good fortune: good fortune by nature, and good fortune by luck. But only the latter really deserves the name 'good fortune'.

Now good fortune by nature is the good fortune whose cause is good natural desire. Suppose that we go on to ask the question whether luck is the cause of that cause; whether luck is the cause of one's desiring what one should when one should. Well, if so, luck will be the cause of everything—not just of the success which is not preceded by reasoning, but also of the success which is so preceded. For deliberation cannot arise from deliberation, nor thought from thought, for ever:

For even if someone deliberated after having deliberated, he did not deliberate in turn about that; there is a certain starting-point. Nor did he think, having thought before thinking, and so on to infinity. (1248ª18–20)[35]

We must come to a stop somewhere; and what should be the stopping-point except luck? In that case everything (sc. in the soul) will be from luck.

The regress argument presented here has been much discussed in modern times, but it is not always realized that it was initially formulated by Aristotle. Alasdair MacIntyre devotes a chapter of his book *Whose Justice? Which Rationality?* to Aristotle's account of practical rationality. In the course of his discussion MacIntyre says that a rational agent has to construct a major premiss which states truly what good it is which is his particular good here and now. He will have to derive this from a set of ultimate first principles and concepts, which specifies the good for human beings as such: the completion of this derivation is the central task of deliberation. But, MacIntyre continues:

There is an initial problem here to which Gilbert Ryle first drew our attention (*The Concept of Mind*, London, 1949, p. 67). If all rational action is to be preceded by deliberation, while deliberation is itself a form of rational activity, as it surely must be on Aristotle's view of it, we seem to be committed to a vicious infinite regress. For any particular piece of deliberation would, in order to be rational, have to be preceded by some further deliberation, and so proceed *ad infinitum*.[36]

MacIntyre then goes on to make a suggestion of his own with a view to exonerating Aristotle from this charge.

[35] At line 18, for δή read εἰ.   [36] *Whose Justice? Which Rationality?*, 131.

Because he concentrates almost exclusively on the *NE*, MacIntyre does not seem to have noticed that this problem was formulated by Aristotle himself. It was, as we shall see, to have a long history for centuries before Ryle. The argument presented here in the *EE* has been criticized by Woods, who says: 'Aristotle is correct in holding that a vicious regress will result if each mental act is held to originate in another act of the same type. But why should it be supposed that each mental act is initiated by another of the same type?'[37] But Aristotle is not making this assumption: he is perfectly ready to accept that a state of desire may precede an act of deliberation. But the question is: What is the cause of this desire itself?

Aristotle answers the question with another one: 'Is there an *archē* [a starting-point or principle] which does not have another principle outside itself and which because it has being of a certain kind can do this kind of thing?'[38] We are looking for nothing less than the ultimate principle of movement in the soul.

This is the same as the principle of the correct desire which lies at the back of intelligence and deliberation. It is the trigger of desire. Well, what is it? The answer, according to Aristotle, has to be God.[39] 'As God moves everything in the universe, so he moves everything here, by intelligence. For what moves in a manner everything is the divine in us' (1248^a26-7).

In *NE* 10 there is a divine element in human beings, which is identified with *nous* or understanding, the power which enables us to philosophize and contemplate. The divine element here in *EE* VIII is something different, something superior to intelligence, which makes use of it. The principle of reasoning is not reasoning, but something superior to it; and nothing is superior to knowledge and intelligence, save God only. Moral virtue is not, for virtue is an instrument of

---

[37] *Aristotle's* Eudemian Ethics, 182.

[38] The MSS at 1248^a24 have: διὰ τί τοιαύτη τὸ εἶναι τὸ τοῦτο δύνασθαι ποιεῖν. Many emendations have been proposed, all with a view to producing a sense equivalent to the Bᶠ text 'quod tale secundum esse tale potest facere'. The simplest way of achieving this is to read διότι τοιαύτη τὸ εἶναι τὸ τοιοῦτο δύναται ποιεῖν.

[39] This is so on any reading; but there is considerable dispute about the correct form of the text. The MSS read, ὥσπερ ἐν τῷ ὅλῳ θεός, καὶ πᾶν ἐκείνῳ. κινεῖ γάρ. Bᶠ reads 'quemadmodum in toto deus et omne illud. movet enim'. πᾶν ἐκείνῳ does not make sense without some kind of emendation. The OCT has κἂν ἐκείνῳ; but this appears to make ψυχή suddenly masculine (hence Spengel emended to ἐκείνη). Jackson's emendation is better inspired: ὥσπερ ἐν τῷ ὅλῳ θεός, καὶ πᾶν ἐκεῖ κινεῖ. κινεῖ γάρ. It is indeed probable that a κινεῖ has dropped out by haplography; but it was a mistake to eliminate the νῳ. We get excellent sense with the reading ὥσπερ ἐν τῷ ὅλῳ θεός, καὶ πᾶν ἐκεῖ νῷ κινεῖ. κινεῖ γάρ.

intelligence; it is intelligence that uses virtue, not virtue using intelligence.[40] The divine element of this *EE* passage most resembles the one described in the common book C, 1153[b]31:

All things, brutes and men, pursue pleasure ... and perhaps they actually pursue not the pleasure they think they pursue nor that they would say they pursue, but the same pleasure; for all things have by nature something divine in them.

In contexts of this type the divine element in humans belongs on the appetitive, not the intellectual, side of the soul.

At this point (1248[a]30) we return for the final time to the topic of *eutukhia*. Up to now we have been talking of those who do have *aretē* and *epistēmē*; in them, as well as in those who lack knowledge, there is the supreme divine *arkhē*. But now we turn back to the fortunate people. These are the people who succeed in what they want without reasoning and who gain no benefit from their deliberation. 'For they have a principle that is better than intellect and deliberation.' What does the 'for' explain? Why are they called lucky? Why deliberation does not benefit them? Neither of these, but simply why they succeed.

But doesn't everyone have this principle, including those with wisdom and understanding? Yes, the *phronimoi* and the *sophoi* do; but not everyone—not the wicked. 'Those who do have reason, but do not have this nor inspiration, cannot do this'[41]—i.e. succeed. What is meant by the reference to inspiration? Aristotle goes on to explain.

They attain to a power of divination which is swifter than the reasoning of the wise and learned; indeed, the divination which comes from reasoning should almost be done away with. But some people through experience and some through habit have this power of using the divine element in their enquiry: and this sees well both what is and what is to come, even in the case of people whose reasoning is thus disengaged. (1148[b]34-9)

This gives us a fuller description of the inspired people who form one category of the fortunate. Whereas the wise and learned have *logos*, these instead have inspiration; and inspiration enables them to do without *logos* and hit the mark at least as fast as the normal wise.

---

[40] The intelligence that uses virtue must be *phronēsis* or wisdom, which cannot be misused. In the first chapter of *EE* VIII Aristotle contrasts it with knowledge, which can be made use of by virtue or vice. See Kenny, *The Aristotelian Ethics*, 184-8.

[41] At line 33 read ὅσοι δὲ τὸν λόγον, τοῦτο δ' οὐκ ἔχουσι οὐδ' ἐνθουσιασμόν, τοῦτο οὐ δύνανται, accepting Allan's emendation ὅσοι, and striking out the second δ' before οὐ δύνανται with B[f]. The bracketing and punctuation of the OCT destroy the sense.

Just as some people by experience, lacking professional training, can do as well as those who possess a skill, so these people can in their practical enquiries do as well as the wise by 'making use of the divine', consulting, as it were, an inner oracle. This oracle can tell of the future as well as the present; and it is more audible in the soul of those who are not distracted by the prattle of reason; just as blind people, so we are told, have better memories because of being undistracted by a constant input of visual data.

It is difficult to be certain what is here being described. It may be that Aristotle has in mind the unreasoned decisions that Socrates attributed to his *daimōn* and that preserved him from wrongdoing. Certainly it seems to be a different kind of divine element, and a different kind of good fortune, from that involved in the initial good impulses of the persons of ordinary virtue.

The long discussion is finally summed up:

It is obvious that there are two kinds of good fortune. One of them is divine, which is why the fortunate person seems to succeed through God. This man is the one who is successful in accordance with impulse, the other is so contrary to impulse; but both are non-rational. And the one kind of good fortune is continuous, and the other non-continuous. ($1248^b3–7$)

Throughout the treatise on good fortune, it is difficult to see which of the many distinctions Aristotle makes are meant to be equivalent to each other, and which are intended to further subdivide classes already divided. But in the light of our previous discussion, we can say that there are four types of candidate for being fortunate.

First, there are those to whom God gives a good nature, which leads, via correct reasoning, to virtuous action. These are the people of normal virtue. Though the original gift of good nature is something outside their power, it is the whole foundation of moral virtue. This is spoken of as true good fortune in the *NE* ($1179^b20–3$); but here, though mentioned at 1248^a17, it is not regarded as a genuine case of luck.

Secondly, there is the case in which God gives good nature, which leads via bad reasoning to a successful outcome (1247^b37). Neither is this really good fortune: it is fortune through nature, and the only real case of good fortune is fortune through luck.

The third and fourth cases are the two that Aristotle regards as the genuine cases of luck, and lists as the two kinds here at the end of the chapter. In the third case, God gives us inspiration that leads from good desire to good outcome: there is no reasoning, but something more valuable than reasoning. It is a kind of luck that is in accordance with impulse. It is this luck that is described as divine in the *EE*. This is continuous good fortune (which means that it too is only doubtfully worthy of the name, since irregularity is taken by Aristotle as one of the characteristics of luck). Finally we have the case in which somebody with bad desires performs good actions, the kind illustrated by Almaviva's lucky escape from adultery, good fortune contrary to one's impulse. This is a genuine kind of luck; it is the non-divine, irregular kind mentioned last of all by Aristotle.

6

MORAL LUCK

In recent years many philosophers have discussed the problem of moral luck.[1] The problem is this. How can a moral matter—such as whether someone turns out virtuous or wicked—depend on luck? Surely only what is in our own power can be a proper matter for praise and blame. On the other hand, the actions on which we are judged are performed in contexts which are at the mercy of luck of various sorts. There is the constitutive luck, of being the kind of person one is at the beginning of one's moral life, well or ill born and bred; there is the situational luck of the kinds of problems and circumstances one has to face, difficult or easy; and there is the executive luck of how one's projects turn out, successfully or unsuccessfully.

Aristotle's discussion of luck and fortune in his ethical treatises addresses some of the same issues; but the overlap is not complete, and there are important differences of approach. One which is particularly striking is this. Aristotle's interest in moral luck is primarily an interest in moral good luck; he wants to know what contribution, if any, fortune makes to moral excellence, to well-doing, and to happiness. Our modern moralists are more interested in moral bad luck. We worry about how to assess the criminal who comes from such a deprived background that we feel he never had a chance to be law-abiding. We are uncertain whether to hold responsible a person who is unfortunate enough to be compelled by terrorists to perform a criminal act. We wonder whether it is fair to punish a drunken driver more heavily because he was so unlucky as to impact on an incautious pedestrian on his homeward journey.

This difference of viewpoint is connected with another more general one. Aristotle in his ethical treatises is concerned with moral excellence: with what it is to be virtuous, to live a good human life at the highest level. Modern students of moral responsibility are much more concerned with moral delinquency: with what it is to violate a moral or legal code, to fall below minimum acceptable standards of

[1] See Williams, 'Moral Luck'; Nagel, 'Moral Luck'; Kenny, 'Aristotle on Moral Luck'.

good living. This may be because we live still under the influence of the Judaeo-Christian concept that the essence of morality is obedience to a divine law, any violation of which is sinful; or it may be for the more secular reason that our interest in morality is an interest in the kinds of sanction, social or judicial, which society is justified in imposing on those whose conduct conflicts with socially accepted norms. To use an academic metaphor: Aristotle's treatment of moral luck is concerned with the influence of fortune on first-class results; contemporary philosophers and jurisprudents are more interested in the influence of luck at the pass–fail line.

Bearing these differences in mind, let us look again at what Aristotle has to say about the three kinds of moral luck which have figured in recent discussions. Constitutive luck is mentioned in the final chapter of the *NE*:

Some people believe that it is nature that makes men good, others that it is habit, and others again that it is teaching. Now, whatever goodness comes from nature is obviously not in our power, but is present in truly fortunate men as the result of some divine cause. (1179^b20-3)

In the *NE*, then, true good fortune is to receive, from a divine source, whatever may be the natural element in virtue. In the *EE*, on the other hand, as we have seen, Aristotle is unwilling to accept that what comes from nature comes from luck. There is one kind of fortune which is the possession of natural good desires: this is indeed regular, and so there is no objection to saying that it is natural, but it is not a matter of luck. 'Not all who seem to have good fortune prosper by luck, and not through nature' (1248^a12 ff.). If we say that there are two kinds of good fortune, namely good fortune by nature and good fortune by luck, we have to say that only the latter really deserves the name 'good fortune'.[2]

There is no doubt, however, that what comes from nature is not in our power; and this implies that human beings, prior to any voluntary desert, have unequal chances of achieving happiness. In *NE* I, 1099^b18-19, Aristotle mentions with sympathy the view that happiness is available, through learning and care, to all those who are not 'maimed with regard to virtue'; but as the treatise progresses the necessary conditions for happiness, whether perfect or imperfect, seem to be such as to be available only to a minority, even among

[2] See above, pp. 70, 74.

Greeks, let alone among the human race as a whole. In *EE* 1, similarly, we read:

If the good life consists in those things we owe to luck or nature, it would be something that many people could not hope for, since its acquisition is not in their power, nor attainable by their care or activity; but if it depends on the individual and his personal deeds being of a certain kind, then the supreme good will be both more general and more divine. (1215ᵃ11-16)

But once again, by the time we have reached the final book we wonder how many of the human race can achieve the status of *kalos kagathos*; even among the Greeks, the Spartans seem by now to have been disqualified (1248ᵇ37)!

The most Aristotle seems entitled to claim is that his account of happiness makes it available to a wider number than some of the rival theories do: the exercise of virtue is not, in itself and of its nature, a competitive good, in the way that riches and power are. Since happiness requires virtue, and since virtue requires the correct natural predispositions, some will by nature be deprived of the possibility of happiness. But these less fortunate people will not be necessarily vicious or wicked; if the presence of certain natural qualities is a necessary condition for virtue, their absence is not a sufficient condition for vice. Someone lacking the natural constitution for temperance, for instance, may none the less achieve the condition of continence.

It is easy to understand Aristotle's reluctance to regard the constitutive luck of good natural dispositions as being strictly speaking a matter of luck. For if we regard our nature as being a piece of good or bad luck, there is the question: To whom does the luck come? That I am a human being and not a god is surely not a matter of luck; there is no 'I' to whom these different options might accede, unless we indulge in the kind of fantasies about possible worlds from which Aristotle's text is blessedly free. Similarly, that I am the kind of person I have been from birth is not something that can be regarded as luck befalling me, whether good or bad.

What of executive luck? Let us first consider first executive good luck. In the *EE* Aristotle considers the case of a good agent whose projects are successful by good fortune rather than good planning (1247ᵇ36); once again, he does not seem to want to consider this really a case of luck, perhaps because it is not a case of an agent getting something better than he deserves. In neither treatise does he seem to countenance the existence of executive bad luck, the case in which a moral agent, pursuing a worthwhile end, fails to achieve his goal because something goes wrong with the execution of his plan. Certainly, if this is something intrinsic to the project it is a case that Aristotle will not count as ill luck at all. According to both *NE* and *EE*, the exercise of virtue involves not only moral excellence but also wisdom; so a person of good intentions who fails to translate them into virtuous deeds will lack wisdom and thus not be really virtuous.

If what goes wrong with the project is something entirely external and incidental, then we have really a case not of executive luck, but of situational luck. This is the position of Priam, unable finally to exercise the kingly virtues because of the collapse of Troy. We have seen Aristotle's account of this situation: Priam loses the capacity for happiness, but he retains his inward virtue and he will not become wretched.[3] In the *EE* situational luck is considered in the form of situational good luck: the luck of Almaviva who is deprived by the action of others of his opportunity to perform bad deeds, just as Priam was deprived by the action of others of his opportunity to perform good deeds.[4]

In the *EE* Aristotle seems more interested in interior, rather than exterior, forms of good fortune. To anyone familiar with the history of Christianity the chapter on good fortune recalls the doctrine of divine grace—a doctrine on whose development, indeed, it had a significant effect. Aristotle's divine fortune, like Christian divine grace, is a gift of God to humans, prior to all desert—the basis on which is built success or failure in the good life, the salvation or damnation of the soul. Grace comes in several kinds, as Aristotle's fortune did. There is the constitutive grace of being born and brought up in a Christian community; this grace, symbolized by baptism, was known as 'sanctifying grace'. The thoughts and inarticulate desires that precede all deliberation and choice and are the expression of the divine in us correspond to what theologians call actual graces. The inspirations received by divinely favoured people such as Socrates correspond to the *gratiae gratis datae* with which some of the saints, such as Joan of Arc, were favoured. Within the Christian Church the emphasis placed on grace has varied greatly from sect to sect, from the predestinarianism of the Calvinist to the libertarianism of Pelagians, ancient and modern.

In the *EE* Aristotle enunciates, in a dialectical passage, the Pelagian view that the gods would only favour someone who was already best and wisest. In his response he insists that the contribution of the divine

---

[3] See above, p. 33.   [4] See above, p. 69.

is prior to any virtue or wisdom acquired by the individual. The author of the *Magna Moralia*, by contrast, appears to accept the Pelagian view at face value:

Can it be then, that good fortune is a sort of care of the gods? Surely it will not be thought to be this! For we suppose that, if God is the disposer of such things, he assigns both good and evil in accordance with desert, whereas chance and the things of chance do really occur as it may chance. But if we assign such a dispensation to God, we shall be making him a bad judge or else unjust. And this is not befitting to God. (1207ᵃ7)

In what way did Aristotle envisage the operation of God in the soul, as described in 1248ᵃ25 ff.? Did he imagine God, as an efficient cause or agent, putting thoughts and desires in our minds by some spiritual and ineffable creative action? This seems a strange suggestion. For Aristotle God's action on the world is in general only as final cause. He is the origin of movement in the soul, according to the *EE* at 1248ᵃ26, in the same way as he is the origin of movement in the universe. But he moves the universe, as we know from *Metaphysics Λ*, 1072ᵇ3, as an object of love. So if God is the first mover in the soul, it is surely because the primary appetite for goodness is seen by Aristotle as a form of love of God.[5]

Yet the matter is not quite so simple. God is introduced not just as an explanation of desire's being for the right object, but also for desire's being at the right time (1248ᵃ17). In the *NE*, at the beginning, we saw Aristotle concerned about a possible infinite regress: a regress about the goods for the sake of which other goods were chosen, a regress in final causes. Here at the end of the *EE*, Aristotle is concerned with another possible infinite regress: a regress in choice itself, a regress in efficient causes. Medieval scholastics made a distinction, in the analysis of human wanting, between the specification and the exercise of volition. The specification of volition is given by saying *what* it is that is the object of wanting. The exercise of volition is explained by ascertaining what brought a particular volition into existence on a particular occasion. Crudely, and not wholly accurately, we could say that the medieval distinction between the specification and exercise of volition corresponds to our contemporary distinction between reasons and causes for action.

---

[5] Those who are under the influence of inspiration, as described in *EE* 1248ᵃ32-8, do perhaps undergo efficient causal activity from a supernatural being, such as Socrates' *daimōn*, but not from the cosmic godhead.

Now the regress threatened in the *NE* is a regress in the specification of volition. The regress threatened in the *EE* is a regress in the exercise of volition. Deliberation and thought, the items which threaten the regress, are datable events in a person's mental history, which appear to stand in relations of efficient causality to each other. So if God is introduced as the starting-point of this causal series, must he too not be acting in the mode of efficient cause?

Whatever may be the correct answer to this question in the Aristotelian system, the discussion so far shows why Aristotle's discussion of good fortune fascinated medieval Christian thinkers. Aquinas, who otherwise exhibits no knowledge of the *EE*, quotes this chapter a dozen times. Thus, in chapter 89 of the third book of the *Summa against the Gentiles* Aquinas argues that God not only gives us the power of free will, but actually causes individual choices, and he calls Aristotle to his support:

In the eighth book of the *Eudemian Ethics* Aristotle argues for this conclusion in the following way. There must be some cause of the fact of someone's understanding, deliberating, choosing, and willing; because every new event must have a cause. But if the cause is another preceding deliberation, and another preceding volition, since we cannot go on for ever in this series, there must be a first item. But this first item must be something which is better than reason. But nothing is better than understanding and reason except for God. Therefore God is the first principle of our deliberations and volitions.[6]

The argument is spelt out more fully in the ninth question of the *Prima Secundae* of the *Summa Theologiae*, where Aquinas is explaining how the will is moved by an exterior principle:

With respect to the will's being moved in regard to the exercise of its activity, here too we must maintain that the will is moved by an external principle. For everything which is at one time in actuality and at another time in potentiality needs to be set in motion by a mover. But it is obvious that the will sometimes begins to will things which it did not previously will. So it is necessary that it should be moved by something so to will. As has been said, it does indeed move

---

6 *Summa contra Gentiles* (1934 edn.), 332: 'Item. Argumentatur ad hoc Aristoteles, in VIII Eudemicae Ethicae, per hunc modum. Huius quod aliquis intelligat et consilietur et eligat et velit, oportet aliquid esse causam: quia omne novum oportet quod habeat aliquam causam. Si autem est causa eius aliud consilium et alia voluntas praecedens, cum non sit procedere in his in infinitum, oportet devenire ad aliquid primum. Huiusmodi autem primum oportet esse aliquid quod est melius ratione. Nihil autem est melius intellectu et ratione nisi Deus. Est igitur Deus primum principium nostrorum consiliorum et voluntatum.'

itself, in that by willing an end it brings itself to will the means to the end. But it can do this only by deliberation. Thus, when someone wants to be healed, he begins to think how this can be brought about, and by thinking he reaches the conclusion that seeing the doctor will help, and then wills to do so. But because he did not always have a volition for health, it must be that he began to want health at the instance of some moving cause. And if the will set itself in motion to willing, it would have had to do this through a process of deliberation based on some preceding volition. But this cannot go on for ever. So it is necessary that the will sets off on its first volition under the impulse of an exterior motive cause, as Aristotle shows in a chapter of the *Eudemian Ethics.*[7]

Aristotle's constant use of the analogy between medicine and ethics provides congenial material for the Christian philosopher. As the recovery of physical health is the goal of someone who turns to medicine, so spiritual salvation is the paradigm goal of practical reasoning for the devout Christian in a sick world in need of healing. 'All the world is our hospital, endowed by the ruined millionaire.' Here, and in other passages, Aquinas exploits the Eudemian solution to the threatened regress in order to establish God as prime mover in the soul, in respect both of nature and of grace.

If Aristotle's treatment of good fortune found echoes in the medieval teaching on divine grace, in the modern secular context it is particularly in discussions of *mens rea* in legal contexts that we have to decide what role to permit to luck in matters of moral responsibility. Recognizing moral luck need not involve holding people responsible for matters in which they had no choice. The law punishes negligent and reckless wrongdoing as well as intentional crime; and what is thus punished is a mixture of choice and luck. We will hold someone guilty of manslaughter if death results from his careless behaviour; if he had

---

[7] *Summa Theologiae* (1970 edn.), 73: 'Sed eo modo quo movetur quantum ad exercitium actus, adhuc necesse est ponere voluntatem, ab aliquo principio exteriori moveri. Omne enim quod quandoque est agens in actu et quandoque in potentia, indiget moveri ab aliquo movente. Manifestum est autem quod voluntas incipit velle aliquid, cum hoc prius non vellet. Necesse est ergo quod ab aliquo moveatur ad volendum. Et quidem, sicut dictum est, ipsa movet seipsam, inquantum per hoc quod vult finem, reducit seipsam ad volendum ea quae sunt ad finem. Hoc autem non potest facere nisi consilio mediante: cum enim aliquis vult sanari, incipit cogitare quomodo hoc consequi possit, et per talem cogitationem pervenit ad hoc quod potest sanari per medicum, et hoc vult. Sed quia non semper sanitatem actu voluit, necesse est quod inciperet velle sanari, aliquo movente. Et si quidem ipsa moveret seipsam ad volendum, oportuisset quod mediante consilio hoc ageret, ex aliqua voluntate praesupposita. Hoc autem non est procedere in infinitum. Unde necesse est ponere quod in primum motum voluntatis prodeat ex instinctu alicuius exterioris moventis, ut Aristoteles concludit in quodam capitulo Ethicae Eudemicae.'

been luckier, and death had not resulted, he would have been guilty, at most, only of a lesser offence.

It is in cases of crimes committed under duress that our intuitions about moral luck are put most severely to the test. If someone is forced by threats to carry out an evil project, should he or should he not be held guilty? Aristotle discusses duress at considerable length in both *EE* and *NE*. The obscurity of the treatment in both treatises is a measure of the difficulty and uncertainty of the topic. In the *NE* Aristotle says that actions performed under duress are in general voluntary; some actions under duress can be excused if the enforcing threats are such as to overstrain human nature; but there are some actions so heinous that no duress will excuse them. In the *EE* Aristotle takes a broadly similar position. In one way, however, the *EE* seems laxer than the *NE*, because it does not specify that there are some acts too wicked to be excused by duress. In another way, on the other hand, the *EE* seems stricter than the *NE*, for it insists that if duress is to excuse at all, the existence of the duress must itself be involuntary.[8]

The problems and hesitations to be found in the *NE* and the *EE* on the topic of duress have currently exhibited themselves in a series of decisions by British judges who have had to adjudicate questions of duress in the context of terrorism. If a man is forced at gunpoint by the IRA to plant a bomb which kills people, is he guilty of murder? A series of cases which came before the supreme courts in the UK in recent years produced incoherent results. In *Lynch*, in 1975 a majority of the House of Lords decided that duress was available as a defence to an accessory or principal in the second degree. The Court of Criminal Appeal of Northern Ireland, in *FitzPatrick*, found that duress was not available as a defence if it was itself voluntary (if it was, for instance, the result of enrolling as an IRA volunteer). In *Abbot*, in 1977, the Privy Council, by a majority, found that duress was no defence if the accused was the actual killer. The resulting situation in English law was unsatisfactory, in that the distinction between principal and accessory would not bear the weight put on it. *Lynch* was eventually overruled in 1987 by the judgement in *Howe*; the House of Lords laid down the rule that duress was no defence to any class of murderer. The court did not accept the moral principle that one who kills an innocent person out of fear for his own life should be exempted from criminal sanction as a concession to human frailty. The distinction between killers and

---

[8] See Kenny, *Aristotle's Theory of the Will*, 29-36, 41-7.

aiders, they decided, in relation to this defence, was a blemish on the law.[9]

At issue here were clearly conflicting intuitions about the relation of luck and morality. It is true that to resist duress may call for heroism. It does not follow that it is morally permissible to do anything else. Most of us most of the time can steer a middle course between wickedness and heroism, but in tragic circumstances—for instance in concentration camps—we may be faced with a stark choice between the two.

To take account of moral luck when we are making legal and moral judgements does not, in fact, involve any injustice. It is true that it involves holding people equally responsible for deeds done under very unequal temptation, as when the victim of duress is punished no less than the cold-blooded murderer. It is true too that it involves holding people unequally responsible who performed equally culpable acts (the lucky vs. the unlucky drunken driver). But in these cases no one gets less than their deserts (though the lucky drunk does better than he deserves) and no one is punished more than he deserves (the coerced killer preferred to take another's life rather than to risk his own, and there is good deterrent reason for the punishment of such a choice).

It is not our sense of justice but our sense of fairness or equality which is offended by the existence of moral luck. Aristotelian morality is explicitly non-egalitarian: the great-souled man needs wealth and power to display the greatness of his soul. Christianity is often contrasted with this: the poor are equal citizens of the Kingdom of God, and the widow's mite counts as much as the munificence of the rich. But if the distribution of terrestrial wealth matters less in Christianity, in the Christian system—whether in the parables of Jesus or the doctrine of the Catholic Church—different human beings have very different chances of achieving heavenly riches. And however much we try, in a secular civilization, to bring up the level of the most disadvantaged members of society to a minimum tolerable standard, there remain ineradicable inequalities in the distribution of the natural gifts which underlie the acquisition and retention of happiness. Neither ancient paganism, nor medieval

---

[9] See Kenny, 'Duress *per Minas*', which set out the details of the judgements in *Lynch*, *Abbott*, and *FitzPatrick*, and urged the overruling of *Lynch*.

Christianity, nor modern secularism has done anything to undermine the conclusion that the world operates on principles quite other than those of equality, and that no human institutions can radically alter the basic unfairness of life.

7

THE CONTEMPLATION AND SERVICE OF GOD

ACCORDING to the *NE*, understanding (*sophia*) is the most perfect virtue, and the activity which is the exercise of understanding, that is to say contemplation (*theōria*), is what perfect happiness consists in. All virtues are chosen for the sake of happiness (for the sake of their activities), but in the case of virtues other than understanding, according to Aristotle (1177^b3), we pursue something other than their activity for its own sake. In the case of understanding we do not seek anything other than the contemplation which is its exercise. According to the definition of perfection of 1097^a30-^b6, a thing's perfection corresponds to the extent to which it is chosen for its own sake. In this sense understanding is the most perfect virtue, and is more perfect than any other virtue. But of course the virtue of understanding is not as perfect as perfect happiness itself, which is not understanding, but the contemplation which is the exercise of understanding.

When from *NE* 10 we turn back to book 1 and read that the good for man is 'activity of soul in accordance with virtue, and if there are more than one virtues, according to the best and most perfect', it is natural to think of understanding as being the best and most perfect virtue. But it is not correct to say that in the passage in *NE* 1 Aristotle is referring to understanding. Rather, he is giving a description which he will show only later, in book 10, to be uniquely satisfied by *sophia*. The clause 'if there are several virtues, in accordance with the best and most perfect' keeps open a place for the eventual doctrine of *NE* 10 that happiness is the activity of the supreme virtue of understanding.

The inclusive interpretation of the description of happiness in book 1, as we have seen, has gained much favour with commentators. It is much more difficult to interpret book 10 in an inclusive sense.[1] One thing seems clear: it is not possible to treat the two books as

---

[1] The best attempt along these lines has been made by Keyt, 'Intellectualism in Aristotle'.

presenting a totally different account of happiness. No doubt we are wise not to take it for granted that *NE* 1 and *NE* 10 were written in a single stint; but there is evidence that when *NE* 1 was written Aristotle was thinking of the topic of *NE* 10 (at 1096^{a}5 he refers to a later discussion of the theoretical life) and that when he wrote *NE* 10 he had in mind *NE* 1 (1177^{a}11, where he refers to an earlier discussion which established that happiness consisted in the exercise of virtue).

In book 10 the argument goes: If happiness is activity which is the exercise of virtue, it is reasonable that it should be activity which is the exercise of the most excellent virtue: and this will be that of the best thing in us (1177^{a}12–13). This is either the understanding (*nous*) or something like it, so the activity of this in accordance with its proper virtue will be perfect happiness.

We have seen that 'perfect' is ambiguous in Aristotle's vocabulary. What does the word mean here? If it means 'final' rather than 'complete', that confirms our claim that it meant the same in the passage of *NE* 1 to which reference has just been made.[2] On the other hand, if it means 'complete' then again it implies that there is no other element in perfect happiness apart from the contemplative activity of *nous*.

Aristotle then goes on to show that theoretic contemplation possesses all the qualities which, according to book 1, were, in popular opinion and in truth, properties of happiness (1177^{a}18). Happiness in *NE* 1 was described as the best activity (1099^{a}30); but contemplation is the best activity, because it is the operation of the best thing in us (the understanding) and concerns the highest objects of knowledge (noble and divine things) (1177^{a}18–21; 1177^{a}15). In *NE* 1 we were told that activities in accordance with virtue were the most permanent and durable of human functions, and those who are blessed spend their life most continuously in them (1100^{b}12–17). Now we are told that contemplation is the most continuous activity, since we can contemplate truth more continuously than we can engage in any action (1177^{a}21–3).

In *NE* 1 we read:

The lovers of what is noble find pleasant the things that are by nature pleasant; and actions in accordance with virtue are such, so that these are pleasant for such men as well as in themselves. Their life, therefore, has no need of pleasure as an ornament, but has pleasure in itself. (1099^{a}13–16)

---

[2] See above, p. 17.

Now are told

We think happiness has pleasure mixed with it, and it is admitted on all hands that the pleasantest of all the activities which are exercises of virtue is the exercise of understanding. (1177^a23-5)

Self-sufficiency, as we have seen, was laid down as a cardinal attribute of happiness in *NE* 1 (1097^b6-20). Self-sufficiency, we are now told, belongs most of all to the *sophos*. He will, like those who specialize in other virtues, need the necessities of life (as already recognized in *NE* 1, 1101^a15); but he will not need others to be the objects of his virtuous activity, and the better he is at his chosen activity of contemplation, the less he will need others as assistants (1177^a27-^b1).

Finally, contemplation is loved for its own sake, much more so than moral virtue, and in contrast to the activities of the statesman which seek a happiness different from political action and sought as being different (1177^b1-15). It is this which gives contemplation the claim to be more perfect, in terms of the conditions laid down in *NE* 1 (1097^a16-30).

In book 1 and book 10 of the *NE* Aristotle behaves like the director of a marriage bureau, trying to match his client's description of his ideal partner. In the first book he lists the properties which people believe to be essential to happiness, and in the tenth book he seeks to show that philosophical contemplation, and it alone, possesses to the full these essential qualities.

The discussion concludes with the following summary:

So if among the actions in accordance with the virtues political and military actions stand out by their nobility and greatness, but are unleisurely and pursue an end and are not desirable for their own sake, but the activity of the understanding, which is contemplative, seems to be both superior in worth, and to pursue no end beyond itself, and to have its own proper pleasure (which augments the activity), and the self-sufficiency and leisureliness and unweariness (so far as is possible for humans) and all the other attributes of the blessed man are evidently proper to this activity, it follows that this will be the perfect happiness of man, given a perfect length of life. (1177^b16-26)

So the concluding section of the *NE*, instead of offering, like the *EE*, a single life containing all the value sought by the promoters of the three traditional lives, offers us a first-class, perfect happiness, consisting in the exercise of understanding. As an alternative, the *NE* goes on to offer a second-class career consisting in the exercise of wisdom and the moral virtues; that too is a form of happiness, but it is not perfect happiness (1178^a9-^b8).

The main reason why interpreters are motivated to reject this intellectualist position is that they do not find the position credible as a piece of philosophy, and as admirers of Aristotle they are unwilling to saddle his mature ethical work with such a strange doctrine. In particular, they find the contemplative who is the hero of *NE* 10 a strange and repellent human being.

A forceful statement of this view is made by Nussbaum:

Throughout books 1–10 Aristotle has indicated that the human good is an inclusive plurality of actions according to excellence, in which intellectual activity will be one component, side by side with other constituents of intrinsic worth, such as activity according to excellences of character and activity benefiting friends. Most of book 10 develops this view. But 10. 7 abruptly shifts to the defense of a life single-mindedly devoted to theoretical contemplation, seeking to maximize this as the single intrinsic good. Interpreters have tried in various ways to minimise this problem but it remains. According to the view expressed in 10. 7 friendship and excellence of character could not have intrinsic value; if we chose to pursue them, it would only be because, and insofar as, they seek to maximize contemplation. But their intrinsic worth is clearly defended in the other books. . . .

Perhaps the best that one can say is that Aristotle, like anyone who has been seriously devoted to the scholarly or contemplative life, understood that, thoroughly and properly followed, its demands are such as to eclipse all other pursuits. Although he tried to articulate a conception of a life complexly devoted to politics, love, and reflection, he also felt (whether at different times or in different moods at the same time) that really fine reflection could not stand side by side with anything else. He would, then, be . . . revising his conception in accordance with a new perception of a conflict between the full demands of one cherished value and all other values.[3]

The specific objection to the position of *NE* 10 may be phrased thus:[4] if Aristotle made contemplation alone a constituent of perfect happiness, then in cases where there is a conflict between the demands of moral virtue and the demands of contemplation, Aristotle must say that the agent should engage in contemplation, even if the alternative is saving his neighbour from a burning house. Even worse, as Devereux has argued, if the contemplative lacks moral virtue there is nothing to prevent him from being quite ruthless in pursuing his goal. For

---

[3] Nussbaum, 'Aristotle', 403.
[4] See Heinaman, 'Eudaimonia and Self-sufficiency', 51.

example, he may by betraying a friend gain a large sum of money and thereby assure himself years of leisure for philosophizing. What would hold him back?[5]

In my own book *The Aristotelian Ethics* I took up the notion of *panourgia* or cunning, as described in the *EE*, where it appears as the vice of excess in a triad in which wisdom appears as the virtue, and foolishness as the vice of defect (1221^a12):

The cunning man pursues a single dominant goal and is ruthless about other values. An intemperate man who pursued pleasure, come what may, would, provided he was intelligent, provide an obvious example of a cunning man. But so, if I am right, would the man who gave himself to the single hearted and unrelenting pursuit of philosophy without regard for the moral virtues. A person who organized his life entirely with a view to the promotion of philosophical speculation would be not wise but cunning . . . The type of person whom many regard as the hero of the *NE*, turns out, by the standards of the *EE*, to be a vicious and ignoble character.[6]

This line of objection is thus answered by Heinaman:

Aristotle's position is that contemplation is the best part of the total life of a person. But that does not mean that there are no other valuable elements in the total life of a person which have value—in part—independently of their contribution to contemplation.[7]

It is wrong to think that if perfect happiness is contemplation, then anything has value only in so far as it contributes to contemplation, and that anything is an intrinsic good only if it is a component of happiness.

Thus moral action too has intrinsic value independently of any contribution it may make to contemplation, even though it is not a component of perfect eudaimonia . . . In a particular case, the thing to do may well be to save one's neighbour from the burning house because in that case as the practically wise man was able to judge, moral action was better than contemplation.[8]

Moreover, it is rash to take for granted that the contemplative will lack the moral virtues. Does Aristotle in fact believe that he will possess them? Some commentators have answered yes, and some have answered no; all have been repelled by the idea of the ruthless,

---

[5] Devereux, review of Cooper.

[6] *The Aristotelian Ethics*, 214. In a footnote I entered a caveat that I was unsure that it was correct to regard the contemplative of *NE* 10 as thus ruthless in pursuit of philosophy.

[7] Heinaman, 'Eudaimonia and Self-sufficiency', 53.   [8] Ibid. 53.

treacherous theorizer, whether or not they regard him as Aristotle's own ideal. But what demands, according to Aristotle, does morality really make of the person of contemplative excellence?

Before answering this question, let us note that there is a distinction, in Aristotle, between failing to possess the moral virtues and falling into moral turpitude. Somebody, without actually being morally virtuous or admirable, may none the less fulfil minimum moral demands such as refraining from murder, theft, and adultery. The moral virtues are concerned with observing the mean among acts which are basically morally acceptable (NE 1107ᵃ8-17). An Aristotelian moral candidate may, as it were, obtain a pass degree in morality without obtaining the honours degree awarded for the excellence of moral virtue.

The position of NE 10 is surely that the contemplative will *possess* the moral virtues, but that their exercise will not constitute part of his happiness. That will be constituted by contemplation alone. None the less, being a human being, and a good human being, he will practise the moral virtues also (1178ᵇ5-7). But the activity of moral virtue is given its definition by the mean, and the mean differs from person to person. The right number of brave actions, for instance, will be greater for the politicians than it will be for the theorizer. Wisdom, which determines the mean, will prescribe differently in the two cases, because of the different overarching end which constitutes the chief happiness of each of the two types of virtuous person. It will diminish the demands of the other fine and noble activities, in order to preserve the maximum room for contemplative happiness.

Is it not a difficulty that on this view it will not be true that the contemplative does everything else for the sake of contemplation? And if he does not do everything else for the sake of contemplation, how can contemplation constitute his happiness? If he really did everything else for the sake of contemplation, why *should* he rescue his neighbour from burning if it distracts from contemplation?

The difficulty can only be resolved by taking a minimalist interpretation of those passages in the first book of the NE which say that happiness is that for the sake of which everything else is done.[9] On the

---

[9] See Broadie, *Ethics with Aristotle*, 31: 'Aristotle does not explain how we are to take the crucial expression "for the sake of (heneka) happiness". To make his claims plausible, we have to stretch this to mean "having regard to happiness". Thus the central good functions sometimes as a constraint rather than a goal in the ordinary sense of a positively aimed for objective.' See p. 20 above.

account just given, the contemplative will sometimes do temperate things for the sake of his philosophy (to avoid the hangover which would impede his research, for instance), but he will also do temperate things for their own sake (he will take precautions not to let himself get soft, for instance).

The objection to the theorizer, on this interpretation, is not that he will let his neighbour's house burn down, or that he will steal in order to get an adequate research fund. It is rather that he will not do such things as volunteering to fight in the course of a just war. He is likely to take a course of action such as that taken by W. H. Auden at the beginning of the Second World War, crossing the Atlantic to nurture his talent in less dangerous surroundings.

Even when the harsh lineaments of the contemplative have been softened in ways such as this, his aspect is still repellent to many commentators, and they seek various ways of absolving Aristotle from excessive intellectualism. Thus Urmson writes: 'It is perhaps not unreasonably charitable to Aristotle to take his verbal identification of contemplation with *eudaimonia* in the later chapters of book X to be the selection of a dominant feature within a life containing other elements necessary to full *eudaimonia*.'[10] John Cooper, in his more recent work, has endeavoured to draw the sting of the intellectualist passages in book 10 in the following manner. When Aristotle says that contemplation is perfect happiness, he is not saying that contemplation is the whole of happiness. He is saying the contemplation is the best part of, the fine flower of, a happiness which contains also the activity of the moral virtues.[11]

This account is unconvincing. First, the account seems to be vulnerable to the arguments of an earlier Cooper, who showed that the crucial passage at 1176^b26 ff. is to be taken as distinguishing between a first-class happiness consisting in the exercise of *sophia*, and an alternative second-class happiness consisting of wisdom and the moral virtues.[12]

Secondly, one argument for saying that understanding is superior to wisdom and the life of the virtues is that it makes its practitioner more self-sufficient: he does not need the money or the cohorts which the pursuer of political happiness does. But if, as Cooper now suggests, the theorizer is also the politician, he *will* need all these things and will lack the self-sufficiency canvassed by book 10.[13]

---

[10] *Aristotle's Ethics*, 66.   [11] Cooper, 'Contemplation and Happiness'.
[12] Cooper, *Aristotle's Man*, 157–60.
[13] This point is made by Heinaman, 'Eudaimonia and Self-sufficiency', 45: 'Aristotle

The argument between the intellectualist interpretation of *eudaimonia* in the *NE* and the inclusive interpretation will no doubt continue. It is noticeable how in the course of the last two decades the positions of the intellectualist interpreters and the inclusive interpreters of the *NE* have come closer and closer together. But no explanation succeeds in the three goals which most commentators have set themselves: (1) to give an interpretation of book 1 and book 10 which does justice to the texts severally; (2) to make the two books consistent with each other; (3) to make the resulting interpretation one which can be found morally acceptable by contemporary philosophers. And even if *NE* 1 and *NE* 10 are reconcilable, the *NE* as a whole seems to have two different heroes: the contemplative of 1 and 10, and the great-souled man of 2–4.[14] Both characters are difficult to make palatable for twentieth-century readers.

But must we judge Aristotle's ethics solely by the Nicomachean position? Those who are prepared to take seriously the *EE* as an expression of Aristotle's mature theory are able to preserve their admiration intact without doing violence to any of the relevant texts of the *NE*.

In the *EE* happiness is clearly a combination of the activities of various kinds of excellence. Like the *NE*, the *EE* argues to the nature of happiness from the notion of function: but unlike the *NE* it takes as its starting-point not the function of man (a doubtful notion) but the function of the soul. As a result of the function argument we conclude at 1219^a35 that happiness is the activity of a good soul. We are then told (line 37) that virtue can be perfect or imperfect. 'Perfect' and 'imperfect' must here be used in the sense of 'complete' and 'incomplete', since we are told that perfect virtue is the whole of virtue, and imperfect virtue is part of virtue. We are told finally that happiness is the exercise of perfect life in accord with perfect virtue; which in the context must mean the virtue which is a whole of parts.

This theme is taken up later in the same book II at 1220^a34: just as the general good condition of the body is compounded of the partial

cannot possibly be intending to say that contemplation plus moral action is perfect eudaimonia because any lack of self-sufficiency attaching to moral action attaches equally to the combination of contemplation with moral action.'

[14] This has been well known for a long time. Thus, Gauthier–Jolif, *L'Éthique à Nicomaque* (1970 edn.), i/1. 81: 'C'est presque un lieu commun de dire qu'il y a dans l'Éthique à Nicomaque deux morales, celle de la vertu et celle de la contemplation, personnifiées l'une dans le magnanime du livre IV et l'autre dans le philosophe du livre X.'

virtues, so also is the virtue of the soul, *qua* end. But of virtue there are two kinds: moral and intellectual.

After the treatment of individual virtues and quasi-virtues is complete, in the final book, we return to the theme: 'About each virtue by itself we have already spoken; now since we have distinguished their natures one by one we must give a more accurate description of the excellence which arises out of their combination, which we now name *kalokagathia*' (1248^{b}8–11).[15] To possess this virtue you have to possess all 'the partial virtues' (*tas kata meros aretas*). This must mean 'the virtues of the parts of the soul', just as the partial virtues of the body are the virtues of the various parts of the body. So it must include the virtues of the intellectual part of the soul, including the supreme or theoretical part.

This is in accord with what was said in the common book B, which is book V of the *EE*, in answer to the objection that understanding (*sophia*) and wisdom are superfluous because unproductive. 'They are indeed productive: not like medical skill in relation to health, but like health itself; it is thus that *sophia* is productive of happiness: for being a part of virtue entire by being possessed and being operative it is productive of happiness' (1144^{a}3–6). The possession of *sophia* is part of perfect virtue (which is the same as 'virtue entire'). Correspondingly, the exercise of *sophia* is part of perfect happiness: it would be pointless of Aristotle to remind us that this virtue is only part of perfect virtue if he wanted to say that it was the whole of perfect happiness. Understanding is one of the virtues which causally produce activities which in their totality are happiness, in the way that health (which is a combination of the healthiness of the various parts of the body) produces the activities of a healthy body.

After *kalokagathia* has been described and contrasted with the Laconian or utilitarian character,[16] the conclusion is drawn in the final chapter of the *EE*: *kalokagathia* is perfect virtue. Here 'perfect' must mean not just complete, but also final. Completeness of virtue was introduced as a defining feature of *kalokagathia*; the ultimacy of virtuous activity as an end is the feature which emerges from the contrast with utilitarianism. So, among virtues, *kalokagathia* is the most final. But it is not the most final human good: because virtues are for the sake of their exercises, not the other way round (1219^{a}32), and so it is the exercise of *kalokagathia* that is the supreme human good which

---

[15] Reading καλοῦμεν, against the OCT.
[16] See above, p. 10.

constitutes happiness. This must include both contemplation and morally virtuous activity.

The final chapter of the *EE* spells out the relationship between these elements within happiness.

Here as elsewhere one should conduct one's life with reference to one's superior, and more specifically with reference to the active state of one's superior.[17] A slave, for instance, should look to his master's and everyone to the superior to whom he is subject. Now a human being is by nature a compound of superior and inferior, and everyone[18] accordingly should conduct their lives with reference to the superior part of themselves.[19] However, there are two kinds of superior: there is the way in which medical science is superior, and the way in which health is superior; the latter is the *raison d'être* of the former.[20] It is thus that matters stand in the case of our intellectual faculty.[21] For God is not a

---

[17] The MSS read: πρὸς τὴν ἕξιν κατὰ τὴν ἐνέργειαν τὴν τοῦ ἄρχοντος. This is usually emended (Ross, Rackham, Dirlmeier, Woods), but is accepted by the OCT. In *The Aristotelian Ethics*, 174, I defended the MS reading by saying 'what is meant is that the slave should help his master to do whatever his master is doing as well as it can be done: he should strive to see that his master's ἐνέργεια has the ἕξις of goodness.' This took ἕξις as attaching to the ἐνέργεια. This now seems to me strained; I think the sentence should be read as if it were equivalent to τὴν ἕξιν τὴν τοῦ ἄρχοντος κατὰ τὴν ἐνέργειαν. The sense comes to much the same. The translation given above is essentially that of Verdenius, who likewise defends the MS reading.

[18] 1249ᵇ11 ἕκαστον. Verdenius, 'Human Reason and God', 287, argues that this means each of the (two) parts of the soul, and has a rather implausible account of why Aristotle did not write ἑκάτερον. Unless it has this meaning, he argues, the text is repetitious. But the point is that we have to live not only in accord with any external ruler, but our internal one (our very own, ἑαυτῶν). (I render the plural 'of themselves'. I think the shift from singular to plural can be natural in both languages, and there is no need to emend with the OCT: Verdenius quotes a Homeric parallel.) With Woods, against Verdenius, I think that the καὶ ἕκαστον introduces an apodosis. After ἕκαστον the MSS have δή; Verdenius defends the MSS, and sees no reason to introduce ἄν with Spengel (and now the OCT).

[19] The genitive is as it were partitive: that part of themselves which is an ἀρχή.

[20] The same point, and the comparison with the intellect, is made in the common book B, at 1145ᵃ6: wisdom is not supreme over understanding or the better part of us, any more than the art of medicine is over health; for it does not use it but provides for its coming into being; it issues orders, then, for its sake but not to it.

[21] The Greek text is οὕτω δ'ἔχει κατὰ τὸ θεωρητικόν, which is ambiguous. Does οὕτω mean 'like the foregoing' (i.e. superior) in being twofold; or like the foregoing (viz. health) in being a *raison d'être*? Does θεωρητικόν mean the intellectual faculty in general (so Düring, *Aristoteles*, 451 n. 125) or the speculative faculty in particular (so Verdenius)? In *The Aristotelian Ethics*, 175, I claimed that the faculty meant was the theoretical intellect, the ἐπιστημονικόν of B. Verdenius, 'Human Reason and God', 291, says this term is chosen 'because the guiding principle God, though relating to the whole of the rational part, is to be apprehended by this special faculty'. In other words, θεωρητικόν anticipates line 17 θεωρίαν and line 20 θεωρεῖν. I now think that it means the broad sense, for reasons given below, p. 98. 'Thus' must therefore be taken in the first of the senses distinguished above.

superior who issues commands, but is the *raison d'être* of the commands that wisdom issues. But '*raison d'être*' is ambiguous, as has been explained elsewhere—this needs saying, since of course God is not in need of anything. To conclude: whatever choice or possession of natural goods—bodily goods, wealth, friends, and the like—will most conduce to the contemplation of God is best: this is the finest criterion. But any standard of living which either through excess or defect hinders the service and contemplation of God is bad. (1249^{b}6–21)

This text incorporates several ambiguities. But what is clear is that Aristotle believes that the intellect is twofold, like the superior, and the theoretical intellect is related to the practical intellect as a *raison d'être*. There is more than one way of getting this sense out of the text, as commentators have exhibited. Moreover, the way in which medicine rules over the patient corresponds to the way in which the rational part of the soul rules over the irrational part. This latter correspondence is not mentioned in the text because this point had already been dealt with a few pages before, where we have been told that wisdom 'uses' virtue as a ruler 'uses' his subject (1246^{b}11).[22]

The most difficult part of the chapter to interpret is the final section setting out the relationship between the soul and God. Von Arnim proposed to replace the word *theos* with the word *nous* wherever it appears in this chapter, attributing the presence of the 'God' to a Christian interpolator. There is no support for this in any manuscript or version, and the proposal is most implausible in itself: what Christian, imbued from childhood with the need to obey the Ten Commandments, would assent to the proposition 'God is not a superior who issues commands'?

However, the mention of God does come as something of a surprise, and many commentators, having rejected von Arnim's proposal as an emendation, have accepted it as an interpretation. Thus, Dirlmeier, citing *EE* 1248^{a}26–9 and *NE* 1177^{a}16, argues that *nous* here is not only regarded as divine but is even called 'God'. The God referred to must be an immanent one, since the relation between God and wisdom as explained at *EE* 1249^{b}13 ff. refers to the *theōrētikon*, i.e. to a part of the soul. If this God were exterior and transcendent, wisdom would be the supreme mental faculty, and wisdom is not appropriate for the contemplation of God. Dirlmeier concludes that the superior and inferior mentioned at 1249^{b}10 are *nous* and *phronēsis* respectively. He takes *theou* at line 17 to be a subjective genitive, so that the

---

[22] So Verdenius, 'Human Reason and God', 288.

contemplation of God must be taken as 'God's contemplation'. At line 20 'the service and contemplation of God' must be taken as 'the service of God, and contemplation'. Thus interpreted, the passage contains a twofold division of the intellectual faculty, one part in which inheres prescriptive wisdom, and another part which is called 'God' and issues in contemplation. The twofold vision will correspond to the division between the *logistikon* and the *epistēmonikon* in B, while the divine status accorded to the contemplative understanding gives this Eudemian passage a close resemblance to *NE* 10.

Dirlmeier's position was adopted by Düring, but Verdenius has shown that it is untenable.[23] It is true that Aristotle calls the human mind 'divine', but he never calls it 'God'. God is superior to the human understanding (1248^a29); God is always in a state of actuality, but the human understanding needs a principle to set it in motion (1248^a17–21). Dirlmeier is wrong to think that the rational part of the soul consists of a superior and inferior; what Aristotle says is that the human being is composed of superior and inferior, that is to say of rational and irrational parts of the soul. The rational part of the soul, however, is itself twofold.

In accordance with the general rule that everyone should live in accordance with their superior part or ruling principle (*arkhē*), a human being should govern his life in accordance with what is required by his rational soul. But while the rational soul is such an *arkhē* or principle, we need to know what kind of principle it is. In matters concerning our body we need to take account of the requirements (i.e. prescriptions) of medical science; we also must take account of the requirements (i.e. needs) of our health. Both medical science and health are *arkhai* in different ways; and the latter is the *raison d'être* of the former. We must apply this to the rational part of the soul: there too there is a principle like medicine and a principle like health. The principle corresponding to medicine is wisdom, which, like medicine, issues commands. So in following the requirements of our *arkhē* we must (1) obey the commands of wisdom and (2) take account of the needs of that which is related to wisdom as health is related to medical science. Well, what is this?

From the discussion in the common book B (1145^a6–11) we might expect the answer to be: understanding. But here Aristotle, instead of giving an immediate answer, goes on 'For God is not a superior who

[23] Verdenius, 'Human Reason and God', 288–91. See also Kenny, *The Aristotelian Ethics*, 175.

issues commands.' This sentence, and especially the 'for', is puzzling, and this is the reason why commentators want to change either the reading or the sense of 'God' so as to make Aristotle refer here to the speculative intellect.

But the sentence becomes clear if we look back to the previous chapter. The cosmic God was the supreme *arkhē* in the soul, superior to *logos*, *epistēmē*, and *nous*. So, it seems, if everyone should live according to the requirements of his superior as a slave lives according to the requirements of his master, we must conclude that in matters of the soul we must live in obedience to the commands of God. But this would be an erroneous conclusion, according to Aristotle: for God is not a ruler who issues commands. To avoid this conclusion, we have to distinguish between senses of *arkhē*: God is indeed the supreme *arkhē* of the soul; but not in the sense in which the analogy of slave and master would suggest.[24]

Aristotle has just said, having explained that there is a twofold *arkhē* in matters of the body, 'It is thus that matters stand in the case of our intellectual faculty.' He means: Our intellectual faculty has likewise a twofold *arkhē*. The term used for the faculty (*theōrētikon*) can be used in a narrower sense; it is used here to denote the broad intellectual faculty, but it is chosen because of the emphasis in the succeeding text on its ability to theorize.

The overall sense of the passage is this: In the same manner there is a twofold *arkhē* in relation to our intellect. God is one *arkhē*, but not, like medicine, an epitactic one which gives commands; wisdom is an *arkhē* which is epitactic, and gives its commands for the sake of God.

In the common book B, at 1145^{a}6-11, we are told:

Wisdom is not in authority over understanding or the better part, any more than the science of medicine is in authority over health; it does not make use of

---

[24] The interpretation given here is set out at greater length in *The Aristotelian Ethics*, 174-8. A very similar interpretation is set out independently by Broadie, *Ethics with Aristotle*, 386: 'In one sense (1) a person is "ruled" by a valuable objective, in another (2) by the practical wisdom that sets about obtaining it. And in one sense (a), that for the sake of which is the good which one aims to achieve, and in another (b) it is the beneficiary of that good. That which *rules* in sense (2) rules by issuing instructions (one part of the soul to the other, for instance, or a doctor to a patient), and *what* is ruled (i.e. managed) in this way is that for the sake of which in sense (b). The good which is aimed for is also *that for the sake of which*, but not in the sense which implies that it is ruled. It is not ruled by anything, but this is not straightforwardly because it is a ruler—as if everything in this area of discourse is either ruler or ruled—for it does not rule in sense (2). Yet even so it conforms to the principle (if such it is) that everything either rules or is ruled; for it does rule in sense (1).'

it, but provides for its coming into being; the orders it issues are not issued to it but issued for its sake.

Are we then to interpret this final passage of the *EE* in the sense that God is like health, which is the *hou heneka* or *raison d'être* of medicine? Surely wisdom does not 'provide for God's coming into being?' Indeed not: there are two kinds of *raison d'être*, and God is not the kind which needs to be brought into existence (like health) or provided with benefits—for God has no needs.[25]

Aristotle is here saying that God is not a *raison d'être* whose good is being aimed at, but a good whose attainment is the *raison d'être* of wisdom's commands. Well then, what is the other *raison d'être* whose good is being aimed at, and what is it for it to attain God? Aristotle gives no explicit reply, but the answer is clear enough from the concluding passage: that which benefits from the commands of wisdom is that which serves and contemplates God; and this service and contemplation is itself the only kind of attainment of God which is possible. And what is it that serves and contemplates God? Either the soul as a whole, or its speculative part: which of the two is intended must depend on what is meant by 'service' here.

Let us look more closely at this final passage of the *EE*:

To conclude: whatever choice or possession of natural goods—bodily goods, wealth, friends, and the like—will most conduce to the contemplation of God[26] is best: this is the noblest criterion. But any standard of living which either through excess or defect hinders the service and contemplation of God is bad. This is how it is with the soul, and this is the best criterion, to be conscious as little as possible of the irrational part of the soul[27] in so far as it is irrational. (1249[b]16-23)

It is not said here that the contemplation of God determines everything in the good person's life; it is the criterion for the choice of

---

[25] At 1249[b]16 read ἐπεὶ ἐκεῖνος οὐθενὸς δεῖται. The ἐπεί is not to explain why God does not issue commands, but why it has to be mentioned that there are two kinds of οὗ ἔνεκα.

[26] MSS τὴν τοῦ θεοῦ θεωρίαν. The OCT, following Robinson, here emends to τοῦ θείου, and at line 20 alters τὸν θεὸν θεραπεύειν to τὸ ⟨ἐν ἡμῖν⟩ θεῖον. It is remarkable how determined scholars are to keep God out of this passage. In this instance, however, the attempt is futile since the OCT has retained θεός at line 14.

[27] Reading Fritzsche's emendation ἀλόγου for ἄλλου (MSS). Verdenius, 'Human Reason and God', 294, argues that there is no need to change: the other part obviously is the irrational part. But the end of the sentence is easier to read with the emendation; it is equivalent to ᾖ ἄλογον; with the other you have to take it, in a very contorted way, as meaning '*qua* hindering from the contemplation of God'.

natural goods like health, wealth, and strength. The noble actions of
the moral virtues are chosen for their own sake and have their own
internal criterion, namely the mean. A good man exercising the virtue
of temperance will indeed be conscious of the irrational part of the
soul: he will enjoy food, drink, and sex in the appropriate measure, and
if he did not he would be guilty of the vice of *anaisthēsia*, insensitivity
(1221^a2, 1231^a26). But he will not be conscious of the irrational part
qua irrational, precisely because it will be obeying the commands of
reason (1220^b28, 1249^b15).

None the less the final chapter of the *EE* does offer a general
standard for the exercise of virtue. The final summary of its content, at
lines 23–5, says 'So much, then, for the criterion of *kalokagathia* and the
point of the prima-facie goods.' We have been offered, then, the
standard of perfect virtue.[28] The prima-facie goods, the natural goods
that are not in themselves praiseworthy, are such things as health,
strength, honour, birth, wealth, and power (1248^b24, 28–30; 1249^a10–
11); they are the subject-matter of the virtues of magnanimity,
magnificence, and liberality (*EE* III, 1231^b28 ff.). The subject-matter of
the virtues of courage, temperance, and meekness is the passions of
the irrational soul mentioned at 1249^b22–5. Thus this last passage in
the *EE* does give a standard for the exercise of the six virtues which
are discussed in *EE* III and which are included in *kalokagathia*. Each
virtue does indeed have its own internal criterion, the mean; but what
the mean is in each case is to be determined by wisdom; and wisdom
gives its commands for the sake of God.[29]

Does this mean that the *kalos kagathos* of the *EE* turns out after all to
be identical with the *theōrētikos* of *NE* 10? Not at all: and indeed it has
been a matter of debate between scholars whether the *kalos kagathos*
will have the virtue of *sophia* at all.[30] Broadie has raised the following

[28] This is denied by Rowe, 'De Aristotelis ... dicendi ratione', 110, and Verdenius,
'Human Reason and God', 295.

[29] In an excellent passage, Broadie emphasizes that the consideration of the 'noblest
criterion' does not imply that *theōria* is the *only* end by which to measure the pursuit of
natural goods: 'Other kinds of noble activity are ends for the noble person; hence wealth
in excess of what is needed for leisure spent in *theōria* would not necessarily be in excess
of the ethical mean, since it could well be needed for other noble practices. This would
not arise, of course, if nothing is noble except the pursuing and engaging in *theōria* or if
no rational choice were wise unless made with this end in view. But there is no ground in
the *EE* for such a monolithic interpretation, and much to suggest that Aristotle
recognises a plurality of noble ends ... Other activities have in common with *theoria* that
they all satisfy A's closing dictum: this is the best limit of the soul: to perceive the non-
rational part of the soul *as such* as little as possible' (*Ethics with Aristotle*, 384).

[30] In favour, Monan, *Moral Knowledge*, 123–31, who says that the *EE* view of reason as

question. If contemplation is one noble activity among others, even if the noblest, why does Aristotle single it out for special attention? Why should he not simply say that it has a high place in the best life, as one of a range of different noble activities, any one of which could be cited as a yardstick for pursuit of natural goods?

Broadie's answer is that Aristotle could not take it for granted that his audience would regard *theōria* as noble at all. So he first sets up a notion of nobility in which natural goods are for the sake of noble practical deeds, which therefore function as a limit. But this makes room for superfluity, and this is incoherent unless there is some new limit, something else for which the extra goods might be too much or too little. '*Theōria* is not only glorious in itself; but is a moral safeguard; it preserves practical nobility in superfluity much as practical nobility preserves sheer basic goodness.'[31] Since contemplation generates no natural goods, its only hope of entry into the good life is via the category of the noble. It is at the supreme point of that category because of the particular form of its superiority, or capacity to rule. *Theōria* can rule only in the way the good rules simply as good; the good as such can cause only as final cause, unlike an efficient cause which rules through power. Hence whatever can affect our lives through final causality alone is closer to perfection of goodness than things which cause by efficiency.

How are the intellectual and practical virtues related to the supreme principle, God? God is related to the intellectual virtue of *sophia* as being the principal object of its activity of contemplation. But how is God related to the practical virtues? Can he be in any way the object of them? The answer to the question cannot be given until we make the enquiry, postponed earlier, into the meaning of 'the service of God' at 1249ᵇ20.

Clearly when Aristotle uses this expression he is not thinking of the liturgies he describes in book 8 of the *Politics*. There is a Platonic

---

part of whole virtue represents a more mature, and therefore later, stage of Aristotle's thought than the intellectualism of *NE*. Against, Verdenius, 'Human Reason and God', 297, who claims that 'The fact that καλοκἁγαθία is called "perfect virtue" does not force us to conclude that it is identical with the "complete virtue" of 1219a39'; it is the perfection only of the moral virtues, and Aristotle does not attempt to rank the life of virtue and the life of contemplation. 'His preference clearly goes out to the latter, but he does not express it in such a radical way as in the EN. This absence of radicalism marks the EE as an early stage of his thought.' It is an interesting idea that people necessarily become more radical as they grow older.

³¹ *Ethics with Aristotle*, 289.

passage whose likeness to the end of the *EE* has struck several scholars, namely *Timaeus* 90 c:

When a man is always occupied with the cravings of desire and ambition, and is eagerly striving to satisfy them, all his thoughts must be mortal, and as far as it is altogether possible to become such, he must be mortal every whit because he has cherished his mortal part. But he who has been earnest in the love of knowledge and of true wisdom, and has exercised his intellect more than any other part of him, must have thoughts immortal and divine, if he attain truth, and in so far as human nature is capable of sharing in immortality, he must altogether be immortal, and since he is ever cherishing the divine power and has the divinity within him in perfect order, he will be singularly happy.

The conclusion drawn by Plato here is that one must feed the divine principle within us upon the harmonies and revolutions of the cosmos. This passage in fact resembles *NE* 10 much more than it resembles *EE*; especially noteworthy is the reference to mortal and immortal thoughts (see 1177^{b}31-4). A closer Platonic parallel to the present passage occurs in Plato's *Euthyphro*. Socrates argues that the notion of the service of the gods is unintelligible: we cannot benefit the gods. *Therapeia* is what slaves give to their masters to help them with their tasks; but what is the task (*ergon*) of the gods? 'Many noble things', says Euthyphro. By the service of the gods Euthyphro has in mind acts of justice, like the attempt to punish a murderer (on which he is currently engaged).

If Aristotle does have the *Euthyphro* in mind here, then the service of God could well include acts of moral virtue. These are the *kalai praxeis* of the *kalos kagathos* which are the subject of the early part of the chapter; they could well be regarded as the many noble things which we, under the *arkhē* of God, find our fulfilment in performing and by which we make our contribution to the splendour of the universe.

8

THEOLOGY, SCIENCE, AND CONTEMPLATION

In both the *EE* and the *NE* the question is raised: Which is the best of the three traditional patterns of life: the life of pleasure, the political life, or the contemplative life? In the *NE* the answer is that the contemplative life is the most perfect life, and the political life is the next best thing; happiness can be found in either life. In the *EE* the answer is that if the three lives are exclusive alternatives, the best is none of the three. The best life is both political and theoretical. As Broadie puts it, 'It is a life of practical wisdom enlightened by nobility and looking towards *theōria*.'[1]

In both systems contemplation plays a crucially important role. It is now time to ask the question: What *is* contemplation? Aristotle tells us tantalizingly little about it. We know that it is the exercise of the intellectual virtue of *sophia* or understanding. We know that it is concerned with the most splendid of knowable objects, and especially, in the *EE*, with God. The most important information we are given about it is that it is related to philosophy as finding is to seeking (*NE* 1177ᵃ27).

We are told a certain amount about *sophia* in the common book B. It is intelligence combined with knowledge—knowledge of the highest objects which has achieved its crown (1141ᵃ17-20). The highest objects are those which are superhuman: most notably, the bodies of which the heavens are framed. The paradigms of *sophia* are famous philosophers like Anaxagoras and Thales. The characteristic marks of the objects of philosophic understanding are that they are remarkable, wonderful, difficult, divine, and useless (1141ᵇ6-8).

It is not hard to recognize the subject-matter of contemplation as being philosophy in the broad sense, including astronomy and theology at least, and perhaps also the study of the necessary

---

[1] Broadie, *Ethics with Aristotle*, 386. She adds: 'This is, I think, more accurate than saying that the best is a *conjunction* of practice and *theōria*, for in the ethics Aristotle's focus never ceases to be practical. He views *theōria* not internally, so to speak, but as a practical objective.'

principles that operate in the physics of the sublunar world. What is more puzzling is to know what it is that the contemplative actually does in the course of contemplating. *What* is it that is related to philosophy as finding is to seeking?

Philosophers spend their lives reading, thinking, puzzling, writing, teaching. Twentieth-century commentators, when discussing *NE* 10, often take the contemporary philosopher to be an example of the contemplative. They talk of research grants, of the publication of papers, of the conducting of seminars, of the promotion of research students, and the like. But the Nicomachean contemplative does not seem to be a researcher. For research is seeking to know, and contemplation belongs to those who already know.

Can Aristotle really mean that the self-satisfied contemplation of the results of one's research is the most important thing in the lives of the most admirable human beings? No: it is a misunderstanding to think that he is telling us that the state of having discovered a truth is pleasanter and more perfect than the activity of enquiry about it. 'This is absurd', says Broadie, 'since pleasure attaches not to states but activities. In fact he is comparing one activity with another: the activity in which we are at one with the developing object, and the less fulfilling activity in which we cast about trying to locate it.'[2]

It is not knowledge (*epistēmē*), the mere possession of correct conclusions, which constitutes the distinguishing mark of the *sophos*. It is knowledge coupled with the intelligence to see how individual items of knowledge fit together with the whole systematic context in which they are embedded. It is this which is the 'crown' of knowledge spoken of in book B; it is this which makes 'understanding' the most appropriate translation for *sophia*.

In mathematics, contemplation is not a matter of congratulating oneself on having produced a proof of a theorem; it is the appreciation of the beauty of the proof itself. In linguistic philosophy, contemplation can be thought of as the goal of analysis. Wittgenstein said, more than once, 'A main source of our failure to understand is that we do not *command a clear view* of the use of our words. Our grammar is lacking in perspicuity.'[3] We aim to establish an order in our knowledge of the use of language, an order which will give us complete clarity about its use. The contemplative, in this field, will be the person who enjoys the clear overview of the use of language.

[2] *Ethics with Aristotle*, 401.
[3] Wittgenstein, *Philosophical Investigations*, i. 122.

What of the contemplation of God? The contemplation of God in the *EE* will include the vision of how the first mover is related to all the levels of motion and causation in the glorious cosmos we inhabit. Following the arguments of *Metaphysics Λ*, assuming those arguments to be successful, will place one in a position to appreciate the cosmic hierarchy with God at its supreme point above the bodies of which the heavens are framed. *Theōria* has been understood, not unreasonably, as being essentially a mystical activity, whose calmness is contrasted with the busy discursiveness of reason. But the contemplation which Aristotle has in mind may be no more mystical than mathematics.

One of the most famous discussions of the contemplative life is in the *Secunda Secundae* of the *Summa Theologiae* of St Thomas Aquinas. In question 179 he makes a contrast between it and the active life, between the life of the contemplation of truth and the life of exterior actions. In 180. 2 he asks whether the contemplative life includes the moral virtues. Essentially no, he answers, but dispositively yes. Contemplation may be impeded by internal passion or external tumult, and the virtues preserve or restore quiet amid these distractions.[4]

It is at 180.3 that he addresses the question of the actual nature of contemplation. He asks whether there is only a single act of contemplation, or whether there are many. His answer is framed in syllogistic terms: there is one concluding act of contemplation, but it is led up to by the grasp of axioms and the deduction of conclusions. When he comes to ask whether the contemplative life consists in the contemplation only of divine truth, the authority of *NE* 10 is explicitly invoked:[5] contemplation is primarily contemplation of God, but secondarily contemplation of God's effects. St Thomas's teaching is summed up in the following passage: 'There are four ordered elements in the contemplative life: first, the moral virtues; secondly, acts other than contemplation; thirdly, the contemplation of divine effects; fourthly, the contemplation of divine truth.'[6]

Thus far the question still seems open whether the contemplation of divine truth is that of the theologian or that of the mystic. The answer

---

[4] Aquinas, *Summa Theologiae* (1952 edn.), 774–5.
[5] 'Philosophus in X Eth in contemplatione optimi intelligibilis ponit altissimam felicitatem hominis.'
[6] Aquinas, *Summa Theologiae* (1952 edn.), 779: 'Quodam ordine quatuor ad vitam contemplativam pertinent: primo quidem, virtutes morales; secundo autem, alii actus praeter contemplationem; tertio vero, contemplatio divinorum effectuum; quartum vero contemplativum est ipsa contemplatio divinae veritatis.'

seems to be that both kinds of contemplation are possible. The supreme grade, it seems, is that experienced by St Paul when rapt up to the third heaven (2 Cor. 12).

The nature of *theōria* seems ambiguous in the *NE* itself, so that it is not strange if later ages wondered whether contemplation is a normal activity like the research of a mathematician, or a paranormal experience like the rapture of a mystic. In *NE* 10. 7 Aristotle seems to be torn between two views. At one time he will say that perfect happiness consists in contemplation because that is the best activity of the most human thing in us (1178^a6). At another time he will say that the life of contemplation is something superhuman (1177^a26). He will contrast the moral virtues, which belong to the human being, compound of body and soul, with the virtue of the understanding, which is, he says tantalizingly, 'a thing apart' (1178^a22). Having claimed, when discussing friendship, that it was incoherent, in deliberating about the good, to think of the good of some other sort of being, such as a god, he now says that we ought to 'immortalize as much as possible', identifying ourselves not with our complex human nature, but only with its intellectual element.[7] And he will offer this as his clinching argument for identifying perfect happiness with contemplation: 'The activity of God, which surpasses all others in blessedness, must be contemplative; and of human activities, therefore, that which is most akin to this must be most of the nature of happiness' (1178^b21-3).

Is there an inconsistency between saying that *nous* is what is most human in us, and also that it is superhuman and divine? Not necessarily. From passages such as these Christian theologians built up the doctrine of the human need for the supernatural. A thorough enquiry into human nature, they claimed, would show that humans' deepest needs and aspirations could not be satisfied in the human activities that were natural for a rational animal; humans could only be perfectly happy if they could share the superhuman activities of the divine, and for that they needed the supernatural assistance of divine grace. Aristotle might have been surprised at some of the uses to which *NE* 10 was put by theologians, but he could hardly complain that they were completely distorting its meaning. The tension between nature and supernature is clearly there for all to read.

When we look at Aristotle's account of contemplation from a modern secular viewpoint, the questions which it poses are rather

---

[7] Nussbaum, *The Fragility of Goodness*, 376.

different. Modern commentators, when they strive to understand Aristotle's text, have in mind not a meditating monk but a philosophical, or more generally, a scientific researcher. It is for this reason that so much recent attention has been focused on the relationship, especially in the *NE*, between contemplative and political happiness. For it is related to the decision, to be made in the actual lives of Aristotle's twentieth-century readers, how much energy and effort to devote to philosophical and scientific research and how much to social and political activity.[8]

The modern equivalent of the question to which Aristotle addressed himself is the problem of the role of science in society. Whatever 'contemplation' exactly meant for Aristotle, one contemporary equivalent of it is the pursuit of basic science. And the Aristotelian issue of the supremacy of contemplation is parallel to the twentieth-century debate about the autonomy of science. The Aristotelian question 'What is the correct attitude for the contemplative *vis-à-vis* the other moral virtues?' has as its modern equivalent 'What are the limits of the autonomy of science?'

Let us set out briefly an answer to the modern question, and then return to relate it to the Aristotelian discussion. Science, I believe, is autonomous with respect to its goal, but not with respect to its means, its conditions, or its consequences. That is to say, the pursuit of scientific truth is an activity which needs no further external good to make it worth while, so that science is an independent value in its own right; but in pursuit of this end the scientist must be answerable to other norms and values in his choice of means for research, in his appropriation of funds for research, and in his concern for the consequences of research. Scientific discovery is an independent goal, and in a sense an absolute goal; but it is not a unique or supreme goal.

Let us consider first science as an end. Scientific discovery is an independent goal, and in a sense an absolute goal. The sense in which it is an absolute goal is the sense in which 'absolute' is contrasted with 'relative'. The quest for scientific truth has been carried out with

[8] Most modern academics see their careers as involving a combination of research and teaching. Is teaching part of Aristotle's contemplative life? The question arose already in the Middle Ages. In his answer to the question Aquinas drew a distinction between two elements of teaching: the object taught (what we would call the subject taught!) and the expression of the object. The object taught may well be an object of contemplation, if the teacher has within himself a scientific truth which he delights in considering; but when we consider the activity of putting these thoughts into audible words for the benefit of pupils, that undoubtedly belongs to the active, not the contemplative, life (Ia IIae 181. 3).

greater energy in some societies than in others; but that does not mean that it is a value which is relative only to a particular social structure (like, say, chivalric honour). There is no conceivable human society for which scientific truth would not be a good.

But if scientific discovery is an absolute goal in this sense, it is not absolute in a different sense with which we have become familiar in our discussion of Aristotle. It is sometimes said that making one single value absolute (be it pleasure, wealth, power, family, fatherland, friendship, beauty, truth, love, religion) would amount to admitting that in pursuing this value anything is permissible. Scientific truth is not a value which is absolute in this sense—but there are no values which are absolute in this sense. There is no value in whose pursuit anything whatever is permissible.

The objection may be made: surely there must be at least one absolute value, morality itself. (This parallels the idea that *eudaimonia* is the motive of everything we do.) If not, are we not all morally adrift in a sea of relativism? No: morality is not an absolute value, because it is not a value at all, though it has an intimate connection with value.

Three elements are necessary for a morality: a moral community; a set of moral values; and a moral code. First, it is as impossible to have a purely private morality as it is to have a purely private language, and for very similar reasons. Second, the moral life of the community consists in the shared pursuit of non-material values, such as fairness, truth, comradeship, freedom: it is this which distinguishes between morality and economics, and between the *kalos kagathos* and the Laconian. Third, this pursuit is carried out within a framework which excludes certain types of behaviour: it is this which marks the distinction between morality and aesthetics.

A common morality, therefore, consists of values and norms. No value is absolute in the sense that its pursuit justifies the violation of every norm. Some norms are absolute in the sense that no value will ever justify their violation. This is simply to say that there are no ends which justify every means, and that there are some means which no end will justify. So if we are asked whether morality is absolute, we must answer with a *distinguo*: moral values, no; moral norms, yes.

Scientific truth, then, is a value which is independent, in the sense that its pursuit needs no ulterior justification. It is a value which is absolute in the sense that it is not relative to particular societies, but it is not absolute in the sense that it trumps all other moral values or overrides all moral norms.

The discovery of scientific truth is not just a permissible goal to pursue: it is an admirable goal; in Aristotle's terms it is something noble. It is a pursuit which it is allowable, and indeed laudable, to devote one's life to. We admire the dedicated scientist more than we admire the dedicated golfer, chef, or banker; and we are right to do so. Why is this? The answer is that the goal which the scientist seeks is a goal which is a good not just for himself, not just for his customers or shareholders, but for the human race as a whole.

Unlike Aristotle's external goods, or goods of fortune, scientific truth is a non-competitive good. It is a good which is indefinitely shareable; it is not a good which is lessened as more people participate in it. When I know a scientific truth, I can share my knowledge with any person qualified to understand it, without in any way diminishing the good I have acquired for myself by my discovery. I cannot in the same way share with other people, without diminishing it, the money I have made. I cannot share my political power with others without diluting it; I cannot distribute throughout the human race the pleasure produced by my culinary skill.

The goal of science is not just truth, but scientific truth. Scientific truth is a value of a higher order than that of truth *simpliciter*. Truth is, of course, always a positive value: if one is to have beliefs on a topic— no matter what the topic, whether important or trivial—it is always better to have true beliefs than to have false beliefs. But there are some topics where it is perhaps better not to have any beliefs at all; some truths which it is better not to know.

Many scientists would argue that it is in principle morally acceptable to know everything, and there are *no morally prohibited truths*. For God, perhaps, it is morally acceptable to know everything; but for human beings? Certainly there are some truths which it would be wrong to make an effort to find out: either because they are private (such as, say, intimate details of the sex life of a neighbouring married couple) or because they are trivial (one should not make a lifetime study of the numbers of winning lottery tickets). If one speaks simply of 'truths' as an important independent value, one puts on a level the enterprise of the research scientist and the muckraking of a gossip-columnist.

It is not easy to specify precisely what makes a truth a scientific truth; many distinguished philosophers of science have failed in the task. But, again taking our cue from Aristotle, we can say that it is clear that it is connected intimately with the notions of necessity and universality, however these notions are to be explained in detail. It is this which makes scientific truth a value which transcends the contingencies of particular historical societies.

The independence of science as an end does not mean that scientific purposes will justify means which would be otherwise immoral. But in addition to the constraints which extra-scientific morality puts upon means of scientific research, the nature of the scientific goal itself rules out certain modes of research behaviour as unworthy of science. When we condemn certain means of research as manipulative, or wasteful, or cruel, we are using criteria which could be used equally well to condemn business practices or military operations. But in the pursuit of scientific truth we may condemn researchers for being secretive, or competitive, in a way which would be quite inappropriate if applied to soldiers or businessmen.[9]

It is because the good sought by science is a good superior to that sought by many other human activities that there are some means which would be justified in the case of science which would not be justified in the case of other areas of human endeavour.[10] Thus, for example, the infliction of harm on animals, or damage on inanimate nature, is much easier to justify if necessary in the pursuit of scientific truth than in the cause of sport, or fashion, or art.

We must make a distinction between the means of scientific research and the conditions for scientific research. While some forms of scientific research—such as pure mathematics—are not in competition with other human activities for the consumption of scarce resources, most forms of natural science are expensive and become increasingly so as science becomes more developed and sophisticated.

When we are considering the allocation of funds for applied science, the decisions to be made resemble the generality of investment decisions: in deciding whether to fund medical research, or to use the funds for providing more hospital beds, we are making comparison between immediate and remote goods, but the goods are of the same kind, namely the health of the community. But when we are deciding how much money should be put into the health service, and how much into pure science such as cosmology, we are faced with a choice

[9] To say this is not to deny that scientists in pursuit of Nobel prizes may, in fact, conceal their results, or try to disadvantage rival researchers; it is simply to say that in so far as they do so they are falling short of their vocation of scientists, which is a vocation which pursues a public, shareable, good, an addition to the patrimony of the human race.

[10] There are some norms which are absolute in the sense that no end will justify them; there are others—and those are the ones here in question—which are capable of being overridden in the pursuit of sufficiently important values.

between incommensurables. Here no principle, whether of welfare economics or of normative morality, offers a clear decision-making procedure, at least in a society where the basic necessities of life are made available to the citizens.[11]

It is in the evaluation of these incommensurables that we rejoin the issue which was our concern in the interpretation of the Aristotelian treatises. For the political problem of the allocation of funds is the social replica of the individual problem of the choice of the ideal life which has been the topic of this book. And if our reading of the texts has been correct, a different answer is given by the two different Aristotelian ethical treatises. The *NE* places a higher value on the autonomy of science in the life of the individual: the highest form of happiness involves locating it entirely in scientific contemplation, even though the scientist will not lose his humanity, and will perform the practical tasks which arise from his living as a human being in the society of others (1178^b6). In the *EE* scientific endeavour is not a totally autonomous goal, but is one element, even though a specially significant element, in a life which is a harmony of several elements. In every action and sentiment, the Eudemian happy person bears in mind not only the contemplation of God, but also the service of God.

Aristotle's ethical treatises, as the intense attention paid to them in the last decades show, provide a magnificent conceptual framework for the discussion of ethical questions. They seem especially attractive to those who have become discontented with Kantian deontologism or positivist emasculation of ethics. They are found attractive both by religious and non-religious people: by non-religious people because so much of the argument seems to proceed on totally secular assumptions; by religious people because many of the finest moralists in the Jewish, Christian, and Islamic traditions were themselves Aristotelians.

But does Aristotle provide any moral guidance? Does he provide

---

[11] Having considered the goals, means, and conditions of science, should we not also consider the consequences of scientific discovery? Clearly the activity of scientists can have evil consequences—not only in the case of applied science, as in the development of nuclear weapons, but also in pure science, as in some research into the characteristics of different racial groups. There are problems of great difficulty and importance here, and though some would argue that the value of science is such that it should be pursued in despite of such consequences (*appareat veritas, ruat caelum*), I do not believe that the pursuit of science will justify ignoring harmful consequences any more than it will justify the choice of immoral means. But in the Aristotelian context it is unnecessary to pursue this in detail, because the objects of research which are likely to have undesirable social consequences are unlikely to have the universality and generality that would qualify them as scientific truths in the same sense as those of biology, chemistry, or physics.

anything more than a framework into which different and incompatible sets of norms and values can be fitted? Can one accept his ethical system? Would anyone be able genuinely to adopt the supreme values of Aristotle or endeavour to practise the moral virtues described in the *EE* or *NE*?

One purpose of comparing closely the two treatises is to exhibit that there are such great differences between them that it is misleading to talk simply of Aristotle's ethical system, even though the conceptual frameworks of the two works are similar. But Aristotelian scholarship is not a merely antiquarian pursuit. Reflection on Aristotle can throw light on first-order moral concerns, though Aristotle himself would have been the first to deny that any genuine moral question can be settled by looking up a book. But the close study of these ancient texts can help us to clarify our own moral concepts, to make explicit our own moral assumptions, and to examine our own concept of human perfection. For 'everyone that has the power to live according to his own choice should set up for himself some object for the good life ... since not to have one's life organized in view of some end is a mark of much folly' (*EE* 1214^{b}6–10).

APPENDIX 1

The Relationship between the *Eudemian* and *Nicomachean Ethics*

I

FOR most of the present century there has been a consensus among Aristotelian scholars that the *EE* is earlier than, and inferior to, the *NE*, which alone can claim to be Aristotle's definitive ethical system. In my book *The Aristotelian Ethics* in 1978 I tried to show that this consensus is ill based. In particular, I argued, it is an error to try to settle the chronological relationship between the two treatises before solving the problem of the three books which make a double appearance in the manuscript tradition, as books 5, 6, and 7 of the *NE* and as books IV, V, and VI of the *EE*. Only if we can settle, independently of chronological hypotheses, the primitive context of those books are we in a position to make non-tendentious comparisons between the treatises.

I went on to argue, on historical, stylistic, and philosophical grounds, that the disputed books, as they stand, belong with the Eudemian and not with the Nicomachean context. Having, as I believed, established this beyond reasonable doubt, I went on to claim that the *EE*, considered as a whole and including the disputed books, had as serious a claim as the *NE* to be considered Aristotle's final and considered system of ethics. Finally, I made some tentative suggestions about the dates of the composition of the treatises and their entry into the Aristotelian corpus.

When reviews of the book appeared, it soon became obvious that I had not expressed myself sufficiently clearly to guard against misunderstanding of my views. An otherwise very careful reviewer, T. Irwin, said at the beginning of his review 'Kenny wants to show that the EE, including the CB [common books] is both later and better than the EN. I want to ask how far he succeeds.' And in summing up, while noting that the book was mostly about the original home of the common books, he claimed that it was all intended to support the view that the *EE* is later and better, and that this view needed more defence than I had given it.[1] That this misunderstanding was more my fault than Irwin's is suggested by the fact that he was not alone in it.

Thus John Cooper, in his review, likewise misstated the scope of the book. He said that I claim that 'the Eudemian Ethics is the last and best ethical

---

[1] Irwin, review of Kenny, 339, 354.

treatise Aristotle wrote, and the Nicomachean should be read as earlier, less polished, more tentative, and more immature philosophically', and he complained that I fail to substantiate this claim.[2] It is true that my book claims that the *EE* dates from the period of Aristotle's maturity and that it has an equal claim with the *NE* to be regarded as the definitive expression of Aristotle's ethical system. But whether the *EE* is later than the *NE*, and whether it is philosophically superior to it, are questions which I deliberately left open. On the very last pages of the book I wrote 'It will only be when the *EE* has been for some time as carefully and widely studied as the *NE* has been for centuries that we shall be able to make an unclouded judgement about their comparative worth . . . I have no strong convictions about the original date of the *NE*'.[3]

What I did try to do in my book was to show that the arguments for the opposite view, that the *EE* is inferior and earlier, were wholly inadequate to support the almost universal conviction which they have carried. There is, I maintained, no evidence which will stand examination that the *NE* is later than the *EE*. There is indeed some evidence, which I present, to suggest that the *NE* is earlier than the *EE*.[4] But the evidence is inconclusive and was presented as such. There is a big difference between saying 'There is no evidence that *p*' and flatly asserting 'Not-*p*'. There is also a difference between saying 'There is some evidence that not-*p*' and going on to conclude that not-*p*. The last section of my book was full of warnings against going on, without further ado, to draw such conclusions. The explanation of the differences between the *NE* and the *EE* may well be other than chronological.

The chronological conclusion which *is* argued for in *The Aristotelian Ethics* is that the *EE* is a late work, dating from Aristotle's final period in Athens, between 335/4 and 322. If the *EE* contains the *AE*, it must undoubtedly (on the basis both of content and of historical allusion) be assigned to Aristotle's later years; we must therefore reject the view that it is early superseded work. In my book this is argued on the following grounds. (1) The *Magna Moralia* appears to be a student's notes of a lecture course by Aristotle, and it contains several topical references which suggest a *terminus post quem* of about 335. But the course of which the *Magna Moralia* is a record is most probably the *EE*, which it follows slavishly in the order of topics and manner of treatment.[5] Moreover, the *Magna Moralia* paraphrases the common books in a Eudemian,

[2] Cooper, review of Kenny.

[3] *The Aristotelian Ethics*, 238–9.

[4] The points I mentioned were (1) possible references to *NE* texts from the *EE*, at 1218^{a}36, 1220^{b}11, and 1244^{b}29–45; (2) the greater distance from which the *EE* criticizes Plato's theory of Ideas; (3) the fact that some virtues and vices which are unnamed in the *NE* are named in the *EE*; (4) the different attitudes to magnanimity, which might be explained by ageing. I no longer think that it is possible to regard 1244^{b}29–45 as a reference to the *NE*; see p. 48 above.

[5] *The Aristotelian Ethics*, 216–21.

not a Nicomachean, context; hence Aristotle was still giving them as lectures in this context in his final years.[6] (2) Though the undisputed *EE* contains no references to anchor it to a particular date, the disputed books, restored to their rightful place as part of the *EE*, contain a reference which fits the final Athenian period.[7] (3) Negatively, a comparison between the two treatments of pleasure, the Nicomachean one in *NE* 10, and the Eudemian one in *AE* C, does not suggest an early dating for the *EE*.[8]

Which of the two treatises, *NE* or *EE*, is the better? No answer to this question can be helpful unless the comparison between the two is made in detail, and unless the methodology of evaluation is made explicit. The *NE* is much easier to read and more conversational in style, so that some have seen it as being an exoteric work; the *EE* is more systematic and more technical, and makes more use of the conceptual apparatus of Aristotelian logic and metaphysics. The structure of the *NE* is often difficult to discern because of the large amount of repetition and the frequent doublets; the *EE* is more economical, and the arguments are often more formalized, but the quest for rigour often results in a very crabbed text. So far as it is possible to discern behind the deficiencies of the manuscript tradition, the *EE* appears to have been more carefully prepared for publication than the *NE*.

From the point of view of philosophical content the most interesting books of Aristotle's ethics, in my own view, are the three books which are in dispute between the two treatises. I have made clear in the present book that I find the overall view of human good and perfection in the *EE* more attractive than the intellectualism of the *NE*. But it is very difficult for a scholar to take a dispassionate view of the two treatises. The *NE* is the most generally familiar of all Aristotle's works and has been the subject of loving scholarly attention for centuries. On the other hand, the text of the *EE* is often corrupt and many of its more difficult passages await not only definitive interpretation but even the most basic elucidation.

It is rash to assume that because a treatise is later in composition it is also philosophically richer in content: I warned against such an assumption both at the beginning and at the end of my book.[9] A comparative judgement of the merits of the two books must in the end be based on a comprehensive and

---

[6] In discussing the *Magna Moralia* in *The Aristotelian Ethics* I did an injustice to Cooper. On p. 219 I attributed to him the view that the *Magna Moralia* is a student's notes of a course given by Aristotle in the 330s as an updating of a juvenile course. In fact, in the article to which I referred ('The *Magna Moralia*') Cooper quite clearly attributed the updating to the student, not to Aristotle; the suggestion of an updating by Aristotle himself, he says, is ludicrous. To me the suggestion that a lecturer might update his lecture-text by inserting contemporary allusions seems in itself no more ludicrous than that a student might insert topical references into his notes of a lecture given long ago. None the less, Cooper was quite right to object, in his review, to my misrepresenting him (Cooper, review of Kenny, 391).

[7] *The Aristotelian Ethics*, 221–4.   [8] Ibid. 233–8.   [9] Ibid. 4, 238.

balanced treatment of the parallel passages in the two treatises. In *The Aristo-telian Ethics* I compared only the passages dealing with wisdom and with happiness; later, in *Aristotle's Theory of the Will* (1979), I undertook a comparison of the passages dealing with voluntariness, choice, and practical reasoning. In this second book I repeated the cautions which I gave in my earlier one: 'The exact chronological relationship between the Eudemian and Nicomachean treatises must await a careful comparison between the texts, taking account of the Eudemian provenance of the disputed books.'[10] My aim in attacking the dogma of the priority of the *EE* was not to set up another dogma in its place, but to encourage agnosticism: an agnosticism that was open to the possibility— no more—that the *NE*, or parts of it, were superseded by the *EE*.

One thing seems clear: that the *EE* plus the *AE* make up a more consistent whole than the *NE* plus the *AE*. This is true even if some of the inconsistencies which we find between the *AE* and the *NE* are to be found between individual books of the *NE*. In *The Aristotelian Ethics* I examined the teaching of the three groups of books on the topics of wisdom and happiness. On the topic of wisdom, there is no great difference between the teachings of the *EE* and the *NE*, so that it is only in matters of detail that one can show that the *AE* resembles the *EE* more than it does the *NE*. But the examination is important none the less, since the difference between the *NE* and the *EE* which Jaeger thought he saw has long been the principal reason for regarding the *NE*, plus the common books, as later than the *EE*. In detail, as I show,[11] the common books resemble the *EE* more than the *NE* on the relationship between wisdom and moral virtue and natural virtue. So too with the other main intel-lectual virtue: philosophical contemplation in the *EE* and in the common book B is an activity of a particular part of the human soul; in *NE* 10 it is the activity of a separable, immortal *nous* which is contrasted with the soul–body compound.

I showed in *Aristotle's Theory of the Will* that in their main lines the accounts of voluntariness, purposive choice, and practical reasoning to be found in the *NE* and *EE* resemble each other closely in substance if not always in terminology. We see also that in almost every case where there is a significant difference between the *NE* and the *EE* the *AE* resembles the *EE* more closely than it resembles the *NE*.

Thus, in the account of voluntariness both the *AE* and the *EE*, unlike the *NE*, make a distinction between its being in our power to do an act, and its being in our power whether to do or not to do an act: the distinction which lies at the origin of the traditional notion of liberty of indifference. The *AE* and the *EE*, in their account of force, unlike the *NE*, allow that some natural processes, though unforced, are neither voluntary nor involuntary, and both offer the same examples of genuine force. In the account of purposive choice the *EE*

---

[10] *Aristotle's Theory of the Will*, p. x.   [11] *The Aristotelian Ethics*, 161–89.

looks forward to the *AE* treatment to a much greater extent than the *NE* does. The *EE* discusses the relationship of virtue to continence, the relationship of virtue to ends and means, the distinction between virtue and wisdom: all of them topics which are to be taken up and developed in precisely similar terminology in *AE* B and C. The *EE* treatment gives us hints, which the *NE* does not, on how we are to relate the early account of technical deliberation with the account of ethical deliberation developed in the *AE*.

Finally, in the treatment of practical reasoning, where the contribution of the *AE* far surpasses that of either the *NE* or the *EE*, it is the *EE* which offers a number of precisions which prepare the way for the full *AE* treatment. Thus, to take just two instances, it is the *EE* and not the *NE* which introduces the distinction between the possession and the exercise of knowledge which is fundamental to Aristotle's solution of the problem of *akrasia* in *AE* C; and it is the *EE* and not the *NE* which works out in complete detail the sense in which the acts of the incontinent are voluntary—a point which is fundamental to the right understanding of the problem which *AE* C sets out to solve.

The third topic on which I have compared the groups of books is that of happiness. In *The Aristotelian Ethics* I compared the dominant, intellectualist Nicomachean view of happiness with the inclusive, organic Eudemian view, setting out briefly the contrast which has been presented at length in the present volume. I showed that the organic view of happiness was to be found in the book on justice (1129^b18) and in the account given in book B of the contribution made to happiness by wisdom and understanding (1144^a3-6). I showed how the treatment of pleasure as the supreme good in book C (1153^b7-24) was, despite superficial appearances, at least as close to the *EE* doctrine as to that of the *NE*.

The one clear sense in which the *EE* is better than the *NE*, then, is that the *EE* taken with the *AE* makes up a more coherent whole than the *NE* taken with the *AE*. If we restrict ourselves to the undisputed parts of each treatise, we must say that a comprehensive and definitive comparative evaluation has yet to be made.

Whatever we, in the twentieth century, may think of the merits of the two treatises, it is a surprising fact that in the early centuries after Aristotle's death most writers gave to the *EE* the primacy which it has long been traditional to give to the *NE*. Unlike the *EE*, the *NE* was not included in the canon of Aristotle's works established by the edition of Andronicus. In *The Aristotelian Ethics* I reviewed the evidence from pseudo-Aristotelian works, from Theophrastus, Cicero, Xenarchus, Arius Didymus, Nicolaus of Damascus, Philo of Alexandria, Favorinus of Arles, and Diogenes Laertius. I found that every writer, from Aristotle himself until the second century AD, who shows a first-hand knowledge of the Aristotelian ethical writings also shows a preference for the *EE* over the *NE*—either in the sense that he refers to it as 'The Ethics', *sans* phrase, or that he quotes it exclusively, or that he prefers its doctrine, or its terminology, or its systematic structure. No author (except the author of the *Magna Moralia*) quotes the *NE* as 'The Ethics'; and the only two authors (Cicero and Diogenes) who show awareness of an Ethics with that title both regard it as the work of Aristotle's son Nicomachus.

Critics of *The Aristotelian Ethics* have contested this account of the ancient evidence in various ways. They have suggested that there are signs in the writings of Epicurus and the Stoics which suggest that they knew the *NE*. The articles by Furley and Long to which they refer, though making interesting comparisons between Aristotle's ethical views and the opposing views of the later schools, do not seem to me to have seriously considered the hypothesis that their knowledge of Aristotle derived from the *EE* or *Magna Moralia* rather than from the *NE*. To the extent that I have made the comparison myself I have found nothing conclusive either way. I continue therefore to believe that what I said in the book is correct, that before the first century AD there is no clear evidence of knowledge of our *NE*, and this is consistent with the evidence that it was absent from the edition of Andronicus.[12]

It has been suggested that the fact that writers before Aspasius cite the *EE* in preference to the *NE* is to be explained by the fact that they were non-scholarly people who preferred a simpler text. But this explanation involves explaining away the use of the text by scholarly authors such as Theophrastus and Xenarchus, and ignores the well-known fact that the *EE* is more scholastic in its treatment than is the *NE*.[13]

The *NE* was very probably known to Cicero, who in *De Finibus* 5. 12, having complained that Theophrastus in his treatise on the happy life made happiness too dependent on good fortune, goes on to say 'Let us therefore follow Aristotle and his son Nicomachus, whose carefully written books on ethics are said to be the work of Aristotle, though I do not see why the son could not have been similar to the father.' Cicero appears here to be alluding to two works here: one, non-Nicomachean, work which he regards as Aristotle's; and one which he is prepared to accept as the work of Nicomachus, which is probably some or all of our *NE*.[14]

John Cooper has argued that the *NE* differs from the *EE* and *Magna Moralia* in that it includes as part of the definition of *eudaimonia* a sufficient equipment of external goods, 1099[a]31 ff.[15] He points to the fact that Cicero, in *De Finibus* 2, when listing theories of happiness, attributes to Aristotle a definition of happiness as the use of virtue accompanied by the prosperity of a perfect life.

---

[12] See Irwin, review of Kenny, 340; Long, 'Aristotle's Legacy'; Furley, *Two Studies*, 184–209. Irwin follows Long in believing that the Stoic conception of pleasure as ἐπιγέννημα may be derived from the *NE* conception of it as a supervenient end (ἐπιγινόμενόν τι τέλος). But the verbal similarity here masks a considerable difference of doctrine.

[13] Cooper, review of Kenny, 366.

[14] It could also be the *Magna Moralia*, known in antiquity as the 'Great Nicomachean Ethics'. See Kenny, *The Aristotelian Ethics*, 16.

[15] This claim has been contested at p. 38 above.

The fact that this contains three elements—the exercise of virtue, the completeness of life, and the presence of external goods—shows, Cooper claims, that it is the *NE* which Cicero has in mind here.[16] This is a proof, he maintains, that the *NE* was read in Hellenistic times and that 'our practice of assigning priority on central questions of philosophical theory to the NE over the other treatises was standard among philosophers already by the beginning of the first century BC at latest'.[17]

This argument depends on seeing in the word *prosperitas* a reference to the goods of fortune, such as wealth and power. But it is not at all clear that Cicero, when he speaks of 'vitae perfectae prosperitas', is referring to two separate elements, long life and material prosperity; the phrase is more naturally read as 'the good fortune of having a complete life'. It would indeed be odd if Cicero here regarded it as characteristic of Aristotle to include the goods of fortune as an element of the happy life, when in a later passage of the same treatise, quoted earlier, he noted it as a mark of Aristotle's superiority over Theophrastus that he did *not* make happiness dependent on good fortune. Both the *NE* and the *EE* include a reference to completeness of life in their account of happiness (1098^a18, 1219^a38-9), and the notion of 'the use of virtue' is much more common in the *EE* than in the *NE*.[18] If Cicero is here exhibiting first-hand knowledge of an Aristotelian text, which must remain uncertain, it is slightly more likely, on the evidence of this passage in isolation, to be the *EE* than the *NE*. The evidence of *De Finibus* 5 remains to show that if he did know the *NE*, he was doubtful whether it was the work of Aristotle.

The position remains that in the four hundred years after Aristotle's death there is more evidence for the existence and authenticity of the *EE* than there is for that of the *NE*.[19] This state of affairs comes to an abrupt end in the second century AD with the work of Aspasius, who left a commentary on *NE* 1-4, and parts of *NE* 8, and the third of the disputed books. For him the *NE* is undoubtedly by Aristotle; the *EE*, by contrast, is doubtful, regarded sometimes as authentic Aristotle, sometimes as the work of his pupil Eudemus.

In *The Aristotelian Ethics* I argued that Aspasius is, none the less, a witness that the original context of the disputed books was the *EE* and not the *NE*. I offered five reasons for concluding that he regarded the disputed books as belonging to the *EE*. (1) In his commentary on C he refers to the *NE* as a different work. (2) He is certain that the *NE* is by Aristotle, but is prepared to consider the possibility that C is by Eudemus, just as he is unsure whether the *EE* is by Aristotle or Eudemus. (3) With one exception, he quotes the *AE*

---

[16] Cicero, *De Finibus* 2. 19: 'Aristoteles virtutis usum cum vitae perfectae prosperitate coniunxit.' Compare the very similar passage in Arius Didymus (ap. Stobaeus 11. 51. 12 Wachsmuth), also discussed by Cooper.

[17] Cooper, 'Aristotle on the Goods of Fortune', 176.

[18] This is documented in detail in Kenny, *The Aristotelian Ethics*, 68.

[19] Between the *Magna Moralia* and Aspasius, the one clear citation of the *NE* is the definition of virtue from 1107^a1 by Arius Didymus. See Kenny, *The Aristotelian Ethics*, 14, 20.

when commenting on the *NE*, and the *NE* when commenting on the *AE*, with the style of quotation he uses for introducing quotations from other works, rather than that which he uses for forward and backward references in the same work. (4) From the *AE* he quotes the *EE* with a form of words he uses for backward reference in the same work. (5) He speaks of the existence of a lacuna in the *NE* as a familiar fact.

This part of my argument has been severely criticized by Cooper and Irwin, and their criticisms have convinced me that I oversimplified the evidence presented by Aspasius. Let me therefore set out afresh the evidence for and against the hypothesis that the text of the *NE* which he had before him lacked the common books.

The most important piece of evidence for the hypothesis is the fact that Aspasius, in commenting on the treatment of pleasure in book C, is willing to attribute it to Eudemus (*CAG* xix/1. 151. 24). This is most plausibly explained if he found the text in the *EE*, which we know independently he was prepared to consider as the work of Eudemus (*CAG* xix/1. 178. 3). In the same passage he writes of the *NE* as if it was a different work from the one on which he was now commenting (*CAG* xix/1. 151. 22).[20]

In his commentary on *NE* 8, where Aristotle says that there has been a previous discussion of the question whether things different in kind can differ in degree, Aspasius remarks that it looks as if this previous discussion took place in the lost parts of the *NE*. The simplest explanation of this is that the *NE* before him lacked the common books, and that either on internal or external evidence Aspasius concluded that there must once have been Nicomachean material in their place.

Cooper dismisses Aspasius' tentative attribution of C to Eudemus, and his reference to a lacuna in the Nicomacheans, as due to concern about the validity of the manuscript tradition. But even on the unlikely hypothesis that Aspasius knew no more about the early transmission of the ethical treatises than we do the question remains why he reacted to the manuscript tradition by saying that parts of the Nicomacheans had got lost, rather than by saying—like Jaeger and Dirlmeier—that parts of the Eudemians had got lost or by saying—like Cooper and others—that nothing had got lost, since the same material was used twice over.

Against this, however, there is evidence to be set that Aspasius did have in front of him our ten-book *NE*. As I acknowledged in *The Aristotelian Ethics*,

[20] Irwin, review of Kenny, 341, says that the fact that Aspasius (151. 22) here refers to *NE* 10 as the 'Nicomacheans' cannot show that he thinks the present passage is non-Nicomachean, because in commenting on *NE* 8 (161. 9-10) he says a topic was discussed 'in the lost parts of the Nicomacheans'. But the parallel is false. If you draw a contrast between the present passage and the Nicomacheans, you imply that the present passage is not part of the Nicomacheans; if you draw a contrast between the present passage and the lost parts of the Nicomacheans, you do not imply that the present passage is not part of the Nicomacheans, but that it is not part of the lost parts of the Nicomacheans.

there is one passage in Aspasius' commentary on *NE* 1 where he discusses an *aporia* which he says Aristotle will resolve 'as he proceeds'. The resolution appears to be given in a passage in *AE* B, and therefore the reference appears to treat B as part of a text continuous with *NE* 1 (*CAG* xix/1. 8. 32).[21]

Again, the passage in the commentary on C which provides major pieces of evidence for the Eudemian provenance of the treatise on pleasure provides one piece of evidence which most commentators take as suggesting a Nicomachean origin. Aspasius expresses surprise that in *NE* 10 there is no back reference to this passage: 'He talks about pleasure as if it had not yet been discussed.' Why should he be surprised if they came from different works?[22]

In *The Aristotelian Ethics* I tried to reconcile these pieces of evidence by saying that Aspasius inherited a text of the *EE* which contained the disputed books, and one of the *NE* without the disputed books, and that he then, having commented on books 1-4 of the *NE*, went on to comment on *EE* IV-VI in order to have a full commentary on Aristotle's ethical system in spite of the lacuna in the Nicomachean version. If it was Aspasius' own act which started the tradition of counting the disputed books with the Nicomachean treatise, then the present *Nicomachean Ethics—NE* plus *AE*—might more aptly be called 'The Aspasian Ethics'.

This conjecture was rightly found implausible by my critics. Thus Irwin asks: why should Aspasius have gone to the trouble of writing about the *NE* and the common books if they were not already parts of a single treatise? If he commented on the common books because he wanted to have a full commentary on Aristotle's ethical system, why should he not have taken the simpler course of commenting on the *EE*, including the common books?[23]

I think it must be conceded that the most natural interpretation of all the evidence is that Aspasius did have before him a text of the *NE* which included the common books. This was the reason why he included them both in a single

---

[21] See *The Aristotelian Ethics*, 34.

[22] Irwin, review of Kenny, 341-2, writes: 'Kenny recognizes that this passage suggests that Aspasius thought the two treatments of pleasure belong to a single work . . . Kenny resists this suggestion, however; he thinks Aspasius is remarking on the lack of cross reference from EN X to the EE. On this view, "not yet" should mean "not in the other, earlier work". Here again Kenny is a good witness against himself: "When he (Aspasius) makes a forward or backward reference within a single book, or from one undisputed *EN* book to another, he uses an expression such as 'as was said before' or 'later'" (*AE* 343). "Not yet" clearly counts as one of those expressions. And so Kenny's own evidence suggests what we would in any case be inclined to infer from Aspasius' remark about the lack of cross reference, that Aspasius took over a ten-book EN.' Irwin and I were both muddled, I now believe. 'Not yet' does indeed mean 'not earlier in the same work': but the point is that Aspasius is here arguing that C cannot be the same work as the *NE*, because if it was Aristotle would indeed have written about pleasure earlier in the same work (so Irwin is confused). On the other hand, if that is what Aspasius means he is not commenting on the lack of cross-references between the *EE* and the *NE* (so I was confused).

[23] Irwin, review of Kenny, 341.

commentary, and is willing to refer forward to a common book from a Nicomachean one.

However, the ten-book treatise must have reached him in a form which raised the question whether the common books did rightly belong with the *NE* and not perhaps with the *EE*; this is made abundantly clear by the discussion of the passage on pleasure in the common book C. For this reason he is generally cautious about cross-referring between the *NE* and the common books. The uncertainty about the provenance of the common books, whatever form it took in the tradition which reached Aspasius, provides the most likely reason for his willingness to recognize a lacuna in the Nicomachean tradition.

We shall return later to enquire about the most likely explanation of these facts. But before doing so, I shall discuss the internal evidence concerning the provenance of the common books.

II

A central part of *The Aristotelian Ethics* was devoted to a study of the style of the disputed books of the *AE* with a view to determining which of the two competing contexts, Nicomachean or Eudemian, they resemble more closely. The study had two parts. In the first, more traditional, section I examined in detail the first chapter of the disputed books (A. 1) and showed that in almost every sentence there were clues of vocabulary, style, or method which suggested that the original environment of the book was Eudemian. This part of my study seems to have been found convincing even by those most unsympathetic to my general enterprise.[24] In the second part of the stylistic study I made use of statistical methods to make a comparative study of the vocabulary of the *NE*, the *EE*, and the *AE*.

The purpose of the statistical study was to discover and compare the regularities within the undisputed Nicomachean books, within the undisputed Eudemian books, and within the books which were disputed. By seeing how far the regularities to be discovered in the disputed books resembled the regularities in each of the treatises, I hoped to obtain an indication of the context to which they originally belonged. The tests which I undertook covered some 60 per cent of the vocabulary of the ethical treatises, and the evidence thus collected showed that there was a very much closer resemblance, in respect of the features studied, between the *AE* and the *EE* than between the *AE* and the *NE*.

A number of critics objected to the statistical method I adopted. Thus Christopher Kirwan complained that my arguments assumed that a regularity once attained in a unitary treatise may be expected to survive throughout it; whereas 'many of the words which pass the test for regularity in NE and in EE

[24] See Cooper, review of Kenny, 383.

are irregular in EE; and if a word behaves irregularly in *any* unitary treatise we ought not to expect its regularity elsewhere to be more than temporary'.[25] Kirwan's assumption seems less plausible than the assumption which I made in my book, namely that if the *AE* was originally part of the *EE* we would expect that those regularities which are displayed in vocabulary use in the *EE* would continue to be regular, and regular at approximately the same rate, in the *AE*; similarly, if the *AE* was originally all of one piece with the *NE* one would expect it to reflect the regularities to be observed there. My assumption was tantamount to saying 'We should expect regularities found in seven books of a ten-book treatise to be found in the other three books; and we should expect regularities found in five books of an eight-book treatise to be found in the other three books.' This might well be regarded as quite a substantial assumption (particularly the second limb of it). But it is an assumption put forward for the purpose of a comparative test; and what is interesting is that when the assumption is tested it is the second, rasher, limb of it which survives the test much better.

Kirwan failed to do justice to the fact that my argument was throughout comparative. I never argued that if there are statistically significant differences between the *NE* and the *AE* the two cannot be from the same treatise; I argued that if the number of statistically significant differences between *NE* and *AE* was (as it is) enormously greater than that between the *AE* and the *EE*, then the more economical and probable hypothesis was that the *AE* belongs with the *EE*.

The problem of the environment of the common books is similar in structure to a problem tackled in one of the best-known classics of statistical stylometry, the study of the Federalist Papers by the Harvard statisticians Frederick Mosteller and David Wallace.[26] The Federalist Papers are a series of articles published in 1787 and 1788 to persuade the citizens of New York to ratify the constitution of the United States. The papers were written by Jay, Hamilton, and Madison; the authorship of most was known, but twelve out of the eighty-eight were contested between Hamilton and Madison. The papers of known authorship provided the material from which features discriminating the two candidates could be extracted.

Mosteller and Wallace studied 'marker words' which were particular likes or dislikes of the competing authors, and also words which were used comparatively frequently by both authors, but at different rates, especially 'function words' such as prepositions, conjunctions, and articles. They identified a set of twenty-eight words with strong discriminating power, and on the basis of comparisons between the rates of use of these words they concluded beyond reasonable doubt that Madison wrote the twelve disputed papers.

My problem was unlike the Federalist problem in that it was not a problem

---

[25] Kirwan, review of Kenny, 52.
[26] Mosteller and Wallace, *Inference and Disputed Authorship*.

of attribution: I have never questioned the modern consensus of scholars that both *NE* and *EE* are to be ascribed to Aristotle. But it resembled the problem in being a simple matter of deciding whether text A resembles text B more than it resembles text C. But the number of features which turned out to discriminate the *NE* from the *EE* was much larger than the number of discriminants between Madison and Hamilton. The very wealth of the material meant that very simple statistical methods were adequate to establish the conclusion with a high degree of probability, whereas Mosteller and Wallace had been forced to use elaborate Bayesian techniques.

In my study significant differences were found in particle use, in the use of prepositions and adverbs, pronouns and demonstratives, in the preference for different forms of the definite article. Having set out these differences, I then identified twenty-four groups of words which were strong discriminators, and used each of these groups as an independent test of the comparative resemblances between the *AE* and its two possible environments. In twenty-three out of twenty-four cases the tests gave an unambiguous answer that the common books, considered as a whole, resembled the *EE* more than the *NE*. The same result was obtained when the *AE* was split into seventeen one-thousand word samples: each individual sample was revealed by these tests to be closer to the *EE* than to the *NE*.

In his review of my book Cooper made some criticisms of my use of statistics in the chapter I devoted to particles and connectives.[27] (He did not discuss the two chapters in which the principal part of the statistical argument is set out.) In particular he objected to my using the frequency of individual words as the unit of statistical study: I should have studied, not particular words, but particular uses of words or particular combinations of words.[28]

It is true that to record the frequency of καί or δέ or οὖν tells nothing about possible different ways of using these particles. It does not follow that the frequencies are uninteresting or that arguments based on them are inconclusive. Cooper's objection is as if one were to argue that the murder rate for a city is a useless statistic, since murder is a category embracing stabbing, poisoning, hanging, and so on. Suppose one is given the murder rate for ten successive years for two cities, one with a high murder rate (say Chicago) and one with a low murder rate (say Oxford). If one is now given the murder rate for the eleventh year for one of the two cities, without being told which, and is asked to assign it to the appropriate city, it is not too difficult to do so with a high probability, and the probability of one's estimate is in no way decreased by the

---

[27] Cooper, review of Kenny, 385.

[28] Elsewhere he says that I should have applied the chi-square test not to individual words, but to particular usage as a whole. It will be seen that his two criticisms point in opposite directions: the first criticism regards the individual particle as too crude a unit to study; the second is tantamount to regarding it as not being crude enough. It might be thought, therefore, that the criticisms cancel each other out.

fact that murder is a rag-bag category. But this is the parallel to the situation when we are trying to decide whether the common books belong with the Nicomachean or Eudemian torso.

In fact the frequency of καί plays no part in my final statistical argument: its occurrence, as explained on p. 94 of my book, is too irregular in both the *NE* and the *EE* to be used as the basis of any rigorous comparison with the *AE*. τε, μέν, and δέ, irregular in *NE*, occur with regular frequency in the *EE*, and with regular frequency in the *AE*; and the homogeneity is in each case preserved if the *AE* is placed in the context of the *EE*. None the less, when at the end of my study I came to assemble Nicomachean and Eudemian indicator-words, I did not include any of these, and their usage plays no part in the final statistical argument which I have summarized above.

The study of the use of combinations and collocations of words is, of course, of value in statistical stylometry. Consider, for instance, occurrences of the particle μήν. In my book (p. 74) they are given as follows: *NE* 25, *AE* 11, *EE* 19. This represents a frequency of 0.06 per cent in the *NE* and *AE*, and 0.07 per cent in the *EE*: a virtually identical frequency in all three works, with the *AE* closer, but insignificantly so, to the *NE*. But the particle μήν occurs in two contexts, οὐ μήν and ἀλλὰ μήν. If we separate out these two uses of μήν, we get the following table:

	NE	AE	EE
ἀλλά μήν	4 (0.01%)	10 (0.06%)	14 (0.05%)
οὐ μήν	21 (0.05%)	1 (0.01%)	5 (0.02%)

It will be seen that the *AE* usage is in fact very much closer to the *EE* one, though the frequencies are so small that in order to base an argument on them they would have to be grouped with others.

The case of μήν illustrates what I said in my book about the crudity of vocabulary-counting. 'The crudity of the classification will do no harm: it may prevent the detection of stylistic differences between texts where a finer analysis might enable us to discriminate; but it cannot have the effect of producing imaginary distinctions where there are none in reality.'[29] It is possible, as Cooper says, that two texts may differ significantly in the overall frequency of a particle simply as a result of the difference of a single usage lumped into the overall count. But this is in no way damaging, since if the single usage in question formed only a small proportion of the overall count the difference in that usage would have to be itself an enormously significant one in order to produce such a result.

In my book I restricted myself to the results of the counting of single vocabulary items because I considered that the differences between the resemblance of *AE* to *EE* and *AE* to *NE* discovered by this method were

---

[29] *The Aristotelian Ethics*, 69.

already so enormous as to make it unprofitable to investigate for more subtle differences.

However, Christopher Rowe in a careful and exhaustive examination of the usage of particles and connectives in the ethical treatises[30] has shown that there is much more to be learnt by distinguishing between different uses, even if in the end this does not disturb the overall stylometric conclusion that the *AE* resembles the *EE* more than the *NE*.

He considers the objection that my computer word-counts are too crude because they fail to make distinctions between homographs (ὅτι 'that', and ὅτι 'because', for instance). In some cases, he says, this need not give grounds for concern, but there are cases where it should. If an item x counted by the computer consists of items x_1 and x_2, there might be a significant leaning on the part of *AE* and *EE* towards x_1, but also a significant leaning on the part of *NE* and *AE* towards x_2; we need only suppose that examples of x_1 are much more numerous than those of x_2, so that the bias of *NE* and *AE* towards x_2 is swamped by the bias of *AE* and *EE* towards x_1. He says 'We cannot strictly judge the strength or weakness of any argument which Kenny bases on counts for any item which possesses two or more distinct uses, unless and until we know the separate counts for those uses.'[31]

Rowe has counted by hand separate uses in *NE* 4, *AE* A, and *EE* III. He gives lists of different senses used in these books; and then specifies regularities vs. irregularities. He sums up as follows:

> Kenny's gross counts for the three sample books made ἀλλα, γάρ, γε, δή, εἰ, ἐπεί, καί, ὅτι, οὐ, οὐδέ, and ὥστε significantly irregular in frequency. Breaking down these and other items in the complete list use by use, we found irregularity located in particular uses of ἀλλά, γάρ, γε, δέ, εἰ, ἐπεί, καί, and ὥστε, irregularities in both uses of ἤ and regularities in both uses of ὅτι and οὐδέ respectively. In addition, we found special considerations affecting the use to be made of counts for δή, μή, οὐ, οὐδέ and οὔτε. I now want to ask whether all or any of the irregularities which remain can straightforwardly be interpreted in terms of stylistic differences.[32]

He goes on to argue that these words are not as topic-neutral as I had suggested. ἀλλά, for instance, is most common in the context 'not A but B'. This type of pattern will increase the more argumentative a context is; and *AE* A is in fact more argumentative than the other two sampled books: it is subject-matter, not style, that accounts for its greater argumentativeness. Again, *AE* A has a lot more instances of εἰ with aorist; this is because of the legalistic aspect of much of the discussion. The relatively high incidence of comparative ἤ in *NE* 4 and *EE* III is accounted for by phrases like μᾶλλον ἤ δεῖ, in connection with discussions of virtues or vices; disjunctive ἤ is more common in *AE* A because the discussion revolves round pairs or groups of opposites. ὡς is

---

[30] Rowe, 'De Aristotelis ... dicendi ratione'.   [31] Ibid. 1: 5.   [32] Ibid. 3: 37.

relatively even in usage in the three books, but this is not so much because of the uniformity but because the differing demands of the subject-matter in different contexts tend to cancel each other out: sometimes it appears in the context of ὡς ὁ λόγος, sometimes in statements of proportions: 'A is to B as C is to D'.

Rowe makes the general observation that in our texts we frequently find much bunching of connectives and particles; this indicates, he claims, a close relationship between the occurrence of a word and the topic being discussed. He also observes that the generally schematic nature of the *EE* is likely to be reflected in use of particles and connectives. It is difficult, however, to see how this is an objection to my method, since being schematic is surely itself a feature of style. He has a more persuasive point when he says that the *AE* may have features of the subject-matter which cause the text to mimic effects of style in *EE*. A higher incidence of καί connecting sentences is an indication of the descriptive nature of the passage in which it occurs. But a systematic treatment of justice will not be descriptive as that of the great-souled man is; justice is a topic which calls for hard analysis rather than detailed description.

When all such points have been taken into account, Rowe allows that significant irregularities are left in the case of γάρ, ἐπεί, and connective ὥστε. In these cases there is no detectable influence from subject-matter; and there is a significant difference between *NE* 4, on the one hand, and *AE* A and *EE* III on the other. *NE* 4 has significantly more sentences with γάρ as connective; while *AE* A and *EE* III are significantly more likely to introduce causal clauses with and to begin sentences with ὥστε. What is more, he says, the total figures for γάρ, ἐπεί, and ὥστε in all books of *NE*, *AE*, and *EE* seem to allow us to extend the argument directly to the three groups of books as wholes, providing only that the incidence of the other uses of the particles is as negligible in the books not tested as it is in the sample books.

Rowe suggests that it might be more profitable to study, instead of the frequencies and proportions of individual particles, the proportions between different idioms for carrying out the same function, such as the drawing of conclusions, the assigning of explanations, the introduction of examples. He lists twenty-seven ways in which Aristotle draws inferences in the three sample books, and groups them into three broad types: 'A, therefore B'; 'B, because A'; 'since A, B'. The distribution of these types in the three books is:

	NE 4	*AE* A	*EE* III
Type 1	57	92	37
Type 2	191	153	120
Type 3	13	18	15

In Type 3 *EE* and *AE* prefer ἐπεί, *NE* prefers the genitive absolute construction. In Type 1 note the high figure for *AE*, representing its argumentative nature. In Type 2, 'B ὅτι A' and causal participial clauses are preferred by *AE* and *EE*. *NE* stands out in preference for 'B, A γάρ'.

Rowe concludes that so far as they are founded simply on raw counts of lexical items, little remains of the arguments I presented in chapter 4 of my book. He says that on the basis of the sample books, only with respect to three of my twenty-four chosen words, γάρ, ἐπεί, ὥστε, do such counts come any-where near to showing anything by themselves. In all the other twenty-one cases, either there are no clearly significant differences in frequency of use, or, where there are significant differences, these are for a variety of reasons unusable for the argument.

Rowe's article contains much valuable information, but his study does not weaken my argument as much as he suggests. The 'twenty-four chosen words' were not words chosen by me to support my argument. They were the twenty-four particles which occurred with sufficient frequency to enable us to make an estimate, from the *NE* and the *EE*, of their likely occurrence in the disputed books, on the assumption of the preservation of regularity.[33] In the case of most of them I agreed with Rowe that for one or another reason they could not be used, individually, as discriminators between the *NE* and the *EE*. Of the twenty-four only nine appear in the discriminating groups in my final statistical argument, namely ἀλλά, δή, διό, καθάπερ, ὅτι, οὖν, ὥσπερ, ὥστε, and ἐπεί.[34] Rowe agrees that ὥστε and ἐπεί are good discriminators. The differences between us, therefore, concern the remaining seven words in the list.

With regard to ἀλλά, Rowe claims that its frequency in *AE* A is not due to style, but to content; it is to be explained by the argumentativeness to be expected in a book on justice. But the particle occurs with great frequency in every one of the disputed books, not just the one on justice. Its frequency in the *NE* as a whole is 0.64 per cent, and in no book of the *NE* is its frequency greater than 0.95 per cent; its frequency in the *AE* as a whole is 1.18 per cent and in no book is its frequency less than 1.02 per cent. If its frequency in the *AE* was the same as that in the *NE*, then it would be expected to occur about six times in every thousand words. In every one of the seventeen one-thousand-word samples of the *AE*, with all their varied subject-matter, it occurs more frequently than this, and in all but four of them its frequency is greater than ten.

δή is a particle which is twice as frequent in the *NE* as in the *EE*; in the *AE* it occurs with the same frequency as in the *EE*. Rowe is unhappy about using it as a discriminator, because there are in some places disagreements between manuscripts as to whether the correct reading is δή or δέ. But this is not a serious problem. It is true that a computer study of an ancient text must depend on the edition available in machine-readable form, so that the material one is studying has passed through the hands of a modern editor. But in this case the effect of editorial decisions can be discounted. The *EE* used for my study was Susemihl's Teubner edition; both the *AE* and the *NE* were taken from the

---

[33] *The Aristotelian Ethics*, 91.   [34] Ibid. 132–3.

same Bywater Oxford Classical Text. If the effect of the preferences of these editors was to make itself felt, therefore, it would be in the direction of making the *AE* seem to resemble the *NE* more than it does, and to resemble the *EE* less than it does. Editorial intervention cannot have had the effect of creating artificial differences between the *AE* and the *NE*; if it has had an effect, it can only have been in masking genuine differences.

Rowe refuses to accept ὅτι as a discriminator, because it breaks down into two units, corresponding to the meanings 'that' and 'because', and when the two units are broken down, then in respect of each of them the group *NE* 4, *AE* A, and *EE* III comes out as a homogeneous whole by the chi-square test. But Rowe here shows that he misunderstands the purpose of grouping when applying tests such as chi-square. In my final statistical argument I used as test items groups of words such as the group consisting of the three words ἕκαστος, τοιοῦτος, τοσοῦτος. This was not, of course, to suggest that all these words had the same meaning; it was because they were all words favoured by the *NE*, but had too low a frequency for reliable predictions to be made on the basis of them as individual items. The prediction which underlies the use of such a group is the prediction of the likelihood of a particular word in Aristotle's text turning out to be *either* a token of the type ἕκαστος, *or* a token of the type τοιοῦτος, *or* a token of the type τοσοῦτος. The event predicted is perfectly determinate, and that is all that is necessary for the statistical argument. Similarly, the occurrence of an ὅτι can, if you wish, be regarded as a disjunctive prediction of the occurrence of ὅτι-because or of ὅτι-that. It in no way weakens an argument based on the expectation of such a disjunctive event if the disjoint events themselves occur with too low a frequency to make accurate prediction possible.

καθάπερ, διό, and ὥσπερ are not discussed by Rowe because in the particular books he chose as samples the frequencies are too low for them to be useful discriminators by themselves. It is for the same reason that they appear in groups in my own statistical tests. In the case of οὖν I agree with Rowe that it is not usable as a discriminator by itself and ungrouped.[35]

Hence, Rowe's study, though it adds much valuable information about Aristotle's use of particles in the three books he studies, leaves my own statistical argument very much where it was. At the end of his article he acknowledges that he is now inclined to accept my solution to the problem of the common books, whether or not my treatment of particles and connectives is sound, on the basis of other material in the statistical study. He was particularly struck by the evidence of a preference in the *NE* for tentative words (like ἴσως and δόξειε) and in the *EE* for dogmatic words (like δῆλον and φανερόν).[36]

In general the statistical discussion in *The Aristotelian Ethics* was more warmly received by statisticians and stylometrists than it was by philosophers and classicists. Mosteller and Wallace, in *Applied Bayesian and Classical Inference*, the

---

[35] See *The Aristotelian Ethics*, 86.   [36] Ibid. 118.

second edition of their study of the Federalist Papers, reported it sympathet-
ically in a survey of recent statistical studies of authorship. Richard Bailey,
doyen of American stylometrists, at an international conference on literary
computing in Israel in 1979, used it as a model to illustrate the general
principles to be applied in statistical studies of literary authorship.[37]

Bailey observed that as long as the scholarly community lacks a formalized
theory of stylistic variation, the choice of particular variables will remain *ad hoc*
and therefore open to dispute:

> Kenny's data provide an illustration of this general proposition. When we examine the
> twenty-four particles and connectives that occur at least ten times in each of the fifteen
> books of the ethical treatises, we can select the following as effective discriminators, ones
> that will distinguish the three groups of books at a significance level of 0.01 or better:
> alla, epei, hoti, and hōste.[38]

Bailey made use not only of the figures I provided for the ethical treatises in *The
Aristotelian Ethics*, but also of figures for a number of particles which I published
in a subsequent article on the *Metaphysics*.[39] Bailey showed that if we add the
fourteen books of the *Metaphysics*, the following emerge from a univariate
analysis of variance routine as discriminators between the four groups of books
at 0.01 or better: ἀλλά, δέ, δή, ἐπεί, ὥστε. At the 0.05 level we get fourteen
particles that contribute to a significant differentiation of the four groups of
books. 'What is the explanation for the differences between the two lists? Why,
for instance, is hoti among the best discriminators of the ethical works but not
of the same importance when the *Metaphysics* is added?'[40] We lack a theory to
explain why particular items behave as they do.

Bailey describes how I compared the *AE* books with their rival contexts by
taking each particle and connective one at a time and measuring the degree of
fit for each word, comparing the *AE* first with the *NE* and then with the *EE*,
and using the parametric method of the standard error of a proportion to show
the number of values that 'stand out' from their context.

An alternative procedure is to make use of the 'best discriminators' identified by the
method of univariate analysis of variance. Like Kenny's standard error technique, the test
assumes that the means derived from each set of books are normally distributed. This
assumption is appropriate to this investigation because of the large number of words in

---

[37] Bailey, 'Determining Authorship in Ancient Greek', 4: 'Besides the elegance and
clarity of his arguments, Kenny is particularly to be commended for providing a complete
and meticulous record of the data, the exact location of the samples from which they
were derived, and the statistical procedures applied at each step of his enquiry. Such care
allows his experiment to be replicated and for the use of his findings in testing some
further hypothesis . . . one can think of only a few cases where the findings of an authorship or chronology study have been presented in such detail.'

[38] Ibid. 5.

[39] Kenny, 'A Stylometric Study of Aristotle's *Metaphysics*'.

[40] Bailey, 'Determining Authorship in Ancient Greek', 6.

each of the fifteen books of the ethical treatises and of the fourteen books of the *Metaphysics*. Note that the direction of discrimination is so far unspecified; the six 'best discriminators' might each pull in a different direction, each separately influencing one or another of the six pairs of documents. If the discrimination tended to cancel differences among the pairs, no significant results would emerge. If the discriminators complement each other, the result will be a grouping of the texts that are distinct.[41]

The result of a multivariate analysis employing the six best discriminators is shown in Table 1, taken from Bailey's article. Instead of cancelling each other out, the discriminators work together towards one result: the *NE* is decidedly different from the three other samples.

TABLE 1. *Best Discriminators: Multivariate One-Way Analysis of Variance*
(ἀλλά, δέ, δή, εἰ, ἐπεί, ὥστε)

	Distance between Stratum Means		
	D-Square	F-Statistics	Significance
NE (versus)			
EE	28.308	11.008	> 0.0001
AE	22.157	6.204	0.0008
Metaphysics	23.794	14.805	> 0.0000
EE (versus)			
AE	1.326	0.332	0.9123
Metaphysics	2.206	1.084	0.4054
AE (versus)			
Metaphysics	2.382	0.785	0.5920

Bailey says that these results show that we can reject the hypothesis that the *NE* is drawn from the same population as the *AE*, *EE*, and *Metaphysics* and can do so with a probability of only 8 in 10,000 of being in error. The hypothesis that *EE*, *AE*, and *Metaphysics* are drawn from the same population must be allowed to stand. Moreover, however we arrange the particles and connectives in *AE* and *EE*, no comparison yields an outcome contrary to the one provided by the 'best discriminators'. Bailey grouped twenty-four particles and connectives into four sets on the basis of the descending frequency of their means in the entire sample. The results are shown in Table 2, also taken from Bailey's article.

[41] Ibid. 7.

TABLE 2. *Multivariate One-Way Analysis of Variance Distance between Stratum Means*

	D-Square	F-Statistics	Significance
I. High-Frequency Particles and Connectives ($\gamma \grave{\alpha} \rho$, $\delta \acute{\epsilon}$, $\check{\eta}$, $\kappa \alpha \acute{\iota}$, $\mu \acute{\epsilon} \nu$, $o\dot{\upsilon}$)			
NE (versus)			
EE	9.159	3.562	0.0145
AE	8.484	2.376	0.0676
Metaphysics	13.276	8.261	0.0001
EE (versus)			
AE	2.260	0.565	0.7531
Metaphysics	2.127	1.045	0.4266
AE (versus)			
Metaphysics	4.613	1.520	0.2226
II. Middle-/High-Frequency Particles and Connectives ($\dot{\alpha}\lambda\lambda\acute{\alpha}$, $\check{\alpha}\nu$, $\epsilon\acute{\iota}$, $\mu\acute{\eta}$, $\acute{o}\tau\iota$, $\dot{\omega}\varsigma$)			
NE (versus)			
EE	8.039	3.126	0.0251
AE	13.363	3.742	0.0117
Metaphysics	9.315	5.796	0.0012
EE (versus)			
AE	1.302	0.326	0.9157
Metaphysics	6.747	3.314	0.0197
AE (versus)			
Metaphysics	9.746	3.210	0.0225
III. Middle-/Low-Frequency Particles and Connectives ($\delta\acute{\eta}$, $o\hat{\iota}o\nu$, $o\dot{\upsilon}\delta\acute{\epsilon}$, $o\dot{\upsilon}\nu$, $o\check{\upsilon}\tau\epsilon$, $\tau\epsilon$)			
NE (versus)			
EE	4.840	1.882	0.1339
AE	6.023	1.686	0.1762
Metaphysics	10.522	6.547	0.0006
EE (versus)			
AE	2.521	0.630	0.7044
Metaphysics	3.340	1.641	0.1878
AE (versus)			
Metaphysics	2.701	0.890	0.5208

	D-Square	F-Statistics	Significance
IV. Low-Frequency Particles and Connectives (γε, διό, ἐπεί, κάθαπερ, ὥσπερ, ὥστε)			
NE (versus)			
EE	15.383	5.982	0.0010
AE	14.828	4.152	0.0072
Metaphysics	14.267	8.877	0.0001
EE (versus)			
AE	0.598	0.149	0.9870
Metaphysics	2.284	1.122	0.3851
AE (versus)			
Metaphysics	3.642	1.120	0.3467

This second approach, though it confirms the first, also brings some surprises. If we accept the 0.05 significance level, the 'middle–high frequency' group forces the rejection of the hypothesis that any of the pairs are drawn from the same population except the *AE–EE* pair. The middle–low group, on the other hand, provides only for the discrimination of *NE* from the *Metaphysics*. This second study demonstrates again that *AE* and *EE* are strongly associated with each other while *AE* and *NE* are distinct by every comparison at that 0.05 level or better.

Our review of Kenny's data presents additional problems for the study of Aristotle's works. The 'best discriminators' support the expected conclusion that the *Metaphysics* belongs to the same population as the EE and the AE. One is tempted to claim that they are all the products of Aristotle's philosophical style. But what of the NE without the common books it shares with EE? No one has ever suggested, as far as I know, that these books are not part of Aristotle's authentic works. Yet the stylistic evidence seems to force a conclusion that they are somehow spurious, drawn from a quite different population of particles and connectives.[42]

It is rash, of course, for a stylometrist to draw the conclusion that because two texts are drawn from different populations in respect of certain features, they are therefore by different authors. All that the statistical study proves is that chance is not an adequate explanation of the differences to be observed between the texts. But a difference of authorship is not the only other possible explanation: differences of content, of audience, of period, of editorial intervention may also provide an explanation. Bailey's work reinforces my own conclusion that no explanation other than chance is needed for the differences

---

[42] Bailey, 'Determining Authorship in Ancient Greek', 11.

in particle use etc. between the *AE* and the *EE*. But it brings out the existence of a special problem in the case of the *NE*, which we must now discuss.

III

If the central argument of *The Aristotelian Ethics* is accepted, that the disputed books had their original home in the *EE*, the question remains: At what time were they included also in the *NE*? The latest date at which this can have been done is the time of Aspasius; from his time onwards our familiar ten-book *NE* is accepted by all scholars and commentators. My own earlier suggestion that the transfer may have been made by Aspasius himself is, I now accept, implausible. So we must ask when, between Aristotle's writing of the *EE* and Aspasius' writing of his commentary, books III, IV, and V of the *EE* were placed together with books of the *NE*, and by whom.

The most widely accepted view among scholars is that they were moved by Aristotle himself, with or without revision, from the Eudemian to the Nicomachean environment. Thus Irwin says: 'Ancient evidence fails to show that Aristotle himself did not intend the CB to be a part of the EN. And so even if we find evidence that the CB are originally part of the EE, we cannot at once infer that they should not also be read as part of the EN.'[43] If it was indeed Aristotle who was responsible for the shift, then the disputed books are indeed common books, Nicomachean as well as Eudemian, and can be read with equal appropriateness in either context, even though there may be more to be learnt about them by studying them within the treatise for which they were first written. But was it, in fact, Aristotle who placed the books with the *NE*?

The hypothesis that he moved them assumes that the *NE* is later than the *EE*. This is something that would be maintained by many scholars in any case. Thus Rowe, even while prepared now to accept that the *AE* belonged originally with the *EE*, regards the *NE* as a reworking of earlier material to be found in the *EE*.[44] But a separate case needs to be made to establish that the *NE* is indeed later. The learned world was convinced of that hypothesis by Werner Jaeger on the basis of the unargued assumption that the disputed books were Nicomachean, and in the context of a theory about the evolution of Aristotle's doctrine concerning wisdom which is now almost universally abandoned. New arguments are needed to show that the *NE* is late. On the other hand, on the evidence of the *Magna Moralia* it seems likely that a course resembling the *EE*, and containing the *AE*, was still being given by Aristotle in Athens in the late thirties of the fourth century; and if we take the *AE* as part of the *EE* we get further confirmation of a late date for the *EE*.[45] The *onus probandi* is now

---

[43] Irwin, review of Kenny, 342.
[44] Rowe, 'De Aristotelis ... dicendi ratione', 5: 74 n. 108.
[45] See above, p. 114.

on those who claim that the *NE* is a later Aristotelian lecture course than the *EE*.

Those who believe that Aristotle moved the *AE* into the *NE* commonly think that at the time of doing so he carried out some revision, so that the books as we have them are to some extent a mixture of earlier and later material. Thus Rowe speaks of a Nicomachean recension of the common books, and Cooper claims that statistics cannot throw light on the hypothesis that the common books, originally written for the *EE*, were rewritten for use with the *NE*, so that as they stand they constitute a patchwork.[46]

It is not correct to say that the patchwork hypothesis could not be tested by statistical methods. Let us consider Cooper's 'cautious version' of the rewriting hypothesis, namely that Aristotle reworded here and there, introduced some new clauses, and sometimes a sentence or two. We may observe first of all that this 'cautious version' is a very tenuous wraith of the full-blooded rewriting hypothesis at one time sustained by Mansion, Gauthier-Jolif, Dirlmeier, and Rowe. But we may go on to ask: do these rewritings add up, in total, to 1,000 words? If they do not, or if they do but we have no idea what the 1,000 words are, then for all practical purposes the books have to be read as Eudemian and not as Nicomachean books. If they do, and if a scholar thinks that he can specify which are the Nicomachean insertions, let him list them, and we can put them end to end and then test the thousand-word sample to see whether it resembles the *NE* more than the *EE*, in precisely the way in which the seventeen thousand-word samples were tested in my book.[47]

Cooper in fact offers only a fragment of thirty-one words as an indication of Nicomachean rewriting: the forward allusion to a discussion of the relation between education and the political art, which he sees as an allusion to *NE* 10 (1130^b26 ff.). If this is the only evidence for Nicomachean rewriting then the hypothesis rests on very slender support indeed: for even those who have maintained the rewriting hypothesis, such as Gauthier and Jolif, agree that the reference may just as well be to *Politics* 3. 4.[48]

There is one strong reason against the view that Aristotle revised and moved the books himself. That is the existence of the treatment of pleasure, which duplicates, and is not cross-referenced to, the treatment in *NE* 10. This, as we have seen, appeared to Aspasius to be a reason for considering the hypothesis that it might not be by Aristotle at all. There is no need to go that far, and there is not the conflict of doctrine between *AE* C and *NE* 10 that Aspasius thought

[46] See Cooper, review of Kenny, 387.

[47] *The Aristotelian Ethics*, 110, 132–3, 155–6. Irwin might perhaps hope to avoid this challenge since he surmises that in rewriting earlier material for the *NE* Aristotle may have been subconsciously influenced by his own earlier style, so that the material ends up looking Eudemian. (Irwin, review of Kenny, 342.)

[48] Gauthier-Jolif, *L'Éthique à Nicomaque* (1959 edn.), ii/1. 349; Cooper, review of Kenny, 387.

there was; but it remains, in the words of Christopher Kirwan, barely credible that these two chapters were intended for the same treatise.[49]

Gauthier and Jolif, likewise, find it inconceivable that Aristotle could himself have meant the two treatments of pleasure to belong to the same work. Since they are committed to the thesis that Aristotle rewrote the common books for inclusion in the *NE*, they put forward the hypothesis that Aristotle inserted only part of his rewritten course in *AE* A, B, and C (ending with the end of chapter 11 of *AE* C) and inserted the remainder of it into *NE* 10, chapters 1–5. The earlier treatise on pleasure, they believe, was inserted after C. 11 by an editor after Aristotle's death.[50] But there is no evidence of style or tradition to support such a hypothesis, and it creates new problems of its own. Why should the treatise on pleasure be singled out for specially drastic revision? If on the other hand the revision of earlier material was carried out throughout with the degree of thoroughness which is represented by the distance between the two treatises on pleasure, why did not the posthumous editor think that the earlier version of the rest of the common books was worth preserving as well?

Gauthier and Jolif believe that the posthumous editor who was responsible for inserting the Eudemian treatise on pleasure into the *NE* was none other than Aristotle's son Nicomachus. There is, indeed, much to be said for the idea that the *NE* was edited by Nicomachus after his father's death. As Gauthier and Jolif convincingly show, it is the most natural explanation of the traditional title of the work.[51] But if Nicomachus was responsible for an edition, may it not be that it was he, and not his father, who removed the common books from their original home in order to transfer them into the *NE*? This is a hypothesis which is more economical than the theory of two separate transfers, one by the father and one by the son; it fits the internal evidence for the homogeneity of book C, and it explains a number of the puzzling features of the external evidence set out in *The Aristotelian Ethics*.

If the *Nicomachean Ethics* was so called because it was edited by Nicomachus,

---

[49] Kirwan, review of Kenny, 52.

[50] Gauthier-Jolif, *L'Éthique à Nicomaque* (1970 edn.), i/1. 86 'La partie la plus délicate de l'œuvre de l'éditeur fut sans doute de résoudre le problème des livres V–VII; si l'insertion des livres IV, V, et VI, ch. 1–11, dans son nouveau cours . . . dont ils forment les livres, V, VI, et VII, ch. 1–11, avait été faite par Aristote lui-même, l'ancien traité du plaisir, entièrement récrite pour former le livre X, ch. 1–5, restait en souffrance, et c'est vraisemblablement [l'éditeur] qui eut la fâcheuse idée de l'insérer dans le cours qu'il éditait pour en faire le livre VII, ch. 12–15.'

[51] Gauthier and Jolif believe that when Aristotle died in 322 the *NE* was merely a notebook. Nicomachus, his son, who was very young when Aristotle died, and died young himself, edited the text, perhaps with the help of Theophrastus, who, according to Aristocles in Eusebius, had a hand in his education. The title does not refer to a dedication; one does not dedicate a notebook, and Nicomachus may not even have been born at the time of Aristotle's course. Gauthier and Jolif date the edition shortly before 300. They think it must have preceded the publication of the *EE* (on the grounds that the latter did not contain the disputed books!).

then the *Eudemian Ethics* was presumably so called because it was edited by Eudemus.[52] The preference shown for the *EE* in the centuries after Aristotle's death may be one instance of the general tendency of scholars to give greater credence to philosophers' posthumous works when they are edited by their colleagues than when they are edited by their widows and orphans. Similar reasons may have accounted for the fact that the Eudemian, but not the Nicomachean, version of the *Ethics* was included in the edition of Andronicus. If the *NE* was edited by Nicomachus, that would explain why Cicero and Diogenes Laertius were inclined to regard the treatise as his work rather than his father's.

The edition of Andronicus, according to our best evidence, contained an eight-book *Eudemian Ethics*; this was also the number of books of the Eudemians according to Diogenes Laertius, commenting on Favorinus of Arles. This shows that the disputed books circulated with the *EE* in antiquity; but of course it does not prove that they did not also circulate with the *NE*, as they have certainly done since the time of Aspasius.

However, there continued for quite a long period to be an uncertainty about the number of books contained in the *NE*. Alexander of Aphrodisias was the first to state explicitly that it contains ten books (*CAG* ii. 1. 8. 31); before his time there was uncertainty about the numbering of the books in Aspasius and Adrastus of Aphrodisias, and there are passages which are attributed to Alexander himself which seem to indicate that he knew eleven Nicomachean books. The confusion continues as late as the *Suda*, which attributes a six-book *Ethics* to Nicomachus.[53]

If we accept the hypothesis that Nicomachus was the first person to add the disputed books to Aristotle's *NE*, the question remains: What exactly did he add these books to? Did he find, among his father's papers, something which corresponded more or less exactly to our *NE* minus the common books? Gauthier and Jolif think that his editorial work, apart from the introduction of the treatise on pleasure, was not extensive: he collected and located (often maladroitly) the doublets of which our text is full; his main contribution was to divide the treatises into books, adding appropriate opening and closing phrases.

There is a different tradition of scholarship according to which Nicomachus' contribution may have been just the opposite: instead of dividing a continuous work into books, he may have collected together a number of self-standing works into a single series. Many years ago Thomas Case, in his celebrated

---

[52] We know from correspondence preserved by Simplicius (*In Phys.* 923. 7) that Eudemus concerned himself with the editing of Aristotle's *Physics*; but because there was no other version of Aristotle's physical teaching current, there was never any need to call the *Physics* the 'Eudemian Physics'.

[53] See *The Aristotelian Ethics*, 31, 36–9, on the confusion in the tradition about the number of Nicomachean books.

Encyclopaedia Britannica article on Aristotle, suggested that 'the probability is that the Nicomachean Ethics is a collection of separate discourses worked up into a tolerably systematic treatise': he argued for this on the basis of the imperfect connection of its several parts, and he believed that he had found traces of the original separate treatises in the list of works in Diogenes Laertius.[54]

Half a century before Case, Rudolf Eucken made the first systematic study of the use of particles in Aristotle's major works. He maintained that the individual books of the *NE* differed so much from each other that they could hardly have been written in a single stint: they fell into four groups, he maintained: books 1 and 2; books 3 and 4; the common books; and books 8–10. I quote Bailey's summing up of Eucken's work:

He noted that [the use of discriminating particles] in the ethical works is considerably more various than in either the *Metaphysics* or the *Physics* and also recognized that EE and AE resembled the canon as a whole. Like Kenny, he was left with the problem of the place of NE; and like most persons who have investigated authorship in ancient Greek, he attributed a result incompatible with authorship to chronology. The NE, he thought, must have been compiled from separate parts written at different times.

Others, more recently, have argued on different grounds that some parts of the *NE* must have started life as separate treatises, but they have not always made up their subdivisions in the same way as Eucken. In 1951 G. Verbeke studied the passages of the *NE* on the ideal of human perfection—the ones which have been the topic of this book—and concluded that they belonged to a very early period in Aristotle's life whatever might be true of the rest of the *NE*.[55] Martha Nussbaum, who takes a very different view from Verbeke of the significance of the passages on perfection in book 1, none the less takes a similar line when it comes to book 10. She relegates 10. 6–8 to an appendix; she thinks it is quite out of keeping with the rest of the *NE* and suggests that it may have been inserted by a later editor.[56]

[54] Much has been written about the ancient lists of Aristotle's writings since the time of Case. My own conjecture is that the earliest list, of Hermippus, contains the *EE* composed of (1) a five-book *Ethics* = *EE* I–III plus *AE* 1 and 2; (2) a book on the influence of the passions (*AE* C); (3) a book on friendship = *EE* VII. The second list, of Hesychius, contains also the seven *NE* books, 1 and 10 and 2–4, grouped with the five *EE* books on ethics, and 8 and 9 grouped with *EE* VII to make three books on friendship. See *The Aristotelian Ethics*, 39–46.

[55] Verbeke, 'L'idéal', 95: 'Soit qu'on essaie de dégager les présupposés psychologiques de l'argumentation aristotélicienne concernant la perfection humaine, soit qu'on compare entre elles l'Éthique Eudémienne et l'Éthique à Nicomaque, on arrive à la conclusion que les passages étudiés de ce dernier ouvrage sont de date très ancienne, c'est à dire de l'époque où Aristote a commencé de prendre position contre son maître Platon, peut-être vers le début de son enseignement à Assos . . . il est généralement admis qu'on traité comme l'Éthique à Nicomaque n'a pas été écrit d'un trait et contient des morceaux d'âge différent.'

[56] Nussbaum, *The Fragility of Goodness*, 372–7. I do not wish to rule out the hypothesis

Rowe concluded his statistical study by drawing attention to the fact that besides the differences between the *NE* and the *AE* + *EE* there were many differences in the use of particles to be found within the groups:

Kenny himself seems hospitable to the suggestion that NE may fall into groups of books; if this were the case, the question would not be whether the style of AE associates it with EE or with NE simpliciter, but whether it associates it with EE or with any of the constituent parts of NE, or perhaps relatively more with some or all of them. The question would change still further if it turned out that either EE or AE as well, or both, were patchworks. On the whole, however, there appear to be no real grounds for raising these latter possibilities. It happens that it is also my intuition, as it is that of many others, that NE is an organic whole, which may or may not have been patched or added to in places. But then it was my intuition that AE belonged to NE (in the sense of being written of a piece with it); a view to which other parts of Kenny's book, if not the part on which I have centred on this paper, deal a near-lethal blow.[57]

If, despite Rowe's intuitions, the conjectures of Eucken, Case, and Verbeke were correct, it would explain a puzzling fact for which no very convincing explanation has ever been offered. We know from Elias (*CAG* xviii. 32. 34) that in antiquity the *Magna Moralia* was known as 'The Great Nicomachean Ethics' and that the *NE* was known as 'The Lesser Nicomachean Ethics'. Since the *NE* is much longer than the *Magna Moralia* this has puzzled commentators. They have suggested that since the individual books of the *Magna Moralia* are larger, they were preserved on rolls which were physically larger than the more numerous but smaller rolls of the *NE*. No doubt this is true; but it is a solution which pushes the question further back. The traditional title of the *Parva Naturalia* suggests that the ultimate solution may be along the lines suggested by Case. The *Parva Naturalia* is not a short treatise, but a collection of only slightly connected treatises. May not the *NE* have been originally, then, the *Parva Moralia* in exactly the same sense? If we add the Eucken–Case conjecture to the Gauthier–Jolif conjecture, we reach a quite plausible explanation for the

that the *NE* may contain writings of Aristotle some of which are earlier and some of which are later than the *EE*. But if we are to parcel up the *NE* then I agree with Verbeke, against Eucken and Nussbaum, that books 1 and 10 must go into the same parcel. They are more closely linked to each other than the pair of them are to books 2–5 or 8–9. The back references in 10. 7 are uncommonly frequent (see above, pp. 19, 87).

Von Fragstein, *Studien*, 417, has suggested that the final chapter of *NE* 10 is out of place, and should really be placed at the end of the *EE*. He claims that *EE* VIII. 3 is not a real ending to a treatise; on the other hand the final chapter of *NE* X has nothing to do with the preceding discussion of pleasure or happiness, but is about education and law: 'Es schliesst mit knappen Worten alles zuvor behandelte ab, unde leitet zur Vorlesung über Politik über, in wohlgesetztem, isokrateischem Stil, geschmückt mit Zitaten aus Theognis und aus der Odysee, schliesslich bereichert um eine milde Auseinandersetzung mit Isokrates. Kurz und gut, was hier unerwartet uns begegnet, ist genau das, was am Schluss der EE fehlt.' He claims to see back references to the *EE* in the reference to nobility and goodness in 1178^{b}10 and the reference to good fortune in 1179^{b}21.

[57] Rowe, 'De Aristotelis ... dicendi ratione', 5: 75.

various pieces of puzzling evidence studied in this appendix and in *The Aristotelian Ethics*. Our *NE* consists of an anthology of genuine but separate Aristotelian treatises, of uncertain date, which were collected together into an anthology of ethical writings after Aristotle's death by his son Nicomachus: an anthology in which Nicomachus included three books which belonged to an existing and more lengthy treatise, the *EE*.[58]

This is, of course, entirely conjectural. But further exploration of the conjecture might throw light on the scanty connections between different books of the *NE*, the doublets within them, and the inconsistencies of doctrine and style which individual books exhibit. But the exploration of the conjecture would involve wide-ranging enquiry. While the relationship between the duplicated books and the *NE* and *EE* is capable of study in isolation, the study of the relative chronology of the two books is not to be separated from the study of the whole corpus, whether from a philosophical or a stylistic point of view.

I referred earlier to the conclusions drawn by Bailey from his study of the statistics from the ethical treatises and the *Metaphysics*: concerning the *NE* books he wrote: 'the stylistic evidence seems to force a conclusion that they are somehow spurious, drawn from a quite different population of particles and connectives'.

Bailey's conclusion, as I have already argued, is premature. Works drawn from a different population in the statistical sense are not necessarily works written by a different author. But the differences he remarks on are striking and cannot be denied. Bailey's work was based on data from the *TLC* only for the *Ethics* and *Metaphysics*. Further word-lists which I have compiled since show that in a number of the features where *NE* differs from *EE* and *AE* and *Metaphysics* it differs from almost all other works in the corpus.[59]

This can be illustrated in a few simple examples. Take, for instance, the rate of καί. If we take a hundred works from the Aristotelian corpus we find variations from about 8 per cent to 2.4 per cent. But the great majority of his works cluster between 4.4 and 6.8 per cent. Three books of the *NE* are over 6.8 per cent: a position they share only with two books of the *Rhetoric* and four undoubtedly spurious works.

[58] Did the publication of the *NE* precede that of the *EE* or follow it (whatever 'publication' may have consisted in)? In either case, there is a problem why the editor who published second included the common books. If the *NE* came first, then Eudemus' inclusion of the common books along with the *EE* is to be explained by the fact that that is where they belong, as the stylistic evidence shows; publication of the *EE* without them would be an incomplete publication of the course. If the *EE* came first, then Nicomachus' inclusion of the common books must stem from the desire to produce an anthology which covered all the major topics of ethics. Modern parallels for posthumous philosophical anthologies which are a mixture of unpublished and already published work are not far to seek (see e.g. Prior, *Objects of Thought*).

[59] Most of these remain unpublished. The statistics quoted below have been published in Kenny, 'A Stylometric Comparison'.

With δέ too the *NE* books are at the outside of the distribution. The great majority of a hundred books are between 3.3 and 4.4 per cent. Five of the *NE* books are over 4.7 per cent: a position they share with half a dozen other authentic books, none of which, however, are at all unusual in their καί frequencies. Something similar emerges if we turn to γάρ. Most of the works are between 1.5 and 2.5 per cent. Two books of the *NE* are 2.5 per cent; two are higher than this, and *NE* 8 at 3.3 per cent is far above any of the other books of the hundred, authentic or spurious.

I take these simply as being the three commonest particles, and to indicate the outlying position of the *NE* with respect to them. They are not particles which were chosen in my *AE* books as particular Nicomachean indicators; it is only since word-lists have been produced for the rest of the corpus that it has emerged that there are eccentricities in the *NE* here. Examples could be multiplied if we turned to specific Nicomachean favourite words (the 'tentative-ness' group, for instance). Time and again we find that when the *NE* stands apart from the *EE* and *AE* it stands apart also from the *Metaphysics*, *Politics*, and other works. The differences between the *NE* and the political and meta-physical writings may no doubt be partly explained by the subject-matter; but they cannot wholly be explained by that, otherwise why should not the *EE* stand apart in the same way and to the same extent?

I do not regard these stylistic differences between the *NE* and the central parts of the Aristotelian corpus as showing that the *NE* is inauthentic, or even as providing evidence in that direction. Nor do I regard them as giving any indication of its chronological location: there is not, so far as I have been able to discover, any particular work or set of works which resembles the *NE*'s idiosyncrasies, and which therefore would provide an anchor to which one might attach a hypothesis of dating: the *Topics*, say, for an early date, the *De Anima*, perhaps, for a later one. Rather, these idiosyncrasies of style suggest that it is wise to keep open the question whether the explanation of the differ-ences between the *NE* and *EE* may not be something quite other than chronological.

If the differences go back to Aristotle himself, in each case, then they may be due to a difference of intended audiences. The *NE* is more fluent, less austerely philosophical, less telegrammatic in its arguments than the *EE*; it may be designed for a less professional audience than the *EE*, just as, throughout history, it has appealed to a wide readership, whereas the *EE* has never appealed to more than a handful of Aristotelian fanatics. But of course the doublets, lacunae, and inconcinnities in both treatises forbid us to think that either of them was brought to anything like publishable form by Aristotle himself.

If the differences between the styles of the two are due, on one side or the other, or both, to the activities of editors, then it seems that we must say that the *NE* has reached us from the hand of an editor different from the one responsible for the edition of Aristotle's other major works. This is, of course, consistent with the fact that the *NE* is the only Aristotelian treatise which we have any reason to believe was edited by Nicomachus. But it would be rash to assume that the peculiarities of the *NE* are personal characteristics of Nicomachus, imposed on a text which without his editing would have resembled, in the features that have been studied, the rest of the corpus. On the contrary, it could even be that in the peculiarities of the *NE* we have preserved, alone among the corpus, some of the stylistic habits of Aristotle himself. Indeed, if it was Nicomachus who transferred the common books from their Eudemian context to keep company with the *NE*, the fact that they retain so many Eudemian features suggests that he was an editor with a very light hand. The *NE* may differ from the other extant works not because it has had more attention from an editor, but because it has had less.

These and other hypotheses seem to me open at the present time. A convincing explanation of those stylistic features that are amenable to statistical study must await a fuller study of the corpus as a whole, and a detailed investigation of the separate parts of the *NE* itself.

APPENDIX 2

Nicomachean Ethics 1. 7, 1097ᵃ15–1098ᵃ20 (Translation)

LET us return once more to the good we are seeking, and ask what it could be. It seems to be different in different actions and crafts: it is one thing in medicine, another in strategy, and something else again in the other crafts.

What then is the good of each? Surely that for whose sake everything else is done. In medicine this is health, in strategy victory, in domestic architecture a house, in other cases something else, but in every action and choice it is the end. For it is for the sake of this that everyone does whatever else they do.

Therefore, if there is some end of everything that is achievable by action, this will be the good achievable by action; if there are several ends, these will be the goods achievable by action.

Our argument has come round, then, to the same point; but we must try to put this even more clearly.

Since there are evidently several ends, and we choose some of them (e.g. wealth, flutes, and instruments in general) because of something else, it is clear that they are not all perfect ends; but the chief good is evidently something perfect. Therefore, if there is only one perfect end, this will be what we are seeking; and if there are several, it will be the most perfect of these

Now something that is pursued for its own sake we call more perfect than what is pursued because of something else; and something that is never chosen because of something else we call more perfect than the things that are chosen both for their own sake and because of the other thing; and what we call unqualifiedly perfect is that which is always chosen for itself and never because of anything else.

Now happiness, more than anything else, seems to be a thing of this kind; for happiness we choose always because of itself and never because of something else; whereas honour, pleasure, understanding and every virtue we choose indeed for their own sake (since we would choose each of them even if nothing resulted from them), but we choose them also for the sake of happiness, supposing that through them we shall be happy. Happiness, on the other hand, no one chooses for the sake of these things, nor, in general, because of anything other than itself.

From self-sufficiency the same result seems to be reached: for the perfect good seems to be self-sufficient. What we mean by self-sufficient is not what is sufficient for a man by himself, living a solitary life, but also for parents, children, wife, and friends and fellow citizens in general; since by nature a human being is meant for society. (Some limit must be set to this: if you proceed to ancestors and descendants and friends' friends the line goes on for ever; but this must be examined on another occasion.) We define the self-sufficient as that which all by itself makes life worthy of choice and lacking in nothing; and such we think happiness to be.

Moreover, we think happiness to be the most choice-worthy of all things without being added to anything else; if so added it is clearly more choice-worthy in conjunction with even the least of goods; for what is added makes an extra amount of good, and the greater of two goods is always most choice-worthy. Thus it appears that there is something perfect and self-sufficient, namely happiness, which is the end of action.

Perhaps, however, to say that happiness is the chief good is a commonplace, and what is missing is a clearer account of what it is. This might be forthcoming if it could be ascertained what is the *ergon* of a human being. For just as for a flautist, a sculptor, or any craftsman, and in general for all things that have an *ergon* or activity, the good and the well seems to reside in the *ergon*, so it would seem to be for a human being, if a human being has an *ergon*. Does the carpenter then have an *ergon* and an activity, and the leather-worker too, and does a human being lack one, being functionless by nature? Rather, just as the eye, the hand, the foot, and in general each of the parts manifestly has an *ergon*, may we not ascribe to the human being some *ergon* distinct from all these?

What, then, could this be? Being alive seems to be something shared even with plants, and we are seeking what is peculiar to humans; so we should set aside the life of nutrition and growth. Next in order there would be the life of sense-perception, but that too seems to be shared by the horse, the ox, and every kind of animal. What remains is an active life of some kind belonging to what has reason (and this contains two parts, one as obeying reason, the other as possessing reason and engaging in thought); and as this too can be spoken of in two ways, we must state that we mean life in exercise, for this seems to be life more strictly so called. Now if the *ergon* of man is an activity of soul in accordance with reason, or not without reason, and if we say the *ergon* of a so-and-so is the same in kind as the *ergon* of a good so-and-so, as for instance of a lyre-player and a good lyre-player, and so in general in all cases, adding the surplus of excellence to the mere *ergon* (for the *ergon* of a lyre-player is to play the lyre, and of a good lyre player to play it well); if this is the case human good turns out to be activity of soul in accordance with virtue, and if there are more than one virtues, according to the best and most perfect.

But we must add 'in a perfect life'. For one swallow does not make a summer, nor does one day; and thus too one day or a short time does not make a man blessed or happy.

APPENDIX 3

Eudemian Ethics VIII. 2 (= VII. 14) (Greek Text)

In the following pages the Oxford Classical Text is reproduced on the left-hand pages. My preferred readings are given on the right.

καὶ ὀρθῶς τὸ Σωκρατικόν, ὅτι οὐδὲν ἰσχυρότερον φρονήσεως.
35 ἀλλ' ὅτι ἐπιστήμην ἔφη, οὐκ ὀρθόν· ἀρετὴ γάρ ἐστι καὶ οὐκ
ἐπιστήμη, ἀλλὰ γένος ἄλλο γνώσ⟨εως⟩.

2 ἐπεὶ δ' οὐ μόνον ἡ φρόνησις ποιεῖ τὴν εὐπραγίαν καὶ *H.* XIV
ἀρετή, ἀλλὰ φαμὲν καὶ τοὺς εὐτυχεῖς εὖ πράττειν, ὡς καὶ
1247ᵃ τῆς εὐτυχίας {εὖ} ποιούσης εὐπραγίαν καὶ τὰ αὐτὰ τῇ ἐπιστήμῃ, σκεπτέον ἆρ' ἐστὶ φύσει ὁ μὲν εὐτυχὴς ὁ δ' ἀτυ-
χής, ἢ οὔ, καὶ πῶς ἔχει περὶ τούτων. ὅτι μὲν γάρ εἰσί 2
τινες εὐτυχεῖς ὁρῶμεν. ἄφρονες γὰρ ὄντες κατορθοῦσι πολλά,
5 ἐν οἷς ἡ τύχη κυρία· ἔτι δὲ καὶ ἐν οἷς τέχνη ἐστί, πολὺ
μέντοι καὶ τύχης ἐνυπάρχει, οἷον ἐν στρατηγίᾳ καὶ κυβερ-
νητικῇ. πότερον οὖν ἀπό τινος ἕξεως οὗτοί εἰσιν, ἢ οὐ τῷ
αὐτοὶ ποιοί τινες εἶναι πρακτικοί εἰσι τῶν εὐτυχημάτων;
νῦν μὲν γὰρ οὕτως οἴονται ὡς φύσει τινῶν ὄντων· ἡ δὲ 3
10 φύσις ποιούς τινας ποιεῖ, καὶ εὐθὺς ἐκ γενετῆς διαφέρουσιν·
ὥσπερ οἱ μὲν γλαυκοὶ οἱ δὲ μελανόμματοι τῷ {τὸ} δεῖν
τοιονδὶ ⟨κατὰ τὸ εἶναι τοιονδὶ⟩ ἔχειν, οὕτω καὶ οἱ εὐτυχεῖς καὶ
13 ἀτυχεῖς.

13 ὅτι μὲν γὰρ οὐ φρονήσει κατορθοῦσι, δῆλον. οὐ γὰρ ἄλο- 4
γος ἡ φρόνησις, ἀλλ' ἔχει λόγον διὰ τί οὕτως πράττει, οἱ δ'
15 οὐκ ἂν ἔχοιεν εἰπεῖν διὰ τί κατορθοῦσι (τέχνη γὰρ ἂν ἦν)· ἔτι 5

34 Σωκρατικόν Bekker (σωκρατηκόν fort. V): σῶμα κρατητικόν Π
36 γνώσ⟨εως⟩ Spengel: γνώσ, tum spat. trium litt. CL: γνώσ, tum spat.
duarum litt. P　　38 ἀρετή C: ἀρετήν PL: κατ' ἀρετήν Jackson ((3),
208–9)　　1247ᵃ 1 {εὖ} secl. Spengel: εὐτυχίας εὖ ποιούσης L: εὐτυχείας εὐποιούσης PC　καὶ Π: κατὰ Spengel　1–2 τῇ ἐπιστήμῃ
Spengel: τῆς ἐπιστήμης Π　4 πολλὰ Π: πολλοί Jackson ((3), 209)
5 ἔτι Spengel: εἰ Π: si Λ²: οἱ Bekker　5–6 πολὺ μέντοι καὶ L:
πολλοὶ μέντοι καὶ PC: multo magis et Λ²　6 ἐνυπάρχει Π: inerit Λ²
7 οὗτοί] τοιοῦτοι Allan (5)　οὐ τῷ Chalc.: aut non Λ¹: non eo quod Λ²:
οὕτω Π　9 πολλοὶ e l. 5 (PC) post γὰρ tra. Allan (5)　11 {τὸ}
secl. Dirlmeier: τῷ τὸ δεῖν Π: τῷ τὸ δεῖνα Langerbeck: an {τὸ} ἀεὶ?: τοδὶ
Spengel　12 τοιονδὶ ⟨κατὰ τὸ εἶναι τοιονδὶ⟩ suppl. Susemihl: eo
quod tale secundum esse tale oportet et habere Λ²: τοιονδὶ L: τοιὸν δεῖ
PC　14 ἡ L, C² sup. lineam: om. PC¹　πράττει Marc. Urb.:
πράττοι Π　15 τέχνη Walzer (cf. φρονήσει 47ᵃ13): τέχνη Π　ἔτι
PC: etiam Λ¹: amplius Λ²: ἔστι L: ὅτι Jackson ((3), 210) (sc. κατορθοῦσι,
47ᵃ13)

1247ᵃ1 {εὖ} ποιούσης] ἐμποιούσης
1247ᵃ1-2 τῇ ἐπιστήμῃ] τῆς ἐπιστήμης

1247ᵃ15 τέχνῃ] τέχνη

δὲ φανεροὶ ὄντες ἄφρονες, οὐχ ὅτι περὶ ἄλλα (τοῦτο μὲν γὰρ
οὐθὲν ἄτοπον· οἷον Ἱπποκράτης γεωμετρικὸς ὤν, ἀλλὰ περὶ
τὰ ἄλλα ἐδόκει βλὰξ καὶ ἄφρων εἶναι, καὶ πολὺ χρυ-
σίον πλέων ἀπώλεσεν ὑπὸ τῶν ἐν Βυζαντίῳ πεντηκοστολόγων) {δι' εὐήθειαν, ὡς λέγουσιν} ἀλλ' {ὅτι} καὶ ἐν οἷς εὐτυ- 20
6 χοῦσιν ἄφρονες. περὶ γὰρ ναυκληρίαν οὐχ οἱ δεινότατοι
εὐτυχεῖς, ἀλλ' ὥσπερ ἐν κύβων πτώσει ὁ μὲν οὐδέν, ἄλλος
δὲ βάλλει καθ' ἣν φύσει ἐστὶν εὐτυχής· ἢ τῷ φιλεῖ-
σθαι, ὥσπερ φασίν, ὑπὸ θεοῦ, καὶ ἔξωθέν τι εἶναι τὸ κατορθοῦν,
οἷον πλοῖον κακῶς νεναυπηγημένον ἄμεινον πολλάκις {δὲ} 25
πλεῖ, ἀλλ' οὐ δι' αὑτό, ἀλλ' ὅτι ἔχει κυβερνήτην ἀγαθόν,
{ἀλλ'} οὕτως ⟨ὁ⟩ εὐτυχὴς τὸν δαίμονα ἔχει κυβερνήτην ἀγαθόν;
7 ἀλλ' ἄτοπον θεὸν ἢ δαίμονα φιλεῖν τὸν τοιοῦτον, ἀλλὰ μὴ
τὸν βέλτιστον καὶ τὸν φρονιμώτατον. εἰ δὴ ἀνάγκη ἢ
φύσει ἢ νόῳ ἢ ἐπιτροπείᾳ τινὶ κατορθοῦν, τὰ δὲ δύο μὴ 30
ἐστί, φύσει ἂν εἶεν οἱ εὐτυχεῖς. 31

8   ἀλλὰ μὴν ἥ γε φύσις 31
αἰτία ἢ τοῦ ἀεὶ ὡσαύτως ἢ τοῦ ὡς ἐπὶ τὸ πολύ, ἡ δὲ τύχη
τοὐναντίον. εἰ μὲν οὖν τὸ παραλόγως ἐπιτυγχάνειν τύχης
δοκεῖ εἶναι, (ἀλλ', εἴπερ, διὰ τύχην εὐτυχής), οὐκ ἂν τοιοῦτον

16 δὲ] enim Λ²: γὰρ Dirlmeier   φανεροὶ Allan (5): φανερὸν Π: ὅτι post
φανερὸν suppl. Spengel   μὲν om. L   17 οὐθὲν L: nihil Λ²: om. PC
Hippocratem Λ¹: Ypocras Λ²   18 ἐδόκει . . . εἶναι] . . . erat Λ²: δόκει
. . . εἶναι Π   19 πλέων] navigans Λ²: πλέον Π   πεντηκοστολόγων L:
πεντηκοστῶ λόγων PC   20 {δι' . . . λέγουσιν} secl. Allan (5)   {ὅτι}
secl. Rowe (3)   ἐν οἷς fort. V: in quibus Λ²: ἐνίοις Π: ἐν ἐνίοις (in
nonnullis) Λ¹   21 δεινότατοι L: peritissimi Λ¹: maxime industrii Λ²:
δυνότατοι P: δυνώτατοι C   23 ἔξ post βάλλει suppl. Jackson ((3),
210–11), πολὺ Susemihl: iacit ex Λ²: multum Λ¹   ἣν (sc. βολήν)
Collingwood (cf. 47ᵇ17)   25–6 {δὲ} agitur Λ¹: navigat Λ²: δὲ πλεῖ
Π: διαπλεῖ Sylburg   26 αὑτὸ C   ἀγαθόν om. Λ²   27 {ἀλλ'}
om. L, secl. Fritzsche   οὕτως Fritzsche: ⟨ὁ⟩ suppl. Susemihl: οὗτος
P²L: sic Λ¹Λ²: ἀλλ' . . . ἀγαθόν om. P¹C   εὐτυχ (spat. duarum litt.)
(εὐτυχὴς P² Marc.) τὸν δαίμονα L: benefortunatum daimonem Λ²
29 δὴ] δὲ Casaubon   30 ἐπιτροπείᾳ C: ἐπιτροπίᾳ PL   κατορθοῦν,
τὰ δὲ δύο Π: dirigentia autem Λ²   33 οὕτω post οὖν suppl.
Bussemaker   34 ἀλλ' . . . ἂν] qui autem propter fortunam benefortu-
natus non utique videbitur Λ²: δόξειε post ἂν suppl. Jackson ((3), 212)

1247ᵃ15-16 ἔτι δὲ φανεροί] ὅτι δέ, φανερὸν

1247ᵃ23 βάλλει] βάλλει ἒξ   εὐτυχής·] εὐτυχής.
1247ᵃ24 κατορθοῦν,] κατορθοῦν;

1247ᵃ27 ἀγαθόν;] ἀγαθόν.

1247ᵃ34 ἂν] ἂν δόξειε

35 εἴη τὸ αἴτιον, οἷον ἀεὶ τοῦ αὐτοῦ ἢ ὡς ἐπὶ τὸ πολύ. ἔτι 9
εἰ, ⟨ἢ⟩ τοιοσδί, ἐπιτυγχάνει ἢ ἀποτυγχάνει, ὥσπερ, ὅτι {ὁ} γλαυκός, οὐκ ὀξὺ ὁρᾷ, οὐ τύχη αἰτία ἀλλὰ φύσις· οὐκ ἄρα ἐστὶν εὐτυχὴς ἀλλ' οἷον εὐφυής. ὥστε τοῦτ' ἂν εἴη λεκτέον, ὅτι οὓς λέ-
γομεν εὐτυχεῖς, οὐ διὰ τύχην εἰσίν. οὐκ ἄρα εἰσὶν εὐτυχεῖς·
1247ᵇ τύχης γάρ, ὅσων αἰτία τύχη ἀγαθὴ ἀγαθῶν.

1247ᵇ   εἰ δ' οὕτως,
πότερον οὐκ ἔσται τύχη ὅλως, ἢ ἔσται μέν, ἀλλ' οὐκ αἰτία; ἀλλ'
ἀνάγκη καὶ εἶναι καὶ αἰτίαν εἶναι. ἔσται ἄρα καὶ ἀγαθῶν
τισιν αἰτία ἢ κακῶν. εἰ δ' ὅλως ἐξαιρετέον καὶ οὐδὲν ἀπὸ 10
5 τύχης φατέον γίνεσθαι, ἀλλ' ἡμεῖς ἄλλης οὔσης αἰτίας
διὰ τὸ μὴ ὁρᾶν τύχην εἶναί φαμεν αἰτίαν (διὸ καὶ ὁρι-
ζόμενοι τὴν τύχην τιθέασιν αἰτίαν ἄδηλον ἀνθρωπίνῳ λο-
γισμῷ, ὡς οὔσης τινὸς φύσεως)· τοῦτο μὲν οὖν ἄλλο πρόβλημ'
9 ἂν εἴη.

9   ἐπεὶ δὲ ὁρῶμέν τινας ἅπαξ εὐτυχήσαντας, διὰ
10 τί οὐ καὶ πάλιν; ἂν διὰ τὸ αὐτὸ κατορθώσαιεν καὶ πάλιν.
τοῦ γὰρ αὐτοῦ τὸ αὐτὸ αἴτιον. οὐκ ἄρα ἔσται τύχης τοῦτο. ἀλλ' 11

35 εἴη Fritzsche: εἶναι Π: esse Λ² τὸ¹] τι Langerbeck ἢ ὡς] aut ut
Λ²: εἰ ὡς PC: ὡς L   35–36 ἔτι εἰ, ⟨ἢ⟩ Langerbeck: ἔτι ἢ Π: ἔτι εἰ
Marc.: adhuc si quia Λ²: ἔτι εἰ, ⟨ὅτι⟩ Fritzsche   36 τοιοσδί Chalc.:
τοῖος δή CL: τοῖος δεῖ P: talis oportet Λ²: post τοιοσδί, δεῖ suppl.
Dirlmeier   ἐπιτυγχάνει ἢ ἀποτυγχάνει Π: accidere Λ²: ἐπιτυγχάνειν ἢ
ἀποτυγχάνειν Dirlmeier   ὥσπερ ὅτι L: sicut quia Λ²: ὅτι ὥσπερ PC   {ὁ}
om. Marc., secl. Bussemaker: ὅτι ὁ Π   37 οὐκ ὀξὺ codd. Λ¹: ὀξὺ
Λ², Ross (cl. GA 779ᵇ12, 35)   ὁρᾷ om. Λ²   1247ᵇ 1 τύχης Π:
fortunati Λ²: εὐτυχεῖς Jackson ((3), 212–13)   ὅσων codd. Λ²: ὅσοις
Jackson: ὅσων ⟨μὴ⟩ Dirlmeier   2 οὐκ¹ Spengel: ἢ codd.: ἢ οὐκ
Jackson ((3), 213)   οὐκ² αἰτία Spengel: οὐκέτι Π   4 ἐξαιρετέον Π:
ἐξαιρετέα Langerbeck   οὐδὲν] μηδὲν dubitanter Susemihl   7 ἄδηλον
Shorey (80; cf. Ph. 196ᵇ6): ἄλογον PC: sine ratione Λ²: ἀνάλογον L:
proportionalem Λ¹   9 ἐπεὶ δὲ C (δὲ sup., eadem manu): quoniam
autem Λ²: ἐπεὶ δή L: ἐπειδὴ P: quandoquidem Λ¹   10 ἀλλὰ post ἂν e
sed Λ²: om. Π   διὰ τὸ αὐτὸ κατορθώσαιεν Jackson ((3), 213): διὰ τὸ
ἀποκατορθῶσαι Π: διὰ τὸ ἀποκατορθῶσαι ἕν, (Susemihl) e propter idem
dirigere unum Λ²   καὶ πάλιν PC: καὶ πάλιν bis L: et iterum Λ²   11 τοῦ
γὰρ αὐτοῦ τὸ αὐτὸ αἴτιον Jackson ((3), 213): τὸ γὰρ αὐτὸ τοῦτ' αἴτιον Π:
eiusdem enim eadem causa Λ²   τοῦτο Jackson: οὐ τὸ Π: hoc Λ²
11–12 ἀλλ' ὅταν PC: sed cum Λ²: ἄλλο τ' ἂν L

1247ᵃ35 εἴη] εἶναι

1247ᵇ1 τύχης] εὐτυχεῖς

1247ᵇ7 ἄδηλον] ἄλογον

1247ᵇ10 πάλιν; ἂν διὰ τὸ αὐτὸ κατορθώσαιεν καὶ πάλιν] πάλιν ἀλλὰ διὰ τὸ αὐτὸ κατορθῶσαι καὶ πάλιν

ὅταν τὸ αὐτὸ ἀποβαίνῃ, ἀπείρων καὶ ἀορίστων, ἔσται μὲν
τῳ ἀγαθὸν ἢ κακόν, ἐπιστήμη δ᾽ οὐκ ἔσται αὐτοῦ ἡ δι᾽ ἐμπειρίαν, ἐπεὶ ἐμάνθανον ἄν τινες εὐτυχεῖς, ἢ καὶ πᾶσαι ἂν
12 αἱ ἐπιστῆμαι, ὥσπερ ἔφη Σωκράτης, εὐτυχίαι ἦσαν. τί οὖν 15
κωλύει συμβῆναί τινι ἐφεξῆς τὰ τοιαῦτα πολλάκις, οὐχ
ὅτι τοιοσδί, ἀλλ᾽ οἷον ἂν εἴη τὸ κύβους ἀεὶ μακαρίαν βάλ-
λειν; 18
      τί δὲ δή; ἆρ᾽ οὐκ ἔνεισιν ὁρμαὶ ἐν τῇ ψυχῇ αἱ μὲν 18
ἀπὸ λογισμοῦ, αἱ δὲ ἀπὸ ὀρέξεως ἀλόγου; καὶ πρότεραι
αὗται; εἰ γάρ ἐστι φύσει ἡ δι᾽ ἐπιθυμίαν ἡδέος {καὶ ἡ} ὄρε- 20
13 ξις, φύσει γε ἐπὶ τὸ ἀγαθὸν βαδίζοι ἂν πᾶσα. εἰ δή τινές
εἰσιν εὐφυεῖς ὥσπερ οἱ ᾠδικοὶ οὐκ ἐπιστάμενοι ᾄδειν, οὕτως
εὖ πεφύκασι καὶ ἄνευ λόγου ὁρμῶσιν, ⟨ᾗ⟩ ἡ φύσις πέφυκε, καὶ
ἐπιθυμοῦσι καὶ τούτου καὶ τότε καὶ οὕτως ὡς δεῖ καὶ οὗ δεῖ
καὶ ὅτε, οὗτοι κατορθώσουσι, κἂν τύχωσιν ἄφρονες ὄντες καὶ 25
ἄλογοι, ὥσπερ καὶ εὖ ᾄσονται οὐ διδασκαλικοὶ ὄντες. οἱ δέ γε

12 ἀπ᾽ ante ἀπείρων suppl. Jackson ((3), 214), dubitanter Collingwood   13 τῳ Jackson ((3), 214, cl. 47ᵇ4): τὸ Π: ὃ Dirlmeier
ἡ Π, Jackson: aut Λ² ἐμπειρίαν Jackson, ex experientiam Λ²: ἀπειρίαν
Π   14 εὐτυχεῖς ΠΛ¹Λ²: εὐτυχεῖν Spengel: ⟨γίνεσθαι⟩ εὐτυχεῖς Allan
((5), cl. 22ᵇ16)   15 Σωκράτης] cf. Pl. Euthd. 279d   εὐτυχίαι L:
εὐτυχείαι PC   16 συμβῆναί τινι L: accidere alicui Λ²: συμβαίνῃ
τινὶ PC   17 τοιοσδί Jackson ((3), 214, cl. 47ᵃ36): τοῖς δεῖ Π: hos
oportet Λ²: οὕτως δεῖ Sylburg   εἴη Sylburg: εἶεν Π: erit Λ²   κύβους
LP²: cubos Λ²: κοίβους P¹C   μακαρίαν Fritzsche (cf. Pl. Hp. Ma.
293a2): μακρὰν Π: longa Λ²   18 ἆρ᾽ Marc.: ἄρ᾽ Π: numquid
Λ²   19 ἀλόγου om. Λ¹   20 αὗται εἰ γάρ ἐστι φύσει ἡ δι᾽
ἐπιθυμίαν Π: ipsi sunt natura quidem. Si propter concupiscentiam Λ²: αὗταί
εἰσι· φύσει γε. εἰ δ᾽ ἡ δι᾽ ἐπιθυμίαν Dirlmeier   ἡδέος L: ἡδέως P: ἡδέου C:
delectabilis Λ²   siquidem naturalis est per cupiditatem iucundae rei
appetitus Λ¹ (i.e. om. {καὶ ἡ²}): hab. Π   21 πᾶσα Allan (5): πᾶν Π:
semper Λ²: πάντοτε Jackson ((3), 215, cl. EN 1166ᵃ28)   22 ᾠδικοὶ
Sylburg (cf. 38ᵃ36): ἄδικοι Π: cantionis imperiti Λ¹: indocti Λ²: ἀδίδακτοι
Allan (5)   ᾄδειν Π: ἃ δεῖ (quae oportet) Λ²   23 εὖ] bene Λ²: οὐ Π
⟨ᾗ⟩ suppl. Jackson ((3), 215): secundum quod Λ²   24 καὶ τότε] et
tunc Λ²: καὶ ποτέ PC: ποτέ L   καὶ οὗ δεῖ om. Λ²   25 κατορθώ-
σουσι] dirigent Λ²: κατορθοῦσι Π   26 ᾄσονται Sylburg: ἔσονται Π
οὐ διδασκαλικοί] cf. Metaph. 981ᵇ7: non docibiles Λ²: οἱ διδασκαλικοὶ Π

1247^b12 ἀπείρων] ἀπ᾽ ἀπείρων
1247^b13 τῳ] τὸ

1247^b17 τοιοσδί] τοιούτοις δεῖ

1247^b20 {καὶ ἡ}] καὶ ἡ
1247^b21 πᾶσα] πᾶν
1247^b22 ὥσπερ] (ὥσπερ
1247^b23 πεφύκασι] πεφύκασι)

τοιοῦτοι εὐτυχεῖς, ὅσοι ἄνευ λόγου κατορθοῦσιν ὡς ἐπὶ τὸ
28 πολύ. φύσει ἄρα οἱ εὐτυχεῖς εἶεν ἄν.

28   ἢ πλεοναχῶς λέ- 14
γεται ἡ εὐτυχία; τὰ μὲν γὰρ πράττεται ἀπὸ τῆς ὁρμῆς
30 καὶ προελομένων πρᾶξαι, τὰ δ' οὔ, ἀλλὰ τοὐναντίον. καὶ ἐν
ἐκείνοις, ⟨ἐν οἷς⟩ κακῶς λογίσασθαι δοκοῦσι, κατορθοῦντας
κατευτυχῆσαι φαμέν· καὶ πάλιν ἐν τούτοις, εἰ ἐβούλοντο ἄλλο
ἢ ἔλαττον ⟨ἢ⟩ ἔλαβον τἀγαθόν. ἐκείνους μὲν τοίνυν εὐτυχεῖν 15
διὰ φύσιν ἐνδέχεται (ἡ γὰρ ὁρμὴ καὶ ὄρεξις οὖσα οὗ δεῖ
35 κατώρθωσεν, ὁ δὲ λογισμὸς ἦν ἠλίθιος· †καὶ τοὺς μὲν ἐνταῦθα, ὅταν μὲν λογισμὸς μὴ δοκῶν ὀρθὸς εἶναι, τύχη δ'
αὐτοῦ αἰτία {οὖσα,} αὐτὴ {δ'} ὀρθὴ οὖσα ἔσωσεν,† ἀλλ' ἐνίοτε
δι' ἐπιθυμίαν ἐλογίσατο πάλιν οὕτω καὶ ἠτύχησεν)· ἐν δὲ δὴ 16
τοῖς ἑτέροις πῶς ἔσται ἡ εὐτυχία κατ' εὐφυΐαν ὀρέξεως καὶ
1248ᵃ ἐπιθυμίας; ἀλλὰ μὴν ἡ ἐνταῦθα εὐτυχία {καὶ τύχη διττὴ}
κἀκείνη ἡ αὐτή, ἢ πλείους αἱ εὐτυχίαι ⟨καὶ τύχη διττή⟩.

ἐπεὶ δ' ὁρῶμεν παρὰ πάσας τὰς ἐπιστήμας καὶ τοὺς 17
λογισμοὺς τοὺς ὀρθοὺς εὐτυχοῦντάς τινας, δῆλον ὅτι ἕτερον ἄν
5 τι εἴη τὸ αἴτιον τῆς εὐτυχίας. ἐκείνη δὲ πότερον εὐτυχία ἢ

---

28 ἄρα P¹L: ἆρα P²C: igitur Λ¹Λ²   ἢ] εἰ (siquidem) Λ¹   30 ἀλλὰ
τοὐναντίον L: sed contrarie Λ²: ἀλλ' οὐ τοὐναντίον C: ἀλλ' οὐ τοὐναν-
τίων P   εἰ post καί² suppl. Rackham   31 εἰ post ἐκείνοις suppl.
Dirlmeier, οἱ Jackson ((3), 216)   ⟨ἐν οἷς⟩] ex in quibus Λ²: om. Π
κατορθοῦντας Ald.: κατορθοῦνται PC: dirigunt (v.l. diriguntur) Λ²: κατορθοῦν τε L   32 κατευτυχῆσαι Bussemaker: καὶ εὐτυχῆσαι Π   εἰ] οἱ
Jackson ((3), 216)   ἐβούλοντο Π: ἐβουλεύοντο Susemihl   ἄλλο Jackson: ἂν Π   33 ἢ¹ Π: secundum quod (i.e., ut vid., ἧ) Λ²   ⟨ἢ²⟩
suppl. Jackson ((3), 216)   ἀγαθόν Spengel   34 δεῖ PL: oportet
Λ²: δὴ C: oportebat Λ¹: ἔδει Susemihl   35 ἦν om. Λ²   35–7 καὶ
... ἔσωσεν susp. Allan (5)   36–7 an ὅταν μὲν λογισμὸς μὴ δοκῇ ὀρθὸς
εἶναι, τύχη δ' αὐτοῦ αἰτία, {οὖσα,} αὐτὴ {δ'} ὀρθὴ οὖσα ἔσωσεν? Mingay
(60–2): ὅταν μὲν λογισμὸς μὴ δοκῶν ὀρθὸς εἶναι, τύχη δ' αὐτοῦ αἰτία οὖσα
⟨ἐπιθυμία⟩, αὕτη ὀρθὴ οὖσα ἔσωσεν Dirlmeier   36 ὀρθὸς Marc. V:
recta (sc. ratiocinatio) Λ²: ὀρθῶς Π   37 {οὖσα,} ... οὖσα] existens
⟨concupiscentia⟩ ipsa recte existente Λ²: αὐτὴ PC: αὐτὴ δ' L: αὕτη
Spengel   ἔσωσεν] salvavit Λ²: ἔξωσεν Π   1248ᵃ 1 ἡ Π: si Λ²: εἰ
Fritzsche: ἢ Spengel   1–2 καὶ τύχη διττή post εὐτυχίαι tra.
Spengel   2 κἀκείνη Π: et ibi Λ²: κἀκεῖ Susemihl: καὶ ἐκεῖ Dirlmeier
ἢ Π: secl. Fritzsche   5 ἡ ante εὐτυχία hab. L

1247ᵇ31 ἐν] εἰ ἐν   κατορθοῦντας] κατορθοῦνται
1247ᵇ32 κατευτυχῆσαι] καὶ εὐτυχῆσαι

1247ᵇ36 τύχη] τύχῃ
1247ᵇ37 {οὖσα}] οὖσα ἐπιθυμία

1248ᵃ1 {καὶ τύχη διττή}] καὶ τύχη διττὴ
1248ᵃ2 κἀκείνη] κἀκεῖ   εὐτυχίαι ⟨καὶ τύχη διττή⟩.] εὐτυχίαι;

οὐκ ἔστιν, ἢ ἐπεθύμησεν ὧν ἔδει καὶ ὅτε †ἔδει τὸ† λογισμὸς
ἀνθρώπινος οὐκ ἂν τούτου εἴη. οὐ γὰρ δὴ πάμπαν ἀλόγιστον
τοῦτο, οὐδὲ φυσική ⟨γ’⟩ ἐστιν ἡ ἐπιθυμία, ἀλλὰ διαφθείρεται
18 ὑπό τινος. εὐτυχεῖν μὲν οὖν δοκεῖ, ὅτι ἡ τύχη τῶν παρὰ
λόγον αἰτία, τοῦτο δὲ παρὰ λόγον (παρὰ γὰρ τὴν ἐπιστήμην   10
καὶ τὸ καθόλου)· ἀλλ’, ὡς ἔοικεν, οὐκ ἀπὸ τύχης, ἀλλὰ
19 δοκεῖ διὰ τοῦτο. ὥσθ’ οὗτος μὲν ὁ λόγος οὐ δείκνυσιν ὅτι
φύσει ⟨τὸ⟩ εὐτυχεῖν, ἀλλ’ ὅτι οὐ πάντες οἱ δοκοῦντες εὐτυχεῖν
διὰ τύχην κατορθοῦσιν, ἀλλὰ διὰ φύσιν· οὐδ’ ὅτι οὐδέν ἐστι
τύχη αἰτία οὐθενὸς δείκνυσιν, ἀλλ’ οὐ τῶν πάντων ὧν   15
δοκεῖ.   16
20   τοῦτο μεντ’ ἂν ἀπορήσειέ τις, ἆρ’ αὐτοῦ τούτου τύχη αἰτία,   16
τοῦ ἐπιθυμῆσαι οὗ δεῖ καὶ ὅτε δεῖ. ἢ οὕτως γε πάντων ἔσται;
καὶ γὰρ τοῦ νοῆσαι καὶ βουλεύσασθαι· οὐ γὰρ δὴ ἐβουλεύσατο
βουλευσάμενος, καὶ τοῦτ’ ⟨αὖ⟩ ἐβουλεύσατο, ἀλλ’ ἔστιν
ἀρχή τις, οὐδ’ ἐνόησε νοήσας πρότερον ⟨ἢ⟩ νοῆσαι, καὶ τοῦτο   20
εἰς ἄπειρον. οὐκ ἄρα τοῦ νοῆσαι ὁ νοῦς ἀρχή, οὐδὲ τοῦ
βουλεύσασθαι βουλή. τί οὖν ἄλλο πλὴν τύχη; ὥστ’ ἀπὸ τύχης
ἅπαντα ἔσται. ἢ ἔστι τις ἀρχὴ ἧς οὐκ ἔστιν ἄλλη ἔξω, αὕτη

6 ἔστιν C: om. PL   ἢ PC: *quae* Λ²: ἢ L: ᾗ Fritzsche: εἰ Spengel
†ἔδει² τὸ† PC: ἔδειτο L: ἔδει, ᾧ λογισμός γε Jackson ((3), 217): maiorem
lacunam subesse susp. Spengel et Dirlmeier: an ἔδει², ⟨καί⟩το⟨ι⟩?
7 τούτου Π: τοῦτο fort. V   εἴη Π: erit causa Λ²   δὴ Chalc.: *utique* Λ²:
δεῖ Π   8 οὐδὲ Susemihl: οὔτε Π: οὗ γε Jackson ((3), 217–18)
φυσική ⟨γ’⟩ Walzer (cf. Denniston, 119 I. 1. ii)   9 οὖν L: *igitur*
Λ²: ἂν PC   10 τοῦτο fort. V: *hoc* Λ²: τούτου Π   11 ἀλλ’ ὡς Π:
aliter Λ²   13 ⟨τὸ⟩ suppl. Bussemaker: εὐτυχεῖν Π: *quod natura
benefortunate agatur* Λ²: εὐτυχεῖται Dirlmeier   14 ἀλλά] ἀλλ’ οὐ
Jackson ((3), 218)   οὐδέν PC: οὐδ’ L: *non* Λ²   14–15 ὅτι οὐδέν ἐστι
τύχη, ⟨οὐδ’ ὅτι οὐκ ἔστι τύχη⟩ ante αἰτία suppl. Jackson ((3), 218)
15 ὅτι post ἀλλ’ suppl. Casaubon   16 ἆρ’ P² Oxon.: *utrum* Λ¹:
ἄρ’ P¹CL   18 δὴ PC: om. LΛ²   19 ⟨αὖ⟩ suppl. Langerbeck:
τοῦτ’ ἐβουλεύσατο Π: *et antequam consiliaretur* Λ², unde πρότερον ἢ
βουλεύσασθαι Bussemaker   19–20 ἀλλ’ . . . τις post ἄπειρον (21) tra.
Rackham   20 ⟨ἢ⟩ e Λ² suppl. Spengel: om. Π   21 ὁ νοῦς
Casaubon: ὁ (?)νοῦς mg. Marc.²: *intellectus* Λ²: συνοῦσα Π   23 ἔσται]
sunt Λ²   ἢ] *aut* Λ²: εἰ Π: *et* Λ¹   αὕτη Π: αὐτὴ Λ²

1248ᵃ6 †ἔδει τὸ†] ἔδει, ᾧ
1248ᵃ7 εἴη] εἴη αἴτιον
1248ᵃ8 οὐδὲ] οὔ γε

1248ᵃ15 αἰτία] οὐδ᾽ αἰτία

1248ᵃ18 δὴ] εἰ

δὲ διὰ τὸ τοιαύτη {τῷ} εἶναι {τὸ} τοιοῦτο δύναται ποιεῖν; τὸ δὲ ζητού- 21
25 μενον τοῦτ᾽ ἐστί, τίς ἡ τῆς κινήσεως ἀρχὴ ἐν τῇ ψυχῇ. δῆλον
δή· ὥσπερ ἐν τῷ ὅλῳ θεός, {καὶ} κἂν ἐκείνῳ. κινεῖ γάρ
πως πάντα τὸ ἐν ἡμῖν θεῖον· λόγου δ᾽ ἀρχὴ οὐ λόγος, 22
ἀλλά τι κρεῖττον· τί οὖν ἂν κρεῖττον καὶ ἐπιστήμης εἴη ⟨καὶ
νοῦ⟩ πλὴν θεός; ἡ γὰρ ἀρετὴ τοῦ νοῦ ὄργανον· καὶ διὰ τοῦτο,
30 ὃ {οἱ} πάλαι ἔλεγον, εὐτυχεῖς καλοῦνται οἵ, ⟨οἳ⟩ ἂν ὁρμήσωσι,
κατορθοῦσιν ἄλογοι ὄντες, καὶ βουλεύεσθαι οὐ συμφέρει αὐτοῖς.
ἔχουσι γὰρ ἀρχὴν τοιαύτην ἢ κρείττων τοῦ νοῦ καὶ τῆς βουλεύσεως
(οἱ δὲ τὸν λόγον· τοῦτο δ᾽ οὐκ ἔχουσι οὐδ᾽ ἐνθουσιασμόν), τοῦτο 23
δ᾽ οὐ δύνανται. ἄλογοι γὰρ ὄντες ἐπιτυγχάνουσι· καὶ τού-
35 των φρονίμων καὶ σοφῶν ταχεῖαν εἶναι τὴν μαντικήν, καὶ
μόνον οὐ τὴν ἀπὸ τοῦ λόγου δεῖ ὑπολαβεῖν, ἀλλ᾽ οἱ μὲν δι᾽
ἐμπειρίαν, οἱ δὲ διὰ συνήθειάν †τε† ἐν τῷ σκοπεῖν χρῆσθαι·
τῷ θείῳ δὲ αὗται. τοῦτο καὶ εὖ ὁρᾷ καὶ τὸ μέλλον καὶ
τὸ ὄν, καὶ ὧν ἀπολύεται ὁ λόγος οὗτος. διὸ οἱ μελαγχο-

24 διὰ τὸ τοιαύτη (τοιαύτη ⟨γε⟩ Jackson (3), 218) {τῷ} εἶναι {τὸ}
τοιοῦτο δύναται ποιεῖν; Walzer: διὰ τί τοιαύτη τὸ εἶναι τὸ τοῦτο δύνασθαι
ποιεῖν; Π: quod tale secundum esse tale potest facere Λ²: ὅτι τοιαύτη ⟨κατὰ⟩
τὸ εἶναι τὸ τοιοῦτο δύναται ποιεῖν; Dirlmeier   26 δή om. Λ²   {καὶ}
secl. Spengel: hab. Π: κινεῖ Ross   κἂν] πᾶν Π, Dirlmeier   ἐκείνῳ Π:
illud Λ²: ἐκεῖνο Dirlmeier: ἐκείνη Spengel   27 οὐ L: non Λ²: om. PC
28 εἴη Spengel: εἴποι Π   28–9 ⟨καὶ νοῦ⟩ suppl. Spengel, ex et
scientia et intellectu Λ²   29 ὄργανον Kenny ((1), 9, adn. 1, cl. Pr.
955ᵇ37)   30 ὃ {οἱ} πάλαι ἔλεγον Jackson ((3), 219; i.e. 47ᵇ21–8): ὃ οἱ
πάλαι ἔλεγον Π: quod olim dicebatur Λ²: ὃ πάλαι ἐλέγετο Dirlmeier   ⟨οἳ⟩
suppl. Smith, ἃ post οἵ Jackson ((3), 219): οἵ, ἂν L, Dirlmeier: qui si Λ²:
οἷαν PC   31 κατορθοῦσιν] dirigunt Λ²: κατορθοῦν Π   βουλεύεσθαι
PC: consiliari Λ²: βούλεσθαι L   32 τοιαύτην ἢ κρείττων τοῦ νοῦ καὶ
(τοιαύτη ἢ κρεῖ post ras.) L: tale (sc. principium) quod melius intellectu et
Λ²: om. PC   βουλεύσεως] consilio Λ²: βουλήσεως Π   33 οἱ Π: ὅσοι
Allan (5)   οὐδ᾽ Langerbeck, e neque Λ²: καὶ Π   ἐνθουσιασμόν Spengel:
divinos instinctus Λ²: ἐνθουσιασμοί Π   34 ἐπιτυγχάνουσι cf. Rh.
1354ᵃ9, ex adipiscuntur Λ²: ἀποτυγχάνουσι Π   τούτων] τοῦ τῶν Sylburg
35 φρονίμων καὶ σοφῶν ironice   36 μόνον L: μόνων PC: solorum Λ²
ὑπολαβεῖν Ross: suscipere Λ²: ἀπολαβεῖν Π   ἀλλ᾽ Π: om. Λ²   37 an
ταύτῃ ἐν?: τε ἐν Π: τε om. Λ²: τοῦ ἐν Spengel: ⟨δοκοῦσι⟩ {τε ἐν}
Dirlmeier   38 θείῳ Spengel: θεῷ Π   αὗται Π: per se Λ²: οὗτοι
v. Arnim   καὶ Π: γὰρ v. Arnim   39 οὗτος Π: an τοῦτο?: sic Λ²:
οὕτως Jackson ((3), 219): οὗτοι Solomon

1248ᵃ24   διὰ τὸ τοιαύτῃ {τῷ} εἶναι {τὸ}] διότι τοιαύτη τὸ εἶναι τὸ

1248ᵃ26   {καὶ} κἂν ἐκείνῳ] καὶ πᾶν ἐκεῖ νῷ κινεῖ

1248ᵃ33-4   (οἱ δὲ τὸν λόγον· τοῦτο δ᾽ οὐκ ἔχουσι οὐδ᾽ ἐνθουσιασμόν),
τοῦτο δ᾽ οὐ δύνανται] ὅσοι δὲ τὸν λόγον, τοῦτο δ᾽ οὐκ ἔχουσι οὐδ᾽
ἐνθουσιασμόν, τοῦτο οὐ δύνανται   1248ᵃ34-5 τούτων] τοῦ τῶν

1248ᵃ38   δὲ αὗται] δύνανται
1248ᵃ39   οὗτος] οὕτως

λικοὶ καὶ εὐθυόνειροι. ἔοικε γὰρ ἡ ἀρχὴ ἀπολυομένου τοῦ 40
λόγου ἰσχύειν μᾶλλον· καὶ ὥσπερ οἱ τυφλοὶ μνημονεύουσι **1248ᵇ**
μᾶλλον ἀπολυθέντες τοῦ πρὸς τοῖς ὁρωμένοις, τῷ ἐρρωμενέστερον εἶναι τὸ μνημονεῦον.   3

24   φανερὸν δὴ ὅτι δύο εἴδη εὐτυχίας, ἢ 3
μὲν θεία (διὸ καὶ δοκεῖ ὁ εὐτυχὴς διὰ θεὸν κατορθοῦν)· οὗτος
δέ ἐστιν ὁ κατὰ τὴν ὁρμὴν διορθωτικός, ὁ δ' ἕτερος ὁ παρὰ 5
τὴν ὁρμήν· ἄλογοι δ' ἀμφότεροι. καὶ ἡ μὲν συνεχὴς εὐτυχία
μᾶλλον, αὕτη δὲ οὐ συνεχής.

H. XV   κατὰ μέρος μὲν οὖν περὶ ἑκάστης ἀρετῆς εἴρηται πρό- 3
τερον· ἐπεὶ δὲ χωρὶς διείλομεν τὴν δύναμιν αὐτῶν, καὶ περὶ
τῆς ἀρετῆς διαρθρωτέον τῆς ἐκ τούτων, ἣν ἐκαλοῦμεν ἤδη κα- 10
2 λοκἀγαθίαν. ὅτι μὲν οὖν ἀνάγκη τὸν ταύτης ἀληθῶς τευξό-
μενον τῆς προσηγορίας ἔχειν τὰς κατὰ μέρος ἀρετάς, φανερόν. οὐδὲ γὰρ ἐπὶ τῶν ἄλλων οὐθενὸς οἷόν τ' ἄλλως ἔχειν.
οὐθεὶς γὰρ ὅλον μὲν τὸ σῶμα ὑγιαίνει, μέρος δ' οὐθέν, ἀλλ'
ἀναγκαῖον πάντα ἢ τὰ πλεῖστα καὶ κυριώτατα τὸν αὐτὸν 15
ἔχειν τρόπον τῷ ὅλῳ.   16

3   ἔστι δὴ τὸ ἀγαθὸν εἶναι καὶ τὸ κα- 16
λὸν κἀγαθὸν οὐ μόνον κατὰ τὰ ὀνόματα, ἀλλὰ ⟨καὶ⟩ καθ' αὑτὰ
ἔχοντα διαφοράν. τῶν γὰρ ἀγαθῶν πάντων τέλη ἐστίν, ἃ
αὐτὰ αὑτῶν ἕνεκά ἐστιν αἱρετά. τούτων δὲ καλά, ὅσα δι'

40–1 ἀπολυομένου τοῦ λόγου Spengel: amissa ratione Λ²: ἀπολυομένους
τοὺς λόγους Π   **1248ᵇ** 2 ἀπολυθέντες τοῦ Π: amissisque hiis Λ²:
ἀπολυθέντος τοῦ Dirlmeier   ὁρωμένοις Ross: visibilia Λ² (cf. Pl. Pm.
130a): εἰρημένοις Π: ὁρατοῖς Fritzsche   τῷ ante ὁρωμένοις Fritzsche,
post μᾶλλον Dirlmeier   ἐρρωμενέστερον suppl. Fritzsche: virtuosius Λ²:
om. Π: σπουδαιότερον post τῷ suppl. Jackson ((3), 219): τοῦ πρὸς τοῖς
ὁρατοῖς εἶναι τὸ μνημονεῦον Ross   3 δή] itaque Λ²: δὲ Π   4 ἡ δὲ
φύσει post κατορθοῦν)· suppl. Spengel   οὗτος L: iste Λ²: οὕτω PC
5 διορθωτικός] κατορθωτικός v. Arnim: ὀρθωτικός dubitanter Dirlmeier
6 εὐτυχία secl. Langerbeck   10 διαρθρωτέον LV: articulatim trac-
tandum Λ³: διωρθωτέον PC   ἐκαλοῦμεν Π: vocamus Λ¹: καλοῦμεν Ross
ἤδη secl. Ross   13 οὐδὲ] neque Λ¹: οὐδὲν Π   14 οὐθεὶς γὰρ ὅλον
μὲν L: nullus enim toto quidem Λ³: οὐθεὶς μὲν ὅλον PC   17 ⟨καὶ⟩
suppl. Bussemaker: καθ' αὑτὰ Spengel: sed et secundum ipsa Λ³: κατ'
αὐτὰ τὰ L: κατὰ ταῦτα τὰ P: κατὰ ταὐτὰ τὰ C

1248^{b}21-3   τῷ ἐρρωμενέστερον εἶναι] εἶναι

APPENDIX 4

Eudemian Ethics VIII. 2 (= VII. 14) (Translation)

SINCE not only wisdom and virtue bring about well-doing, but we say also that the fortunate do well, on the assumption that fortune produces well-doing and the same results as knowledge, we must enquire whether it is by nature, or otherwise, that one man is fortunate and another unfortunate, and how matters stand on this topic. That there are some people who are fortunate is a matter of observation. For people who lack wisdom succeed in many things where luck rules; and also in areas which are the province of skill, but where there is also scope for luck, for instance in the case of generalship and steersmanship. Are people like this as a consequence of some disposition, or do they achieve their fortunate results not because of any quality of their own? At the present time people take the following view, that some people are fortunate by nature, and that nature gives people certain qualities, so that they differ from each other from birth: just as blue-eyed and black-eyed people differ because someone who is a certain kind by nature must be of a certain kind in disposition, so too fortunate people differ from unfortunate people.

For that they do not succeed by wisdom is clear. For wisdom is not unreasoning, but can give an account of why it is acting as it does; but these people would not be able to say why they succeed (that would be art). That they succeed is clear, though they are lacking in wisdom—not just about other things (there would be nothing strange in that case: Hippocrates, for instance, was a geometer but in other matters he was thought silly and foolish, and once on a voyage was cheated of much money by the customs men at Byzantium, because of his unworldliness, they say), but lacking wisdom in the very things in which they are fortunate. For in navigation it is not the most skilled who are fortunate, but it is as in dice where one man throws a blank and another throws a six in accordance with his natural good fortune.

Or is it through being loved, as they say, by a god so that success is the result of something external? Just as a badly constructed ship often sails better, not on its own account, but because it has a good helmsman; in this way the fortunate man has a good helmsman in the shape of a supernatural being. But it would be strange for a god or supernatural being to favour such a man rather than the best and wisest. If, then, success must be due either to nature or intelligence or some kind of guardianship, and two of these are ruled out, then the fortunate must be so by nature.

Nature, however, is the cause of what occurs either universally or generally, whereas luck is the opposite. Now if prosperity contrary to expectation seems to belong to luck—but if someone is fortunate he is so by luck—the cause would not seem to be the kind of thing that is the cause of what is universally or generally the same. Further, if a man prospers or fails to prosper because he is the kind of man he is, just as a man sees poorly because he is blue-eyed, then not luck but nature is the cause. Such a man, then, is not so much fortunate as gifted by nature. So we shall have to say that those whom we call fortunate are not so by luck. In that case they are not fortunate at all, for the fortunate are those whose goods are caused by good luck.

If this is so, will luck not exist at all, or will it exist, but not be a cause? No, it must both exist and be a cause. It will, then, also be a cause of good to some people and bad. Should it be eliminated altogether, and should it be said that nothing happens by luck, but that we merely say that luck is a cause, when there is some other cause, because we do not see it? (It is for this reason that when they define luck some people lay down that it is a cause which is opaque to human reasoning, on the assumption that there is a natural factor.) That would set us a different problem.

Since we see people being fortunate once only, why do we not see them succeeding again through the same cause and yet again? For the same cause has the same effect. So this will not be a matter of luck. But when the same event results from antecedents which are indeterminate and indefinite, the result will be good or bad, but there will be no empirical knowledge of it, as otherwise some fortunate people would have learnt it. Or would all the sciences be types of good fortune, as Socrates said? What, then, prevents such things from happening to somebody often in succession, not because he is the kind of person he is, but like a long run of success in throwing dice?

What follows then? Are there not impulses in the soul of two kinds: some from reasoning, and others from unreasoning appetite? And are these not prior? For if the impulse which comes from the desire of the pleasant, and also the appetite, are by nature, then by nature everything will march towards the good. If then there are some people well endowed by nature (as musical people without professional knowledge of singing are well endowed in that respect) and who without reasoning are impelled in accord with nature, and desire what they ought and when they ought, these persons will succeed even though they lack wisdom and reasoning, just as men will sing well who are incapable of teaching singing. People of this kind are fortunate, people who without reasoning succeed most of the time. It will follow that the fortunate are so by nature.

Or is there more than one sense of 'good fortune'? For some actions come from impulse and from people who choose to act, and others do not, but quite the contrary. And in those cases if people succeed in things in which they seem to have reasoned badly, we say that they have also been fortunate. So again in these cases, if they wanted a different, or a lesser, good than they have received.

In the case of those people it is possible for them to be fortunate through nature, for the impulse and the appetite, being for the right thing, prospered, though the reasoning was futile. In the case of these other people, when reasoning seems not to be correct, but desire happens to be present as a cause, the desire being rightly directed comes to the rescue. (And yet, on some occasions, a man again reasons in this way under the influence of desire and is unfortunate.) But in the other cases, how can there be good fortune in accordance with a good endowment of appetite and desire? But then if in this case fortune and luck are twofold, is there in the other case just one and the same fortune, or are there more than one?

Since we see some people succeeding against all sciences and correct reasonings, it is clear that something else is the cause of the good fortune. But is this or is it not good fortune, the desiring of the right thing at the right time in a case where human reasoning is not the cause? For that of which the desire is natural is not altogether without reason, but the reasoning is distorted by something. So such a person is thought to be fortunate, because luck is the cause of things contrary to reason, and that is contrary to reason since it is contrary to knowledge and the universal. But, as it seems, it is not really the result of luck, but it appears to be so for this reason. Consequently this argument does not show that good fortune is by nature, but that not all those who seem to be fortunate succeed by luck, but by nature. Not that luck is nothing, or is not a cause of anything, but that it is not the cause of all the things it seems to be.

But this further question might be put: Is luck the cause of the very fact of desiring what one should when one should? If so, will it be the cause of everything? For it will be the cause also of thought and deliberation. For even if someone deliberated after having deliberated, he did not deliberate in turn about that; there is a certain starting-point. Nor did he think, having thought before thinking, and so on to infinity. So intellect is not the starting-point of thinking, nor is counsel the starting-point of deliberation. What else is there then save luck? Thus everything will be by luck.

Or is there some principle with no other principle external to it which, because it is the kind of thing it is, can produce this kind of effect? This is what we are looking for: what is the starting-point of motion in the soul? The answer is plain: as in the universe, so here, God moves everything by mind. For in a manner the divine element in us moves everything. Reason is not the principle of reason, but something superior. But what can be superior to it, and to knowledge and to intellect, except God? For virtue is an instrument of intellect.

And for that reason, as I said earlier, people are called fortunate who, lacking reason, succeed in what they attempt. Deliberation is not useful to them. For they have a principle of a kind which is superior to intellect and deliberation; while those who have reason, but not this principle, nor inspiration, have not the same ability. And they attain to a power of divination which is swifter than the reasoning of the wise and learned; indeed the divination which comes from reasoning should almost be done away with. But some people through experience, and others through habit, have this power of using the divine element in their enquiry: and this sees well both what is and what is to come, even in the case of people whose reason is thus disengaged. Thus those of a melancholic temperament also have good dreams. For the principle seems stronger when reason is disengaged, just as blind people remember better when released from having their memory fixed on visible objects.

It is obvious that there are two kinds of good fortune. One of them is divine, which is why the fortunate person seems to succeed through God. This man is the one who is successful in accordance with impulse, the other is so contrary to impulse; but both are non-rational. And the one kind of good fortune is continuous, and the other non-continuous.

BIBLIOGRAPHY OF WORKS CITED

ACKRILL, J. L., *Aristotle on EUDAIMONIA* (London, 1974).

AQUINAS, ST THOMAS, *Summa contra Gentiles* (Leonine edn.; Rome, 1934).

—— *Summa Theologiae* (Rome, 1952).

—— *Summa Theologiae* (Blackfriars edn., vol. 17; London, 1970).

BAILEY, R. W., 'Determining Authorship in Ancient Greek', in *Proceedings of the International Conference on Literary and Linguistic Computing* (Israel, Apr. 1979).

BARNES, J., *The Complete Works of Aristotle* (Revised Oxford Translation; Princeton, 1984).

BROADIE, S. W., *Ethics with Aristotle* (New York, 1991).

CASE, T., 'Aristotle', in *Encyclopaedia Britannica*, 11th edn. (1910–11).

CLARK, S. R. L., *Aristotle's Man* (Oxford, 1975).

COOPER, J. M., 'The *Magna Moralia* and Aristotle's Moral Philosophy', *American Journal of Philology*, 94 (1973), 327–49.

—— *Reason and Human Good in Aristotle* (Cambridge, 1975).

—— 'Aristotle on Friendship', in A. Rorty (ed.), *Essays on Aristotle's Ethics* (Los Angeles, 1980).

—— review of A. Kenny, *The Aristotelian Ethics*, in *Nous*, 15 (1981), 366–85.

—— 'Aristotle on the Goods of Fortune', *Philosophical Review*, 94 (1985), 173–96.

—— 'Contemplation and Happiness: A Reconsideration', *Synthese* (1987), 187–216.

DÉCARIE, V., *Aristote, Éthique à Eudème* (Paris, 1978).

DEVEREUX, D., 'Aristotle on the Active and Contemplative Lives', *Philosophy Research Archives* 3 (1977), 834–44.

—— 'Aristotle on the Essence of Happiness', in D. J. O'Meara (ed.), *Studies in Aristotle* (Washington, 1981).

DIRLMEIER, F., *Aristoteles, Eudemische Ethik, übersetzt und kommentiert* (Berlin, 1969).

DÜRING, I., *Aristoteles* (Heidelberg, 1966).

EUCKEN, R., *De Aristotelis Dicendi Ratione* (Göttingen, 1866).

FRAGSTEIN, A. VON, *Studien zur Ethik des Aristoteles* (Amsterdam, 1974).

FURLEY, D. J., *Two Studies in the Greek Atomists* (Princeton, 1967).

GAISER, K., 'Zwei Protreptikos-Zitate in der Eudemischen Ethik des Aristoteles', *Rheinisches Museum*, NP 110/4 (1967), 314–45.

GAUTHIER, R. A., and JOLIF, J. Y., *L'Éthique à Nicomaque*, 2 vols. (1959; 2nd edn. of vol. i/1: Paris–Louvain, 1970).

HARDIE, W. F. R., 'The Final Good in Aristotle's Ethics', *Philosophy*, 40 (1965), 277–95.

HARDIE, W. F. R., *Aristotle's Ethical Theory* (Oxford, 1968).

HEINAMAN, R., 'Eudaimonia and Self-sufficiency in the *Nicomachean Ethics*', *Phronesis*, 33 (1988), 31–53.

IRWIN, T. H., review of A. Kenny, *The Aristotelian Ethics*, in *The Journal of Philosophy*, 77 (1980), 338–54.

—— *Aristotle*, Nicomachean Ethics (Indianapolis, 1985).

—— 'Permanent Happiness', *Oxford Studies in Ancient Philosophy*, 3 (1985), 89–124.

—— 'Stoic and Aristotelian Conceptions of Happiness', in M. Schofield and G. Striker (eds.), *The Norms of Nature* (Cambridge, 1986).

JAEGER, W., *Aristotle: Fundamentals of the History of his Development*, trans. Robinson (Oxford, 1948).

KENNY, A., 'Happiness', *Proceedings of the Aristotelian Society*, 66 (1965–6), 93–102.

—— *Will, Freedom, and Power* (Oxford, 1975).

—— *The Aristotelian Ethics* (Oxford, 1978).

—— *Aristotle's Theory of the Will* (London, 1979).

—— 'Duress *per Minas* as a Defence to Crime', in M. A. Sewart (ed.), *Law, Morality and Rights* (Boston, 1979).

—— 'A Stylometric Study of Aristotle's *Metaphysics*', *Journal of the Association for Literary and Linguistic Computing* (1982).

—— 'A Stylometric Comparison between Five Disputed Works and the Remainder of the Aristotelian Corpus', in P. Moraux and J. Wiesner (eds.), *Zweifelhaftes im Corpus Aristotelicum* (Berlin, 1983).

—— 'Aristotle on Moral Luck', in J. Dancy, J. M. E. Moravcsik, and C. C. W. Taylor (eds.), *Human Agency* (Stanford, 1988).

KEYT, D., 'Intellectualism in Aristotle', *Paideia* (1978), 138–57.

KIRWAN, C., review of A. Kenny, *The Aristotelian Ethics*, in *Classical Review*, 30 (1980), 50–2.

KNOX, R. A., *Enthusiasm* (Oxford, 1950).

KRAUT, R., *Aristotle on the Human Good* (Princeton, 1989).

LONG, A. A., 'Aristotle's Legacy to Stoic Ethics', *Bulletin of the Institute of Classical Studies*, 15 (1968), 72–85.

MACINTYRE, A., *Whose Justice? Which Rationality?* (Notre Dame, 1988).

MONAN, J. D., *Moral Knowledge and its Methodology in Aristotle* (Oxford, 1968).

MOSTELLER, F., and WALLACE, D. L., *Inference and Disputed Authorship: The Federalist* (Reading, Mass., 1964).

—— —— *Applied Bayesian and Classical Inference* (New York, 1984).

NAGEL, T., 'Moral Luck', *Proceedings of the Aristotelian Society*, suppl. 50 (1976), 137–51.

NUSSBAUM, M. C., 'Aristotle', in T. J. Luce (ed.), *Ancient Writers*, i (New York, 1982).

—— *The Fragility of Goodness* (Cambridge, 1986).

PRICE, A. W., 'Aristotle's Ethical Holism', *Mind*, 89 (1980), 338–52.

PRIOR, A. N., *Objects of Thought*, ed. P. T. Geach and A. Kenny (Oxford, 1971).

ROCHE, T. D., 'ERGON and EUDAIMONIA in *Nicomachean Ethics* I: Reconsidering the Intellectualist Interpretation', *Journal of the History of Philosophy*, 26 (1988), 175–94.

ROWE, CHRISTOPHER, 'De Aristotelis in tribus libris Ethicorum dicendi ratione', *Liverpool Classical Monthly*, 8 (1983), 1: 4–11, 3: 37–40, 4: 54–7, 5: 70–4.

URMSON, J. O., *Aristotle's Ethics* (Oxford, 1988).

VERBEKE, G., 'L'idéal de la perfection humaine chez Aristote et l'évolution de sa noétique', *Fontes Ambrosiani*, 25 (1951), 79–95.

VERDENIUS, W., 'Human Reason and God in the *Eudemian Ethics*', in P. Moraux and D. Harlfinger (eds.), *Untersuchungen zur Eudemischen Ethik* (Akten des 5. Symposium Aristotelicum; Berlin, 1971).

WHITE, S., 'Is Aristotelian Happiness a Good Life or the Best Life?', *Oxford Studies in Ancient Philosophy*, 8 (1990), 103–44.

WILLIAMS, B. A. O., 'Aristotle on the Good', *Philosophical Quarterly* (1962), 289–96.

—— 'Moral Luck', *Proceedings of the Aristotelian Society*, suppl. 50 (1976), 115–31.

WITTGENSTEIN, L., *Philosophical Investigations* (Oxford, 1953).

WOODS, M., *Aristotle's Eudemian Ethics, Books I, II, and VIII* (Oxford, 1982).

WRIGHT, G. H. VON, 'The Good of Man', in id., *The Varieties of Goodness* (New York, 1963).

INDEX